Mathematics Education at Highly Effective Schools That Serve the Poor

Strategies for Change

Mathematics Education at Highly Effective Schools That Serve the Poor

Strategies for Change

Richard S. Kitchen
University of New Mexico

Julie DePree
University of New Mexico–Valencia

Sylvia Celedón-Pattichis
University of New Mexico

Jonathan Brinkerhoff
University of New Mexico

2007

LAWRENCE ERLBAUM ASSOCIATES, PUBLISHERS
Mahwah, New Jersey   London

Lawrence Erlbaum Associates, Inc., Publishers
10 Industrial Avenue
Mahwah, New Jersey 07430
www.erlbaum.com

Cover design by Tomai Maridou

Library of Congress Cataloging-in-Publication Data

Mathematics education at highly effective schools that serve the poor : strategies for change / Richard S. Kitchen ... [et al.].
  p. cm.
Includes bibliographical references and index.
ISBN 0-8058-5688-9 (cloth : alk. paper)
ISBN 0-8058-5689-7 (pbk. : alk. paper)
ISBN 1-4106-1454-9 (E book)
1. Mathematics—Study and teaching. 2. People with social disabilities—Education—Case studies. I. Kitchen, Richard S.
QA11.2.M2778 2006
510.71'2—dc22   2006001822
                                                       CIP

Books published by Lawrence Erlbaum Associates are printed on acid-free paper, and their bindings are chosen for strength and durability.

Printed in the United States of America
10 9 8 7 6 5 4 3 2 1

*For my mother, whose strength, love,
and compassion continue to inspire me. —RK*

*For my family, especially my husband,
who has always supported me, and my mother,
whose spirit still guides me. —JD*

*To my familia, especially my mother, who has been
the pillar of each goal I accomplish. —SCP*

Contents

Foreword

Walter G. Secada
University of Miami, Florida

This book adds to the ever-growing body of research into the organizational features of schools and, in the case of secondary schools, of mathematics departments that support student learning of and achievement in mathematics (Gamoran et al., 2003; Gutierrez, 1996; V. E. Lee & Smith, 2001; Newmann & Associates, 1996). Beyond replicating earlier studies (a much underappreciated educational-research activity), this particular effort extends our knowledge by providing three, complexly constructed and very well-defined department- or school-level characteristics that support achievement. What is more, this effort elucidates how schools can succeed within the policy context of high-stakes testing.

THE THREE THEMES

One of the most important contributions of this effort lies not just in its three themes, but also in how it (re)constructs them as complex entities.

"High expectations," the first part of Theme 1, are a commonly cited requirement for student achievement found in the multicultural education and student expectations literatures. However, without "sustained support for academic excellence," Theme 1's second component, high expectations, can become little more than expecting students to sink or swim within an elitist set of unreachable goals. Similarly, "sustained support for academic excellence" without the expectation that students actually achieve something with that support can morph into the wasting of resources and the sanctioning of failure.

Not only are this study's students expected to do well, they are supported and even pressed to do so. Students are provided with extended time to do mathematics, afterschool tutoring, remedial as well as enhanced course content, and access to their teacher's cell phone number.

The second theme combines "challenging mathematical content" and "high-level instruction." Their juxtaposition reminds us that, unfortunately, it is all-too-common for students to waste their time on content that is not worth learning or that classy content can be stripped of what makes it interesting through instructional techniques that suck the life blood out of student engagement and leave even the most willing students squirming in their seats, waiting for the bell to end math class.

Whereas student success on standardized tests is very important to this study's teachers, we are reminded that the most successful teachers do not limit themselves to simply preparing students for what is on the test. Instead, in a manner that is reminiscent of Knapp and Associates (1995) results, the most successful teachers range through the entire curriculum.

Finally, the relationships that teachers build among themselves (Theme 3) are created from and support the achievement of shared purposes. In some cases, this study's teachers' shared-sense-of-purpose found articulation in their efforts to improve their curricular offerings; in others, on creating collaborative student-learning environments; and in others, on shifting from teaching only the mechanics of mathematics to also deepening student understanding of mathematical ideas. In all cases, teachers' shared purpose pressed them to work together, to create and maintain supportive relationships, and to focus their efforts on ensuring that their students would learn mathematics and achieve.

A QUESTION OF BALANCE

Interestingly, throughout this book, this study's teachers did not abandon basic skills, traditional content, and direct instruction. Rather, they sought to create a new balance between those practices and problem solving and applications; new content, such as found in the NSF-funded curricula; and more open-ended forms of instruction that seek to foster higher order thinking skills. In my own work (e.g., Secada & Adajian, 1997), I have been impressed by teachers' pragmatic search for "what works." Seldom, if ever, do mathematics teachers swing from one extreme to another as is so often portrayed in the math wars. Rather, teachers want their students to learn a breadth of mathematical content and they seek tools that will help them succeed at ensuring student learning.

SOCIAL CLASS

Another striking feature of this study is that actions taken by this study's schools and teachers seemed targeted not at overcoming differences inherent in their students. Instead, their actions seemed to ameliorate the persistent real-world inequities that can be traced to social class (Lubienski, 2003). The example of students (at the Yes College Preparatory School and the

KIPP Academies) being given their teachers' cell phone numbers is particularly telling in this regard.

The most common complaint that I have heard from mathematics students at all levels is that when they encounter problems or tasks that they do not understand, they need and want help immediately and in real time. One only need walk into a mathematics class during seatwork to see the hands up in the air, almost demanding immediate assistance from the teacher. As any vendor of any technology will attest, if the buyer cannot get something up and running without major problems, then the buyer will quit in frustration, re-box the item and return it; computer vendors call this the buyer's "out of the box experience (OOBE)." Mathematics students are not that different from the person who demands a positive OOBE. If their initial experiences with a mathematical concept are negative, then they will often close their books and quit in frustration.

Middle- and upper-class students have access to a wide range of extra-school resources that allow them to access help immediately and in real time. Wealthier students can ask their better educated parents or other family members; they have cell phones to call one another; they have access to the Internet to Google their questions or to IM one another. By providing students with their teachers' cell phone numbers, schools began to level the playing field. Not only did students have immediate access to help, but teachers' knowledge that their students would call them pressed the teachers to develop their lessons carefully so as to minimize the number of late-night phone calls that they received.

FINALLY

Although there are many other (and some very provocative) ways of reading this book, I would encourage teachers, curriculum specialists, and district administrators to spend some time understanding the three cases. Each school and its mathematics department operates as an organic whole. Within that school's everyday workings can be seen the characteristics that Richard Kitchen and his colleagues suggest are critical to student achievement. I hope that these case studies could help schools and their mathematics teachers to develop a set of strategies that would help them become more successful in their own teaching of mathematics within the current high-stakes testing environment.

REFERENCES

Gamoran, A., Anderson, C. W., Quiroz, P. A., Secada, W. G., Williams, T., & Ashmann, S. (2003). *Transforming teaching in math and science: How schools and districts can support change.* New York: Teachers College Press.

Gutierrez, R. (1996). Practices, beliefs, and cultures of high school mathematics departments: Understanding their influence on student advancement. *Journal of Curriculum Studies, 28*(5), 495–529.

Lee, V. E., & Smith, J. B. (2001). *Restructuring high schools for equity and excellence: What works*. New York: Teachers College Press.

Lubienski, S. T. (2003, November). Celebrating diversity and denying disparities: A critical assessment. *Educational Research, 32*(8), 30–38.

Knapp, M. S., & Associates. (1995). *Teaching for meaning in high-poverty classrooms*. New York: Teachers College Press.

Newmann, F. M., & Associates. (1996). *Authentic achievement: Restructuring schools for intellectual quality*. San Francisco: Jossey-Bass.

Secada, W. G., & Adajian, L. (1997). Mathematics teachers' change in the context of their professional communities. In E. Fennema & B. S. Nelson (Eds.), *Teachers in transition: Mathematics and reform* (pp. 193–219). Mahwah, NJ: Lawrence Erlbaum Associates.

Preface

This book presents research findings about both school-level characteristics and classroom-level characteristics that distinguish nine public schools—all serving low-income or high-poverty communities in the United States—as highly effective, particularly in mathematics. In spring 2002, these nine schools were selected in a national competition to participate in the Hewlett-Packard (HP) High-Achieving Schools (HAS) Grant Initiative. As part of this initiative, the nine schools participated in the research study described in this book. These schools from across the United States were specifically selected because they demonstrated: free or reduced lunch rate of 50% or higher and sustained exemplary academic achievement, particularly in mathematics, over a minimum of 3–5 consecutive years.

The study employed both qualitative and quantitative research methodologies to examine school-level factors and classroom-level factors that contributed to high achievement, particularly in mathematics. During the 2002–2003 academic year, researchers from the University of New Mexico visited each of the nine participating schools twice to conduct classroom observations in mathematics, conduct individual and focus group interviews with mathematics faculty, conduct focus group interviews with students, and interview and administer surveys to school administrators.

We believe that the schools described in this book have much to teach us about creating powerful learning environments that empower all students to learn challenging mathematics. We want to stress that the nine schools are not presented as final products; indeed, the teachers and administrators at these schools often spoke about their schools as dynamic learning places engaged in a continual process of improving and evolving. Rather, these nine schools are merely examples from which we can all learn. What makes these schools unique and worthy of extensive study are the populations they serve, high-poverty and racially/ethnically diverse communities in both inner-city and rural areas, and their innovative approaches to create powerful learning communities.

Our goal is that this book will be a unique contribution to the mathematics education research literature because no books currently exist that focus exclusively on the characteristics that distinguish highly effective schools in mathematics that serve poor communities. The book includes both the theory and practice of creating highly effective schools in communities that have historically been underserved by public education institutions. Given the very real accountability measures of the No Child Left Behind legislation, we believe that this book is extremely timely for administrators, district mathematics coordinators, teachers, graduate students, and others who are searching for exemplary schools that serve high-poverty communities.

ORGANIZATION OF THE BOOK

In the first chapter, the goals of the research study are initially provided. Research literature is then presented to familiarize the reader to schooling in high-poverty communities and to the literature on school restructuring and effective teaching. A further review of research literature in mathematics education and diversity and equity in mathematics is provided as a means to introduce a conceptual framework for the study.

In chapter 2, each of the nine participating schools is introduced. The sources of the information presented in this chapter include an extensive survey completed by a school administrator and the applications that the schools submitted in the spring 2002 when the schools applied for possible inclusion in the High-Achieving Schools Initiative.

In chapters 3, 5, and 7, Richard Kitchen summarizes the primary research findings about the salient characteristics that distinguish the nine participating schools as high achievers in mathematics. Because the research findings from the classroom about teachers' conceptions and practices with regard to mathematics curriculum, instruction, and assessment also provided insights into the school-level characteristics that distinguished the schools as high achievers, these findings are also integrated throughout chapters 3, 5, and 7. All the research findings were grouped within three major themes that were predominant at all participating schools: (a) high expectations and sustained support for academic excellence, (b) challenging mathematical content and high-level mathematics instruction that focused on problem solving and sense making (as opposed to rote instruction), and (c) the importance of building relationships. In chapter 3, the initial theme about high expectations and sustained support for academic excellence is explored. Chapter 5 considers the second theme of challenging mathematical content and high-level mathematics instruction. Finally, chapter 7 explores the importance of relationship building.

As a means to provide a more in-depth perspective of the school-level characteristics and classroom-level (teachers' conceptions and practices) characteristics that distinguished the nine schools as highly effective, case studies are provided in chapters 4, 6, and 8. First, in chapter 4, Julie DePree presents a comprehensive case study on the mathematics teachers at YES College Preparatory School in Houston, Texas. This exemplary school follows chapter 3 precisely because it is a model of high expectations for student success and takes very seriously the work of sustaining support for the academic excellence of its students. In chapter 6, Julie DePree and Jonathan Brinkerhoff give a comprehensive case study of Emerald Middle School in El Cajon, California. This public middle school is highlighted immediately following chapter 5 because it exemplifies the second theme of challenging mathematical content and high-level mathematics instruction. In chapter 8, Sylvia Celedón-Pattichis provides a comprehensive case study of the Young Women's Leadership School in East Harlem, New York, that offers insight into a unique school, one of a handful of public, single-sex public schools in the United States. The case study on the Young Women's Leadership School is provided after chapter 7 because this school so powerfully modeled what it meant to value building relationships among teachers and students. In all three case study chapters, exemplary classroom lessons are included as a means to understand more intimately highly effective mathematics teachers' lessons. Lastly, in chapter 9, Richard Kitchen offers a final discussion and recommendations for further research.

ACKNOWLEDGMENTS

The study described in this book, the HP High-Achieving Schools (HAS) Initiative, was supported by a grant from the Hewlett-Packard Company. The authors would like to thank Hewlett-Packard Company for its commitment to education and the success of all students. HP established the HP High-Achieving Schools Grant Initiative, which gave the University of New Mexico (UNM) and the nine public, secondary-level schools that were studied the resources to conduct and disseminate this research, and to further integrate technology at the schools and at UNM.

The authors thank Jeff Hale, formerly from the College of Education Office of Development at UNM. Jeff was instrumental in developing a strong proposal that ultimately led to HP selecting the University of New Mexico to be its university collaborator on the HP HAS Initiative. We would also like to thank Sue Lloyd and Pauline Goolsby, who helped with gathering the classroom observation data and interviewing the teachers. We are eternally grateful to Sue Lloyd, who transcribed almost all of the interviews that were audiotaped. This was a monumental task, which Sue completed in a timely and competent manner.

We would like to thank Walter Secada and Okhee Lee of the University of Miami. Aspects of the research design were influenced by a study devised by Professors Secada and Lee for a study of Urban Systemic Initiative (USI) districts funded by the National Science Foundation. In addition, some of the research instruments used in the research project described herein were modified versions of instruments used for the USI project. We thank Francine Roy of the University of Rhode Island for her thoughtful suggestions and assistance with organizing parts of the research literature reviewed. We are also grateful to Jon Berman from Albuquerque, New Mexico, for his competent review of the statistical analysis completed during the study.

We would like to thank our editor, Naomi Silverman, and her assistant, Erica Kica, for their timely assistance and enthusiastic support for the duration of this project. We are also indebted to the following scholars who provided invaluable reviews of the book project: Jacqueline Leonard of Temple University, and Francine Cabral Roy of the University of Rhode Island. Finally, we would like to thank Walter Secada for his kind foreword. We are extremely honored to have Professor Secada, one of the preeminent mathematics educators of our time, introduce this book.

Lastly, and most importantly, we would like to thank the teachers who welcomed us into their classrooms to be observed and generously participated in numerous interviews. We are honored and privileged to try and represent the remarkable work that these individuals are doing for their students.

1

An Overview of Schooling
in High-Poverty Communities

Richard S. Kitchen

> Although performance in mathematics is generally low [in the United States], there are signs from national assessments that it has been improving over the past decade. In a number of schools and states, students' mathematical performance is among the best in the world. The evidence suggests, however, that many students are still not being given the educational opportunities they need to achieve at high levels.
>
> —*National Research Council* (2001a, p. 4)

In the fall 2005, Hurricane Katrina focused national attention on the poor of New Orleans. This city has a child poverty rate that, at 41%, is among the highest in the nation (Annie E. Casey Foundation, 2004). Hurricane Katrina exposed the hidden America and reflected badly on how one of the richest countries in the world treats its poor.[1] The flood waters also revealed how poverty disproportionately affects racial and ethnic minorities. As was clear from the media images of Katrina, African Americans were particularly hard-hit by the devastation in New Orleans, where they comprised 67.9% of the city's population (McKinnon, 2001). More generally, Hurricane Katrina made transparent injustices that continue to plague this nation's poor and people of color in education, health, employment opportunities, and housing (Wallis, 2005).

---

[1]At the end of the 20th century, the United States had the highest per capita national income in the world after Luxembourg (Bradbury & Jantti, 1999). Nevertheless, in 2003, more than one out of every six American children lived in poverty (Children's Defense Fund, 2004). Moreover, an American child is more likely to be living in poverty than a child living in any of the other 18 wealthy industrialized nations for which data exists.

In education, school districts are struggling to meet mandates required by the No Child Left Behind (NCLB) legislation. Proponents of the NCLB legislation hope to achieve educational equality through high-stakes testing. They argue that by holding low-performing schools (i.e., schools that predominantly serve low-income students and students of color) accountable through high-stakes testing, student learning and achievement will improve at these schools (U.S. Department of Education, 2002). Of course, little mention is made by NCLB promoters of the huge profits earned by the corporations that produce the test preparation materials and tests (Meyer, 2005). Needless to say, the accountability measures of NCLB have changed the educational landscape; states, entire districts, and schools have taken extraordinary actions with the sole purpose of improving test scores. In this high-stakes testing climate, educators are searching for the magic formula that leads to test success.

What is the relationship between testing and poverty in the United States? Analyses of mathematics scores for both Grades 4 and 8 on the 2003 National Assessment of Educational Progress (NAEP) found average scores were lower for students who qualified for free or reduced-price lunch in comparison to students who did not qualify (National Center for Education Statistics, 2005). Achievement gaps highlighted through analysis of NAEP scores and other standardized tests (e.g., comparing low-income and high-income students, Blacks and Whites, etc.) have put a national spotlight on the inequities that exist in schools across the United States.

Certainly, the achievement gaps that exist in the United States are a national disgrace; diminishing and, ultimately, eliminating such gaps should be a national priority. Interestingly, one of the primary reasons for the poor performance of students at schools that serve the poor has been the extraordinary focus at these schools on preparing students for success on "the test." Long before NCLB, research documented how urban and rural schools serving high-poverty communities in the United States generally focus instruction on the rote learning of low-level skills (see, e.g., Haberman, 1991; Knapp & Woolverton, 1995). Instead of stressing high-level thinking and the development of students' critical thinking skills, the focus has been on instruction of rote skills for success on standardized tests. This has led to low educational expectations, which has catastrophic consequences for students from these communities, many of whom are also people of color. To claim that wide-scale standardized testing has been disastrous for high-poverty communities is putting it mildly.

Class-based achievement disparities persist in the United States because opportunities to learn are based on where students attend school. Research has consistently demonstrated over the past several decades that students from more affluent neighborhoods have greater access to high-quality educational opportunities than students from low-income communities (Atweh, Bleicher, & Cooper, 1998; Oakes, 1990a; Tate, 1997).

Nationwide differences in educational opportunities are reflected in huge discrepancies in test performance between schools that serve low-income and middle/upper-middle-class neighborhoods and schools serving wealthier communities. These differences in educational opportunities can be attributed to the fact that schools serving the poor have historically had far fewer resources, both human and capital, than their middle-class counterparts (Kozol, 1967, 1991, 2005). Frankenstein (1995) directly connects social class inequities that exist in the United States and how they "perpetuate inequities in schools" (p. 165). Put in mathematical terms, a student's access to a high-quality education has historically been a function of the student's social class.

In this book, we celebrate nine exceptional public, secondary-level schools that have overcome injustices associated with poverty, while elucidating characteristics that distinguish the schools from their low-performing counterparts. These schools have much to teach us about creating powerful learning environments that empower all students to learn challenging mathematics. All of these schools demonstrated high achievement on standardized tests and on other indicators, while serving high-poverty communities (also referred to as low-income or poor communities throughout the book) that have historically been inadequately served by public schools. Research will be presented to elucidate how these schools surmounted historical, cultural, economic, and social class barriers to transform themselves into "highly effective" schools, particularly in mathematics.[2] Through stories told by teachers, students, and administrators, and analyses of classroom observations, light will be shed on the goals and policies at the schools, and in the mathematics classrooms, that shaped and sustained exceptional learning opportunities.

The following nine public, secondary-level schools participated in the study described herein and were among a very elite group of high-achieving schools nationally at the time of the study:

1. Emerald Middle School, El Cajon, California.
2. J. D. O'Bryant School of Mathematics and Science, Boston, Massachusetts.
3. KIPP Academy Bronx, South Bronx, New York.
4. KIPP Academy Houston, Houston, Texas.
5. Latta High School, Latta, South Carolina.
6. Rockcastle County Middle School, Rockcastle, Kentucky.
7. YES College Preparatory School, Houston, Texas.
8. The Young Women's Leadership School, East Harlem, New York.
9. Ysleta Middle School, El Paso, Texas.

---

[2]This work of authorship represents the sole efforts and opinions of the authors and does not represent Hewlett-Packard Company or its opinions in any manner.

These schools were selected from an applicant pool of more than 200 public, secondary-level schools that were applying for a grant from Hewlett-Packard (HP) Company. The goals of the HP grant included sponsoring research that would identify the factors that contribute to success, particularly in mathematics achievement, at schools serving low-income students; rewarding the selected high-achieving schools and contributing to their future success by giving them equipment and services to bring the benefits of technology to the students and teachers; and communicating findings to other educators serving low-income students. In chapter 2, additional information about the application process is described. Suffice it to say, however, when this study was initiated, the schools that participated formed a unique group of "highly effective" schools that served high-poverty communities throughout the United States.

The sections that follow review the research literature to familiarize the reader with schooling in high-poverty communities and with the literature on school restructuring and effective teaching. This is followed by an introduction to the goals of the research study described in this book and a further review of research literature that is pertinent for providing a conceptual framework to make sense of the study's goals.

POVERTY AND SCHOOLING IN POOR COMMUNITIES IN THE UNITED STATES

In 2003, 35.9 million Americans lived below the poverty line, which was about 12.5% of the total U.S. population (U.S. Census Bureau, 2003). Poverty levels in the United States vary depending on the location. For example, poverty rates are much higher in metropolitan, inner-city neighborhoods than in surrounding suburbs (Institute for Research on Poverty, 2005). Poverty in the central city of U.S. metropolises increased steadily from the 1960s until the early 1990s (Goldman & Blakely, 1992). In 1979, inner-city poverty averaged 15.7%. By 1993, an average of 21.5% of inner-city households were poor (Institute for Research on Poverty, 2005). In 2003, the average central city poverty rate was 17.5%, almost twice the 9.1% rate in the suburbs. According to Rury (1993), given the high concentration of students living in poverty in urban areas, it is little wonder that big-city schools exhibit low levels of achievement, high dropout rates, and a diversity of other problems. Poverty in rural areas is also not negligible. In 2003, 14.2% of people living in the countryside and small towns, outside metropolitan areas, lived in poverty (Institute for Research on Poverty, 2005).

Of course, it is important to recognize who is most adversely affected by poverty in the United States. Although poverty cuts across race and ethnicity, people of color have historically been impacted more by poverty than non-Hispanic Whites. Data from the U. S. Census Bureau (2001) reveals that poverty rates for Blacks and Latinos typically exceed the national average (National Poverty Center, 2005). In 2001, 22.7% of Blacks and 21.4% of Latinos lived in poverty, as compared to 11.7% of the total population. A particularly sinister side of poverty is that it tends to have an even greater impact on the most vulnerable in society, our children. In 2003, 34.1% of Black children, 29.7% of Latino children, 12.5% of Asian American children, and 9.8% of non-Hispanic White children were poor (Children's Defense Fund, 2004).

Given this data, it is not difficult to make the logical leap that poverty in the central cities of the United States disproportionately affects Blacks and Latinos more than Asian Americans and Whites. Moreover, in the rural south and southwest, high rates of poverty exist for African Americans and Latinos, respectively (Guzman, 2001; McKinnon, 2001).

Given the high rates of poverty in inner-city America and in the rural south and southwest that overly affect African Americans and Latinos, schools in these parts of the country face specific challenges not found in more affluent communities. For instance, at schools that serve poor communities, students often attend classes in dilapidated facilities, have higher percentages of novice teachers, teachers without a teaching credential, and teachers who are teaching subjects in which they have neither a major nor a minor (Ingersoll, 1999; National Research Council, NRC, 2001b). Additionally, schools that serve high-poverty communities are also characterized for their highly bureaucratic organizational structures (Kaestle, 1973); lack of support for change, particularly to personalize and individualize education (Louis & Miles, 1990); and standardized and uncoordinated instructional programs that encourage a custodial attitude toward children (Winfield & Manning, 1992). At high-poverty schools, the focus of the classroom tends to be on managing students and the transmission of low-level skills (Haberman, 1991; Knapp & Woolverton, 1995). Many scholars (see, e.g., Kozol, 1967, 1991, 2005) have highlighted similar characteristics of schools that serve diverse populations, that is, those serving a majority minority population. For example, these schools have fewer resources and poorly trained teachers in contrast to predominately White schools, particularly White suburban schools.

Policymakers, national organizations, politicians, and others have recognized the special needs of students who have been underrepresented in mathematics. In the *Principles and Standards for School Mathematics* (PSSM; NCTM, 2000), students who "live in poverty," non-native English speakers, students with disabilities, females, and "many non-White students" are identified "to be the victims of low expectations" (p. 13) in mathematics. Whereas strategies are identified in the PSSM document to support the mathematical learning of non-native English speakers, students with disabilities, and students with special interests or exceptional talent, no recommendations are provided about how to accommodate the unique needs of students who live in poverty. Thus, teachers are left to sort out for themselves how to mathematically empower poor students.

Perhaps part of the reason so little attention is given to the specific educational needs of the poor is that social class differences are taken as inevitable in a society that considers itself class-less. As Secada (1992) pointed out, there is little outrage in the United States about social class achievement differences in mathematics education:

> Social class differences are not as problematic in the literature as are racial, ethnic, or other disparities. For example, while the research literature and mathematics education reform documents (e.g., National Council of Teachers of Mathematics, 1989, 1991) at least mention women and minorities, issues of poverty and social class are absent from their discussions. Frankly, the literature does not bristle with the same sense of outrage that the poor do not do as well in mathematics as their middle-class peers as it does with similar findings along other groupings. ... It is as if social class differences were inevitable or that, if we find them, the results are somehow explained. (p. 640)

Few studies have been conducted to investigate how teaching mathematics at schools in high-poverty areas may differ from teaching in more affluent communities. However, at one study conducted at high-poverty schools in rural New Mexico (Kitchen, 2003), mathematics teachers described how an overwhelming workload, poorly defined work conditions, and resistance to change by administrators, colleagues, parents, students, and others hampered their efforts to implement standards-based curriculum and instruction in their classrooms. Teachers' work conditions at high-poverty schools may differ significantly from the work conditions of teachers at more affluent schools. For instance, teachers at high-poverty schools may be required to take on multiple duties outside of the classroom because of a lack of qualified personnel (Kitchen, 2003). Such extra duties place additional burdens on teachers that make it more difficult for them to plan and implement quality mathematics lessons. The intensification of teachers' work has become a distinguishing characteristic of U.S. schools, particularly at schools that serve the poor (Apple, 1990).

Realizing the vision of the mathematics education reform movement (see NCTM, 2000; NSF, 1996) at schools in high-poverty areas requires policymakers and reform advocates to identify barriers to reform in these communities and then to craft strategies to overcome these obstacles. For instance, the intensification of teachers' workloads points to the need for the mathematics education community to make improving teachers' work conditions a priority as a means to support teachers who implement reforms at schools serving high-poverty communities (Kitchen, 2003). In addition, the few teachers at rural schools that served high-poverty communities in New Mexico who attempted to implement standards-based mathematics curricula in their classrooms met great resistance from administrators, colleagues, and parents, as well as from their own students

(Kitchen, 2003). Resistance to changes in mathematics education is an ongoing challenge at all schools, not only at those serving the poor. Teachers will need ongoing support from policymakers, researchers, reform advocates, and others to deal with such resistance.

Ultimately, bringing to fruition the reform vision for those who have historically been excluded (e.g., the poor) requires mathematics educators to consider the larger sociopolitical context of education. This will necessitate a fundamental transformation of the mathematics education culture to think beyond changing classroom curricula and instruction to connect with broader movements that promote mathematical literacy and equity. One example of such a movement is Robert Moses's Algebra Project (Moses & Cobb, 2001) that has worked to "drive a broad math literacy effort [for] the Black and poor students and the communities [in] which they live, the usually excluded" (p. 19). Acknowledging that mathematics education is a political endeavor would compel the mathematics education community to recognize how the reform movement should be viewed as part of a larger social project for social and political justice.

SCHOOL RESTRUCTURING/REFORM, EFFECTIVE TEACHING, AND STUDENT RESISTANCE

The schools effects (e.g., Goodlad, 1983) and the effective schools literature (e.g., Edmonds, 1979; Purkey & Smith, 1983), dating back to the late 1970s and early 1980s, found that most schools provide very similar instructional settings. These studies also indicated that there is a set of school-level characteristics, such as orderliness and safety, that discriminates more from less effective schools. In an update of those studies, M. O. Martin, Mullis, Gregory, Hoyle, and Shen's (2000) analyses of the Third International Mathematics and Science Study (TIMSS) data found that opportunities provided to students at home, such as access to reading materials, were the most common characteristics that discriminated schools whose students achieved at a high level from those scoring at a low level on the TIMSS mathematics and science assessment. Interestingly, the nature of mathematics and science instruction that was provided to students was important, but it was not found to be as strong a characteristic in distinguishing high-performing from low-performing schools.

In contrast to the schools effects and effectiveness literatures, the effective teaching literature (Brophy & Good, 1986; for mathematics, see Good & Grouws, 1979; Good, Grouws, & Ebmeier, 1983) has consistently found that students taught by mathematics teachers whose practices structure the lesson, maintain a decent pacing, and focus on the development of its main points outperform students whose teachers do not engage in a similar set of practices. In research on school restructuring and its relationship to student performance on high-level tasks, Newman and Associates (1996; Newmann & Wehlage, 1995) found that students enrolled in classes where the curriculum content and instruction focused on depth over mere coverage, analytic reasoning over mere memorization, and the construction of value over doing tasks as ends in themselves, outperformed students whose classrooms lacked these instructional features. For more on these tasks and instruction, see Newmann, Secada, and Whelage (1995).

One possible explanation for these divergent research findings is that teachers whose practices are effective are distributed unevenly. That is, a school may have a highly effective teacher, but the rest of its teaching staff is more typical. In such a case, the impact of effective teaching lasts a year and is not cumulative. Support for this hypothesis can be found in V. E. Lee and Smith's (2001) study of secondary schools. Secondary schools where mathematics and science course offerings were predominantly academic, where teachers as a whole tended to report instruction that focused on depth, analytic (or higher order) thinking, and value were schools whose students achieved more highly, and began to close the social-class-based gap in achievement, as compared to schools where either of these instructional characteristics was missing (a focused curriculum and instruction that resembled what was reported by Newmann et al., 1996).

More than a few researchers have found that high-poverty schools have struggled to implement and benefit from school reform efforts meant to enhance an entire faculty's capacities to teach effectively (A. Jackson & Davis, 2000; Little & Dorph, 1998; Olsen, 1994). A. Jackson and Davis (2000) found that barriers to such change included a loss of passion and focus by the leaders of the reform efforts, high turnover of school leaders, and political issues within and beyond the campus. In a large survey study completed by J. Johnson, Duffett, Vine, and Moye (2003), district administrators and school principals complained that most of their time was devoted to district politics and bureaucracy. This made it difficult for them to support the implementation of standards-based reforms in schools.

Newmann, King, and Rigdon (1998) defined a school's organizational capacity to include: "Teachers' professional knowledge and skills, effective leadership, availability of technical and financial resources, and organizational autonomy to act according to demands of the local context" (p. 40). Newmann and his colleagues conjectured that the strength of a school's organizational capacity correlates with its capacity to deliver high-quality instruction, which in turn impacts student achievement.

Other researchers have also addressed how a school must possess a certain level of prerequisite organizational capacity if school reforms are to be successful (Darling-Hammond, 1993; O'Day, Goertz, & Floden, 1995). As previously discussed, it is not uncommon at high-poverty schools for teachers to be underqualified and teaching out of discipline, or for the schools to possess poor facilities and lack financial resources.

From this perspective, for mathematics education reforms to be supported at high-poverty schools, they must first possess a minimum threshold level of organizational capacity, including strong administrative support for change.

Another area that is often neglected in the mathematics education literature is student resistance to learning. For example, Willis (1981) wrote about working-class students' resistance to schooling that prepared them for the monotony of the production line. Through disruptive behavior, high truancy rates, disproportionate dropout rates, and passive disengagement (McKay & Wong, 1996; U.S. Department of Education, 1998), students manifest resistance. Studies have demonstrated how the sociocultural context of schools can contribute to student resistance in both intended and unintended ways (McNeil, 1986; Powell, Farrar, & Cohen, 1985; Wehlage, Rutter, Smith, Lesko, & Fernandez, 1989). Although student resistance to learning occurs across disciplines, Lubienski (2000) found that poor students, particularly poor female students, demonstrated greater resistance to a challenging, problem-solving approach to learning mathematics than their peers. Student resistance to teaching and learning is a challenge to the implementation of mathematics education reforms, yet it is rarely considered in the preparation of prospective mathematics teachers (Rodriguez & Kitchen, 2005).

Research in school restructuring and reform, effective teaching, and student resistance make obvious just some of the significant challenges faced by schools serving high-poverty communities. The schools presented in this book have all overcome such challenges. In order to better understand this accomplishment, research findings will be reported based on individual interviews conducted with teachers at each school, an interview conducted with the mathematics faculties at all nine schools, an interview conducted with a randomly selected group of students at each of the nine schools, an interview conducted with an administrator at each participating school, and a comprehensive survey completed by one of the nine schools' administrators (see appendix A for a detailed description of the research methodology). The goals of the research undertaken were twofold: (a) to investigate the salient characteristics that contributed to each school's academic success, particularly in mathematics; and (b) to explore participating teachers' beliefs and knowledge (conceptions) and practices with regard to mathematics curriculum, instruction, and assessment.

As part of this study, we also looked for the instructional features described by Newmann and his colleagues (1995, 1996) by using classroom observational scales (provided in appendix B) developed by Newmann et al. (1995). According to our hypothesis, we would be more likely to find instruction in the highly effective schools that matched these features than in typical schools.

From the initiation of this research project, a tacit belief of the UNM research team[3] was that high-achieving schools, commonly referred to as "highly effective schools" in the research literature, have or do something that distinguishes them from typical or low-achieving schools. The dual research goals reflected the research team's objective of investigating these distinguishing characteristics at both the school and classroom levels.

CONCEPTUAL FRAMEWORK

Two areas of the research literature provide background information relevant to the study's two research questions. First, a review of the research literature on teachers' conceptions and practices with regard to mathematics curriculum, instruction, and assessment is provided. This review is intended as a means to understand participating teachers' conceptions and practices described in the study. This is followed by a review of the research literature pertinent to promoting high academic achievement and effective learning environments for culturally and linguistically diverse students. Because all but two of the nine schools that participated in this study had majority populations of students of color, the literature review focuses on the notion of "teaching for diversity" (Rodriguez & Kitchen, 2005), that is, teachers of mathematics working effectively with ethnically and racially diverse student populations.

TEACHERS' CONCEPTIONS AND INSTRUCTIONAL PRACTICES IN MATHEMATICS

In the past several decades, notions about teachers' conceptions and practices of mathematics content (Ma, 1999), instruction (Ball & Cohen, 1999), and assessment (Kulm, 1994) have dramatically changed. Reforms in mathematics education stress the need for problem-solving approaches to promote students' reasoning and communication skills (National Council of Teachers of Mathematics, NCTM, 1989, 2000; National Science Foundation, 1996). The incongruity between this vision, referred to throughout this book as "standards-based" curriculum and instruction, and the conceptions and practices of many practicing teachers of mathematics (e.g., mathematics as a sequential, rule-based discipline in which memorizing facts and following procedures is highly valued) is well documented. In the following sections, literature on teachers' conceptions and practices of mathematics content, instruction, and assessment is reviewed.

---

[3]The UNM research team consisted of Jonathan Brinkerhoff, Sylvia Celedón-Pattichis, Julie DePree, Pauline Goolsby, Richard Kitchen, and Sue Lloyd. The UNM research team had disciplinary training in mathematics education and English to Speakers of Other Languages (ESOL).

Mathematics Content

A. Thompson (1992) identified three possible views of the nature of an academic discipline. The first, which he referred to as instrumentalist, views a discipline as an isolated body of discrete skills. The second, called Platonist, regards a discipline as a body of connected and unified knowledge, and the third, which A. Thompson called problem solving, deems a discipline as a process of inquiry that is continuously expanded by human creation. These three distinctions have also been cast as a duality between absolute (e.g., instrumentalist) and fallible (e.g., problem-solving) views that take shape in beliefs about mathematical knowledge and legitimate mathematical activities (Romberg, 1992; A. Thompson, 1992).

Teachers who embrace an instrumentalist view often present mathematics as a sequence of fixed skills or concepts (Brown, Collins, & Duguid, 1989). Mastery of prerequisite skills is deemed necessary for subsequent learning. This view assumes that "rules are the basic building block of all mathematical knowledge and all mathematical behavior is rule governed" (A. Thompson, 1992, p. 136). The teacher's role is to demonstrate procedures, and the students' role is to practice them.

In contrast, teachers who adhere to a Platonist view of mathematics emphasize the logic connecting concepts. These relationships are assumed to be fixed and often require explanations by the teacher. Although emphasis on developing students' reasoning is highlighted as part of standards-based curriculum and instruction, the Platonist view models a top-down approach in which instruction begins with the knowledge of the expert, rather than that of the learner (Hiebert & Carpenter, 1992).

Alternatively, teachers who adopt a problem-solving, or inquiry, view of mathematics see their role as posing questions and challenging students to think and reason. Instruction is student-centered, beginning with an understanding of the learner. Teaching from the problem-solving perspective also values interpreting the learner's mathematical ideas and misconceptions (Ball & Cohen, 1999). Students are encouraged to actively engage in mathematics learning by constructing their own meanings of the content. This view is compatible with the goals of standards-based curriculum and instruction, as well as with a constructivist view of learning.

Mathematics Instruction

A. Thompson (1992) showed a consistent relationship between teachers' beliefs and instructional practices in mathematics. Teachers who embrace the instrumentalist view teach in a manner that contrasts most distinctly with the ideals of mathematics reform and teaching mathematics for understanding (Hiebert & Carpenter, 1992; Lampert & Ball, 1999; NCTM, 1989, 1991, 2000; NSF, 1996; Romberg, 1992; Schifter & Fosnot, 1993). Mathematics is characterized as static and predetermined in the instrumentalist philosophy, but those who adhere to this view emphasize mathematical facts and pursue a drill-and-practice approach to teaching (Schifter & Fosnot, 1993). Such mathematics instruction is characterized by a focus on teaching mathematical procedures and a preoccupation with students memorizing facts.

An example of teachers who embrace the Platonist view of mathematics is provided in Ma's book, *Knowing and Teaching Elementary Mathematics* (1999). Ma provides numerous examples in her book of how Chinese teachers promote conceptual understanding of mathematics, although their instruction is characterized as top-down and authoritarian. A theme throughout Ma's book is that teachers must possess a deep and broad knowledge of mathematics to make conceptual connections between mathematical ideas. According to Ma, "limited subject matter knowledge restricts a teacher's capacity to promote conceptual learning among students" (p. 36). Ma's research demonstrates that a strong understanding of mathematics is necessary to teach in a manner consistent with either the Platonist or problem-solving view.

Teachers whose primary objective is to advance mathematical problem solving demonstrate the style of teaching and learning that reformers advocate—"doing of mathematics" (Davis & Hersh, 1980; Ernest, 1991; Lakatos, 1976; Tymoczko, 1986). From this view, "learning is primarily a process of concept construction and active interpretation—as opposed to the absorption and accumulation of received items of information" (Schifter & Fosnot, 1993, p. 8). Pedagogy inspired by this view engages students in posing and solving problems, making and proving conjectures, exploring puzzles, sharing and debating ideas, and contemplating the beauty of ideas in an academic discipline. Students engaged in such active mathematical learning develop "mathematical power" (NCTM, 1989, 1991; Parker, 1993).

In classrooms in which the focus is on mathematical exploration, less emphasis is placed on showing students how to solve problems. Instead, students are given opportunities to devise computational procedures that directly model the actions and relations of a word problem (Carpenter, Fennema, & Franke, 1996; Fennema & Franke, 1992; Resnick, 1992). Students who are provided support to develop their own mathematical strategies to solve computational problems perform significantly better than those who are regularly taught to memorize algorithms to solve similar problems (Kamii, Lewis, & Livingston, 1993).

To transform the culture of mathematics education to more highly value the Platonist or problem-solving views, mathematics educators must address teachers' deeply held conceptions in which the instrumentalist view is predominant (Richardson & Placier, 2001; Schifter & Fosnot, 1993; C. L. Thompson & Zeuli, 1999; Wilson & Berne, 1999). Not surprisingly, teachers who may want to promote these perspectives might not be able to do so because of a lack of conceptual mathematical knowledge (Ma, 1999). For instance, teachers may introduce manipulatives during mathematics instruction, but teachers with limited mathematical knowledge often use manipulatives only to illustrate procedural-level knowledge (e.g., that 1 ten equals 10 ones). Thus, although teachers may want to adopt a Platonist or a problem-solving view, their lack of conceptual knowledge of mathematics inhibits their capacity to align their teaching with either of these philosophical views.

Mathematics Assessment

Assessments relying primarily on paper-and-pencil basic skills computations and the evaluation of recall of isolated facts align with the instrumentalist view of mathematics. Alternative assessments that do not simply assess facts and skills in isolation, but that also require students to apply their knowledge in real-life contexts, align more with the Platonist or problem-solving view. According to Kulm (1994):

> Alternative assessment approaches that include open-ended questions, presentation of solutions in both written and oral form, and other performances send very different messages to students about what is important in mathematics learning. The thinking and reasoning approaches and the way mathematical thoughts are presented can receive high marks even if the answer may not be complete or correct. The shift from an emphasis on producing correct answers to the expectation that students think and communicate is a major one for many students and teachers. (p. 6)

This shift in emphasis corresponds to the philosophical change necessary for an instrumentalist to adopt either a Platonist or problem-solving view. Such a shift is supported by researchers who advocate revising assessment practices to bring about changes in instruction based on how children learn (O'Day & Smith, 1993). Another goal of alternative assessment is to promote higher order thinking among students (Kulm, 1991). In addition, alternative assessment approaches and the use of multiple assessment formats require students to communicate their thinking and elicit a range of student responses (Wiggins, 1993).

TEACHING FOR DIVERSITY

It is clear from research that teachers' beliefs and knowledge (conceptions) about mathematics and teaching are strongly linked to classroom practice and student learning in interesting and complex ways (National Research Council, 2001b). What remains underrepresented in the literature on teachers' conceptions and practices is research examining the role of teachers' views with respect to race, culture, and language on the development of their mathematics instruction (Rodriguez & Kitchen, 2005). As a result, the existing knowledge base for promoting academic achievement within a culturally and linguistically diverse student population is limited and fragmented, in part because disciplinary knowledge and student diversity have traditionally constituted separate research agendas (O. Lee, 1999). The literature in multicultural education emphasizes issues of cultural and linguistic diversity and equity, but gives little consideration to the specific demands of the different academic disciplines (Banks, 1993; Ladson-Billings, 1994; O. Lee, 1999). Realizing the vision of current reform efforts aimed at "academic achievement for all students" requires integrating disciplinary knowledge with knowledge of student diversity (McLaughlin, Shepard, & O'Day, 1995).

Currently, teachers are being asked to teach in ways they may never have experienced, while supporting the learning of all students. In essence, teachers of mathematics have two enormous challenges: to implement standards-based curriculum and instruction and to promote high academic achievement and learning for all students as opposed to just the very best students. Implementing challenging, standards-based curriculum and instruction that is accessible for all students requires moving mathematics education away from functioning to legitimate a select few deemed as the mathematically talented through selecting, sorting, and certifying students (Apple, 1985). Mathematics education has played an especially pivotal role in sorting people in schools (e.g., through ability grouping) by denying them access to challenging coursework (D'Ambrosio, 1983; Gerdes, 1988). This is particularly true for students of color and students from high-poverty communities. In the following three sections, additional research will be explored to further understand the complexities involved in transforming mathematics education to truly support the learning of all students.

Standards-Based Curriculum and Instruction and Equity

Although little research in mathematics education centralizes notions of equity, many studies have been conducted in mathematics classrooms in districts and schools that serve sizable populations of students of color and poor students (Roy & Kitchen, 2005). Much of this recent research considers whether standards-based curricula or instruction is effective with all students, particularly with students of color and those living in poverty. The results are promising. For example, J. Riordan and Noyce (2001) report that Massachusetts' students who learned from *Everyday Mathematics* and *The Connected Mathematics Project* achieved higher standardized tests scores in Grades 4 and 8, respectively, than those using traditional curricula. These results held for all student subgroups, including African American, Hispanic, poor, and low ability. Schoenfeld (2002) found similar results in a review of studies of standards-based curricula in the United States: "In those cases where authors conducted studies to address the issue, the data suggest that the new curricula, although hardly eradicating performance differences between Whites and underrepresented or linguistic minorities, do tend to mitigate those differences" (p. 19).

These studies are also supported by Boaler's (2002a, 2002b) investigation that compared two high schools in England serving students from high-poverty backgrounds. One school relied heavily on ability grouping and teachers mostly utilized traditional teaching methods. A second school used heterogeneous groupings and teachers emphasized open-ended mathematics projects. Despite finding equal levels of student engagement, students from the project-based school outperformed students receiving traditional instruction and tended to possess more positive attitudes toward mathematics (Boaler, 2002a, 2002b).

These studies demonstrate that students from marginalized groups can engage and learn from standards-based mathematics curriculum and instructional practices (Roy & Kitchen, 2005). These curricula and instructional practices show some promise for mitigating existing achievement gaps and contrast sharply with rote instructional practices, promoted by those holding instrumentalist perspectives that historically have dominated the teaching of students of color and poor students (Haberman, 1991; Knapp & Woolverton, 1995; Oakes, 1990a). However, as discussed in the next section, the implementation of standards-based instruction may not be equitably distributed.

Centralizing Equity in Standards-Based Curriculum and Instruction

Mathematics education reform documents promote the need for teachers to be prepared to teach in culturally sensitive and responsive ways (NCTM, 1989, 2000; NSF, 1996). An explicit goal of the reform movement is to improve access to challenging mathematics content and instruction to students who have historically been denied such access. For practicing P–12 teachers of mathematics, the goal of this work is to promote achievement among culturally, linguistically, and socioeconomically diverse students.

Many scholars have identified the establishment of high academic expectations as a primary means to improve the teaching of students who have historically been underserved by schooling (Ladson-Billings, 1994; Lipman, 1998; Sheets, 1995; Zeichner, 1996). Although high expectations are necessary for effective teaching and learning, they are far from the norm—especially with minorities and students from high-poverty communities. It is well-documented that many teachers hold lower expectations for students of color and the poor than they do for White, middle-class students (Ferguson, 1998; Grant, 1989; Knapp & Woolverton, 1995; Winfield, 1986; Zeichner, 1996). Knapp and Woolverton (1995) found that teachers of high-poverty students focus more on classroom control than on fostering students' high-level thinking and, in the process, teach their students that little is expected from them except compliance to a rigid classroom environment. This "pedagogy of poverty" (Haberman, 1991) is particularly prevalent in urban and/or high-poverty schools.

Research has also consistently demonstrated that teachers are less likely to deliver high-level content and standards-based mathematics instruction to students of color and those from poverty (Atweh et al., 1998; T. M. Johnson, 1994; Szatjn, 2003). For instance, T. M. Johnson (1994) studied calculator usage in two 12th-grade mathematics classes taught by the same teacher. The classes differed in level; students in one class were studying pre-calculus and many were college bound, whereas students in the other class studied technical mathematics and most were technical school bound. Johnson's study documented that the teacher did not use graphing calculators in technical mathematics as he did in pre-calculus. Furthermore, the students in technical mathematics did not study high-level function topics found in pre-calculus. Johnson explained that this disparity of instruction was a function of the teacher's perceptions of the technical college expectations, the school district, technical mathematics students, and their parents.

Roy (2002) similarly studied two high school mathematics teachers working in a working-class community. The teachers, who were instructing students placed in low-ability classes in a highly tracked system, began the academic year implementing some practices aligned with standards-based instruction. As the year progressed, students resisted these strategies and both teachers responded by reverting to more procedural and rote ways of teaching mathematics. Lubienski (2000) also struggled to engage poor female students in problem solving and mathematical inquiry using a standards-based curriculum. Her lack of success in engaging some students in standards-based instruction led her to question the appropriateness of such practices with students from high-poverty backgrounds, even though she valued the problem-solving approach afforded by the curriculum.

These studies show that implementing standards-based mathematics instruction is influenced by student demographics such as race, ethnicity, gender, or class. More specifically, teachers may not institute standards-based mathematics instruction with students from diverse racial, ethnic, linguistic, or socioeconomic backgrounds because of their inability to engage them or because of preexisting (low) expectations (Roy & Kitchen, 2005). This insight complements more mainstream studies of mathematics teacher change (e.g., Fennema & Nelson, 1997), which cite the need to change teachers' conceptions of how children learn or increase teachers' pedagogical content knowledge (e.g., Carpenter, Fennema, & Franke, 1996; Schifter & Fosnot, 1993) but ignore the influence of students and their socio-demographic backgrounds on teachers' decision making.

Sociocultural Context, Equity,
and Problematizing Mathematical Content

Much has been written about the need to implement standards-based curriculum and instruction in mathematics classrooms, but little emphasis has been placed in the mathematics education community on preparing teachers of mathematics to implicitly and explicitly incorporate socially, culturally, and politically equitable instructional strategies in their classrooms, that is, "teach for diversity" (Rodriguez & Kitchen, 2005). For progressive educators, a potential role of the mathematics education reform movement is to promote more egalitarian and democratic societies in which all students have the opportunity to develop mathematical literacy (Kitchen, 2005). Because prospective mathematics teachers primarily experience mathematics as devoid of social, cultural, and political considerations (see Hersh, 1979; Lakatos, 1976, for perspectives on how mathematics is in fact value-laden and fallible), it is highly unlikely that multiculturalism and issues related to equity are modeled or discussed in their mathematics coursework. However, many teachers of mathematics work in schools with racially and ethnically heterogeneous student populations that are located in high-poverty communities. These schools have unique sets of problems that distinguish them from their more affluent, suburban counterparts (Ingersoll, 1999; National Research Council, 2001b).

Although reform documents have little to say about the mathematical preparation of students from high-poverty communities, there is a developing body of inquiry into the social, cultural, and political context of the teaching and learning of mathematics (see Atweh, Forgasz, & Nebres, 2001; Gutstein, 2003; Kitchen, 2005; D. B. Martin, 2000; Roy & Rousseau, 2005; Secada, 1995; Tate, 1995). Research and teaching in mathematics education that takes seriously the social, cultural, and political context of learning examines how tracking affects learning, whether diverse students have equitable opportunities to learn challenging mathematics, and how race and class play out in the classroom.

Other studies show how teachers use mathematics as a means to build critical consciousness in students (Frankenstein, 1995; Gutstein, 2003; Kitchen & Lear, 2000; Ladson-Billings, 1995; Tate, 1995). Some scholars have employed a multidisciplinary framework to investigate the interaction between mathematics and students' linguistic and cultural practices (see Adler, 1995, 1998; Brenner, 1998; Civil & Andrade, 2002; Gutiérrez, 2002; Khisty, 1997; Lipka, 1994; Moschkovich, 1999). Still other scholars have applied a social reconstructionist orientation in their teaching to prepare prospective teachers to incorporate equitable and socially just instructional strategies in their classrooms (see Dunn, 2005; Leonard & Dantley, 2005).

In addition to working to provide greater access to all students—particularly poor and diverse students—to opportunities to learn mathematics, what mathematics students actually study needs to be problematized. For example, some scholars believe that teachers can evaluate the values implicit in various mathematical contexts by selecting mathematical problems and topics that motivate critical reflection among students (Abraham & Bibby, 1988; Mellin-Olsen, 1987). Kitchen and Lear (2000) created a series of lessons that inspired a group of young Mexican American girls to reconsider their views about body image after measuring Barbie dolls. If teachers are going to take equity seriously, then they need to engage in and create lessons that incorporate students' socioeconomic and political realities.

Critical mathematics educators (see, e.g., Ernest, 1991; Frankenstein, 1987; Gutstein, 2003; Skovsmose, 1994) posit that mathematics can promote mathematical literacy as a means to achieve social, political, and economic justice for all. From this point of view, the study of mathematics should promote a critical perspective among students of the discipline. Such an approach also challenges students to question the use of mathematics as a mainstream tool of destruction and violence.

For instance, during the invasion of Iraq, the U.S. military engaged in a "shock and awe" campaign to frighten the Iraqi people into subservience. Mathematics was an essential component of this campaign, because the weapons used were designed with sophisticated mathematical ideas. In the United States, for the most part, little consideration was given to the moral and ethical implications of this campaign (Kitchen, 2003). Viewed from a critical perspective, the role of mathematics in this immoral campaign must be acknowledged and made problematic. The uses of mathematics are not always benign and students should learn to question mathematics from a moral and ethical perspective as they learn about its many powerful applications.

The significance of these studies is that they redefine traditional notions of "effective pedagogy" (Roy & Kitchen, 2005). Effective teaching is viewed as more than engaging students in constructivist-based mathematics activities. In particular, effective teaching of diverse and poor students supports cultural identity, empowerment, and social justice. These ideals are beyond that of the equity vision put forth in the PSSM document (NCTM, 2000), which largely supports learning dominant, albeit reform-based, mathematics (Gutiérrez, 2002; Rodriguez & Kitchen, 2005; Roy & Kitchen, 2005) with little attention to issues of culture and social criticism.

Finally, the challenges inherent in preparing prospective teachers to work in high-poverty, diverse schools need to be acknowledged (Jordan, 1995; Scott, 1995; Tatum, 1992). Moreover, coursework in multicultural teacher education has been relatively ineffective at challenging prospective teachers' beliefs about racism, White privilege (Sleeter, 1994), and their belief that through hard work, it is possible to be successful in school and in mathematics. Given the ever-increasing volume of research on teachers' resistance to teaching for diversity, it is clear that this work is complex and teachers will need ongoing professional development to build capacity to teach for diversity (Jordan, 1995; Scott, 1995; Tatum, 1992; Rodriguez & Kitchen, 2005).

In this study, we investigated teachers' knowledge and beliefs (conceptions) about mathematics and the teaching of mathematics. We hypothesized that teachers in highly effective schools would articulate well-developed, coherent views of their conceptions and practices and those views would be consistent with theoretical perspectives found in various reform documents. We also hypothesized that the teachers would articulate ideas associated with the construct of teaching for diversity as integral to their conceptions and practices.

2

Introduction to the Participating Highly Effective Schools

Richard S. Kitchen

This chapter introduces the nine public, secondary-level schools (Grades 5–12) that participated in the study. The primary sources for this chapter are a survey completed by a school administrator and the two applications submitted by the schools in the spring 2002 as part of the Hewlett-Packard High-Achieving Schools Grant Initiative. Achievement data for all the participating schools, also provided in the schools' applications, is included in appendix D. First, there is a summary of the process for selecting schools to participate in this study.

HP HIGH-ACHIEVING SCHOOLS GRANT INITIATIVE

In January 2002, faculty from the College of Education at the University of New Mexico (UNM), in collaboration with the College of Education Office of Development, submitted an application to the Hewlett-Packard Company (HP) as part of a national competition to work with them in the HP High-Achieving Schools Initiative (HAS). Immediately after the UNM was selected to work with HP in the HP HAS project, a Request for Proposals was distributed by HP, soliciting proposals from public, secondary-level schools (Grades 6–12) to apply to be part of the HAS project. Those schools selected to participate in the project would receive an HP Wireless Mobile Classroom that included a mobile cart of 30 laptop computers, an all-in-one printer/copier/scanner/fax, a wireless access point, digital camera and accessories, instructional delivery software, a cash award of $7,500, support with integrating technology in the classroom provided by UNM, opportunities to network with teachers from other high-achieving schools, and participation in the research study described in this book.

To be considered, schools needed to demonstrate (a) a free or reduced lunch rate of 50% or higher; (b) sustained exemplary academic achievement, particularly in mathematics, over a minimum of from 3 to 5 consecutive years across a variety of indicators; and (c) technical infrastructure at the school to support the maintenance and use of the HP Wireless Mobile Classroom. Typically, schools submitted testing data to demonstrate exemplary academic achievement. Schools were also encouraged to describe unique characteristics of their schools, such as high parental involvement, a cohesive faculty, low student-to-teacher ratio, implementation of standards-based curriculum, and use of alternative assessments.

In the spring 2002, 231 schools from across 32 states, the District of Columbia, and Puerto Rico submitted applications in the first round of the HP High-Achieving Schools Grant competition. Each application was reviewed by a minimum of three members of the research team and rated across multiple criteria. The 88 schools that met the basic requirements of the competition (free/reduced lunch rate of 50% or higher, sustained exemplary academic achievement, and availability of technical infrastructure) were then invited to respond to a second Request for Proposals from HP in late spring 2002. In their applications, schools were asked to provide specific information, such as the percentage of students who attended the school by race/ethnicity; mathematics teachers' average number of years of teaching experience; the school's admissions process and requirements (if any); and the number of teachers who taught at least one mathematics course and, of those, how many had a minor or degree in mathematics. Schools were required to analyze their past 3 years of testing data, comparing their results with other schools in their district and state and in the nation to demonstrate how their students were high achieving relative to others. In a separate section, they also could list additional characteristics that contributed to high achievement at their respective schools, particularly in mathematics, such as administrative support, parental involvement, standards-based curriculum and instruction, cohesive faculty, student-to-teacher ratio, use of alternative assessments, high percentage of students matriculating in advanced placement (AP) courses, extra academic support available to students, and anything else that the schools identified as important to their academic success. Schools also needed to describe their progress and vision toward integrating technology and learning. Lastly, two mathematics teachers and one administrator were required to submit letters of support for the project.

In May 2002, applications of the 88 finalists were reviewed by both the UNM research team and a team assembled by Hewlett-Packard. An identical weighted rubric was used by both the HP and UNM teams to rate schools across multiple indicators, principally with respect to each school's ability to demonstrate sustained exemplary academic achievement, particularly in mathematics, over a minimum of 3 to 5 consecutive years. We also rated schools with respect to (listed in descending order of importance): (a) percentage of students who qualified for free/reduced-price lunch; (b) vision and administrative support for integrating technology and learning; (c) additional evidence of school programs and/or characteristics that promoted high achievement (e.g., high percentage of students enrolled in AP courses); and (d) commitment of administration and teachers to the project. There was high agreement among the ratings completed by the UNM and HP teams and nine public, secondary-level schools were selected to participate in the High-Achieving Schools Initiative. They were notified of their inclusion in the project in June 2002. These nine unique "highly effective" schools that serve high-poverty communities will now be introduced.

EMERALD MIDDLE SCHOOL, EL CAJON, CALIFORNIA

Emerald Middle School is a Title I, public, urban, neighborhood school and technology magnet for the Cajon Valley Union School District in eastern San Diego County. The percentage of students who qualified for free or reduced-price lunch at Emerald in the 2001–2002 academic year was 78%.

During this school year, Emerald Middle School demonstrated sustained multiyear improvement in Stanford Achievement Test (SAT-9) scores with an ethnically and socioeconomically diverse student population (see appendix D for achievement data provided by all participating schools). As part of the application, an administrator wrote that the school's academic goals were that "all students were expected to master the state curriculum standards for their grade and subjects. [In addition, students were expected to] improve 6 points on the state assessment tests. The school's mission is to work together with our community to help students achieve to their fullest potential" (administrator survey, 8/02). In support of this mission, an afterschool tutoring program existed at Emerald Middle School to support student learning.

To enroll at Emerald, students were required to show proof of California immunizations, demonstrate legal residency within school boundaries, or document an approved intradistrict transfer. The school's student population at the time the study was undertaken was 44% White, 31% Latino (primarily of Mexican descent), 10% Chaldean/Arabic, 10% African American, 2% Asian, 1% Pacific Islander, 1% American Indian/Alaskan Native, and 1% Filipino. Emerald students spoke 16 different first languages during the 2001–2002 school year.

At this time, Emerald Middle School employed 45 regular and special education teachers with an average of 9 years teaching experience. Of these teachers, 16 taught at least one section of mathematics (8 general education, 8 special education). During that same period, none of these teachers held a degree or minor in mathematics. However, of these teachers, 3 held supplemental mathematics credentials in California in addition to their other teaching credentials. An administrator indicated that many professional development opportunities existed for the mathematics faculty, such as "district sponsored workshops and summer academies, K–12 Math Alliance, summer workshops, and University workshops on mathematics" (administrator survey, 8/02). Also, 50% of the teachers at Emerald Middle School engaged in 10 hours or more of staff development focusing on mathematics curriculum and/or instruction. Emerald Middle School's web page is located at http://www.cajon.k12.ca.us/schools/ems/home.htm

JOHN D. O'BRYANT SCHOOL OF MATHEMATICS AND SCIENCE, BOSTON, MASSACHUSETTS

The J. D. O'Bryant School of Mathematics and Science is one of three urban examination schools in the Boston Public School District. The school serves students in Grades 7–12 who are selected based on results of an entrance exam. The mission of the J. D. O'Bryant School of Mathematics and Science is to enable every student to become prepared for college, advanced learning, and a highly skilled career. This school is also a School-to-Career School and, as such, provides a rigorous academic program using specialized curricula to help students make connections between school activities and skills and competencies required in the career marketplace of the 21st century. Eleventh and 12th graders have the option of enrolling in one of three career pathways: informational technology, biotechnology, and engineering. Some of the specialized courses offered within these pathways include pre-calculus for engineering using CAD, honors physics for engineering, English 11 and 12 incorporating *Microsoft* MOUS, AP calculus, Cisco networking, and web design.

In 2001–2002, 1,260 students attended the J. D. O'Bryant School of Mathematics and Science, of which 62% received free or reduced-price lunch. The school's student population was 48% African American, 28% Asian, 15% Latino, and 9% White. During the academic year, 68 teachers taught at the school with an average of 22 years of teaching experience. Fourteen of these teachers were responsible for teaching at least one mathematics course, and 12 of these teachers held a major or minor degree in mathematics. The web page of the J. D. O'Bryant School of Mathematics and Science is located at http://boston.k12.ma.us/obryant

KIPP ACADEMY, BRONX, NEW YORK

KIPP Academy Bronx is a college preparatory, public charter middle school (Grades 5–8) located in the South Bronx that admitted students through a lottery. KIPP is an acronym for the Knowledge Is Power Program. The school's mission is to equip students with the academic, intellectual, and character skills necessary for success in high school, college, and the competitive world beyond. An administrator wrote that the academic goals at the school are that "90% of all students will attain mastery in all subjects. 90% of all students will attend college or a 4 year university" (administrator survey, 8/02).

During the 2001–2002 school year, all (100%) of the students at KIPP Academy Bronx represented ethnic or racial minorities; 53% of the school's population was Latino, 46% was African American, and the remaining 1% was Other. Of the 240 students enrolled in Grades 5 through 8, 93% qualified for free and reduced-price lunch.

During this school year, there were 19 full-time teachers at KIPP Academy Bronx. On average, the teachers had 10 years of teaching experience. Five of these teachers taught at least one mathematics class; none held a degree in mathematics. Additional information can be found about KIPP Academy Bronx and other KIPP Academies throughout the United States at http://www.kippny.org

KIPP ACADEMY, HOUSTON, TEXAS

KIPP Academy Houston is a public charter school serving predominantly low-income, minority students in Grades 5 through 9. Like KIPP Academy Bronx, its mission is to prepare students with the academic, intellectual, and character skills necessary for success in high school, college, and the competitive world beyond.

KIPP Academy Houston has been recognized by the Texas Education Agency as an Exemplary School every year since its inception in 1995. Approximately one half of the students that enter KIPP Academy Houston in fifth grade pass the state's basic skills test, the Texas Assessment of Academic Skills (TAAS). But, after a year at KIPP Academy Houston, nearly 100% of students pass the test. The schoolwide TAAS passing rate for the 2001–2002 school year was 99.8%.

As an open-enrollment charter school, KIPP Academy Houston students are chosen by lottery. Like all KIPP Academies throughout the United States, all enrolling students, their parents, and teachers are required to sign a Commitment to Excellence Form that specifies attendance from 7:30 a.m. to 5:00 p.m. Monday through Friday, 4 hours most Saturdays, and 1 month each summer. The agreement obligates parents to reinforce the students' commitment, ensure attendance, and make sure the homework (2–3 hours per day) is completed each evening.

In 2001–2002, approximately 75% of KIPP Academy Houston's 330 students were Latino, 20% were African American, 3% were White, and 2% were Asian American. During this period, 90% of these students qualified for the federal free or reduced-fee breakfast and lunch program. The Hispanic population at KIPP Academy Houston was predominately from Mexico and El Salvador.

The school had 17 full-time teachers on staff, averaging just over 5 years of teaching experience. Four of these teachers taught mathematics. These teachers had a combined 18 years experience teaching mathematics, but none held a major or minor in mathematics. KIPP Academy Houston has a web page located at http://www.kipphouston.org

LATTA HIGH SCHOOL, LATTA, SOUTH CAROLINA

Latta High School is a rural, public secondary school serving Grades 9–12 in Dillon County, South Carolina. The sole admission requirement to attend Latta High School is that students must live within the district boundaries. In April 2002, Latta High School served 404 students, of which 58% received free or reduced-price lunch. In Latta's application, it was noted that "We believe this number [58% who receive free or reduced lunch] is somewhat misleading given the number of applications that are never returned and the fact that our elementary and middle schools both have 74% and 70% participating in the Free/Reduced Lunch program, respectively." The student population at Latta High School at the time this study was initiated was 53% White, 46% African American, and 1% Latino. The staff at Latta in the 2001–2002 academic year consisted of 29 teachers with an average teaching experience of 8 years. Of those 29 teachers, 5 taught at least one mathematics course and all 5 of these teachers had an undergraduate degree in mathematics. The mathematics teachers were paid a stipend to meet during the summer to "align textbooks and standards and to create curriculum guides" (administrator survey, 8/02).

Latta High School demonstrated a high level of student achievement during the years immediately prior to applying to participate in this project. Among the academic goals at Latta High, an administrator wrote, "We want to average 1000 or better on the SAT, scores above 90% passing on each area of the South Carolina Exit Exam, 100% passing on all areas of the Exit Exam by the time seniors are ready to graduate, a 60% passing rate on the AP exam" (administrator survey, 8/02). The following was included in the Latta High School application: "Even though we are proud of our achievements, we recognize that we must continue to develop and evolve as a school to meet our students' needs." The Latta High School web page can be found at http://www.dillon3.k12.sc.us/lhs/index.htm

ROCKCASTLE COUNTY MIDDLE SCHOOL, ROCKCASTLE, KENTUCKY

Rockcastle County Middle School is located in a rural, southeastern Kentucky county that has a population of about 16,000 people and includes some of the poorest and most isolated areas in Kentucky. The Rockcastle County school district consists of the middle school, a high school, and three elementary schools. Rockcastle County Middle School is a public school with no admissions process or requirements other than residence in the county. Among the academic goals at the school, as described by an administrator, included: "To write and implement a curriculum that meets or exceeds state and national standards and prepares students to be successful and productive members of society. [In addition, to] Write and consolidate plans for school improvement and track our academic goals" (administrator survey, 8/02).

In 2001–2002, Rockcastle County Middle School had a student population of 715 students. At that time, most of the student population at Rockcastle County Middle School was White (98%), whereas less than 1% were African American and less than 1% were Latino. Of the 715 students, 67% qualified for free or reduced-price lunch. During this time, the school had a staff of 52 certified teachers with an average of 9.94 years teaching experience. Six of these teachers were responsible for teaching at least one mathematics course. Of the 6 mathematics teachers, 4 held Kentucky certification for teaching mathematics in the middle school, which requires 24 hours of undergraduate credit in mathematics classes. Six special education teachers also collaborated with the 6 mathematics teachers in at least one mathematics course. None of the 6 special education teachers held a degree in mathematics. The mathematics teachers at Rockcastle regularly engaged in staff development, at which time they examine "test results, determine area of weakness and adjust curriculum and teaching styles appropriately. Staff gives feedback on type of PD desired" (administrator survey, 8/02). The school district's Web site is located at http://www.rockcastle.k12.ky.us

YES COLLEGE PREPARATORY SCHOOL, HOUSTON, TEXAS

YES College Preparatory School is an open enrollment, state charter school for Grades 6–12. Situated on 25 acres in southeast Houston, YES is the only state-chartered secondary school in Houston that provides inner-city students with a rigorous college preparatory curriculum. In 2001–2002, YES College Preparatory School drew its 450 students from over 40 zip codes throughout the city of Houston. YES provided free transportation for any student that required bussing. YES's mission is to provide at-risk students with a rigorous college-preparatory curriculum that prepares them for matriculation and success in college. In order to graduate from the school, students must first be admitted to a 4-year college.

YES students spent 65% more time in school than the national average for public school students. All YES students in Grades 7–10 were required to participate in any one of a variety of extracurricular activities from 4 p.m. to 5 p.m. Students also had opportunities every year to visit college campuses, major U.S. cities, and national parks. To fund these trips and the many other activities offered at the school, the development officer "must raise $700,000 a

year" (administrator survey, 8/02). The school had developed multiple partnerships with corporations, foundations, and individuals to provide some of
the needed financial resources. Expectations of the staff were extensive. For
instance, each teacher was given a school-sponsored cell phone to be accessible to their students after hours. In 2001 and in 2002, every YES senior graduated and matriculated to a 4-year college. Most significantly, over 85% of
these graduating seniors were the first in their family to attend college.

At this time, there were approximately 300 students enrolled in the middle school and 150 students enrolled in the high school. YES plans to reach
its target population of 600 students by 2005. In the 2001–2002 school year,
88% of the student body was Latino, 8% was African American, and the remaining 4% was Asian and White. The majority of the Latino student population came from Mexico and Central America. In addition, approximately
85% of YES students were economically disadvantaged and received either
free or reduced-price breakfast and lunch.

By law, YES College Preparatory School could not deny anyone acceptance to the school as long as space was available. In 2001–2002, there were
approximately 300 students on the school's waiting list. Families who wished
for their children to attend YES submitted their child's name to an open lottery. The first 120 names drawn became the following year's sixth-grade
class. Openings in other grade levels were also selected via lottery. YES teachers conducted home visits with each student selected in the lottery, during
which the teacher, parents, and student all signed a Commitment to Excellence contract. This contract stipulated that the family would do "whatever it
takes" to pursue the goal of college matriculation and success.

During this academic year, YES employed 31 teachers who averaged 5
years of teaching experience. Six teachers were responsible for teaching at
least one mathematics course. Of these 6 teachers, 2 held a bachelor's degree in mathematics, 2 held a minor in mathematics, and 1 held a master's
degree in mathematics. One teacher also held a bachelor's degree in business administration and was a certified public accountant. Also, 100% of the
teachers at YES College Preparatory School spent at least 10 hours in staff
development focusing on mathematics curriculum and instruction. According to an administrator at the school: "Teachers design their own [pro-
fessional development goals] to meet their goals for instruction and goals
for curriculum implementation. NCTM conference is required for all math
staff" (administrator survey, 8/02). YES College Preparatory's Web site is
located at http://www.yesprep.org

THE YOUNG WOMEN'S LEADERSHIP SCHOOL, EAST HARLEM, NEW YORK

The Young Women's Leadership School of East Harlem (TYWLS) was
founded in 1996 in collaboration with the New York City Board of Education, Ann and Andrew Tisch, and the Center for Educational Innovation—

Public Education Association. The school was a collaboration between Community District 4 (East Harlem) and the Manhattan High School Superintendency, and served girls from across New York City. In 2001–2002, TYWLS was the only all-girls public school in New York State. At that time, there were only 10 other public, single-sex schools in the country. The school is housed in the 7th to 11th floors of an office building in East Harlem. During that period, the school's mission was to prepare young women for college and to increase their opportunities for careers in mathematics, science, and technology. An administrator wrote that the academic goal at the school was to "help our girls excel in mathematics and science using small classroom sizes so that girls' experiences are personalized" (administrator survey, 8/02).

Enrollment at TYWLS in 2001–2002 was 360 students in Grades 7 through 12. It is a college preparatory school and 100% of the first (2001) and second (2002) graduating classes were accepted to college. Ninety percent of graduates are the first in their families to attend college. At the time of this study, the student body was 63% Latina (primarily Dominican and Puerto Rican, but also Mexican, Honduran, and Guatemalan) and 37% African American. The Young Women's Leadership School also enrolled a small number of Muslim students and students from East Africa. At this time, over 84% of students qualified for free or reduced-price lunch.

There were 27 teachers employed, with an average of 4.3 years teaching experience. Five of these teachers were responsible for teaching at least one mathematics course, and all of them held a major or minor in mathematics or were certified in Math 7–12. In 2001–2002, 100% of the teachers at the school participated in 10 or more hours of professional development focusing on mathematics curriculum and instruction.

The admissions policy required applicants to submit essays, assessment tests, report cards, citywide exam scores, and to participate in an interview. Applicants from District 4 (East Harlem) were given priority for admission. In addition, TYWLS eighth graders were given priority consideration for acceptance into the TYWLS high school. In 2001–2002, approximately 25% of admits came from outside the district. Also, there were approximately 1,250 applications for three ninth-grade openings. The school selected average to above average students who were committed to the school's mission and who school personnel believed would benefit from the extra support and resources provided by the school. Through the school's advisory system, each girl admitted received individual advisement. TYWLS was also committed to reduced class size (18–22), and inquiry-based cooperative and applied learning. The school's web page is located at http://www.tywls.org

YSLETA MIDDLE SCHOOL, EL PASO, TEXAS

Ysleta Middle School (YMS), which opened in 1976, is located in the lower valley urban community of El Paso County, Texas, approximately one-half mile from the U.S.–Mexico border. The school is located within a federally designated "Empowerment Zone," characterized as the sixth poorest area in the country in average per capita income, with 27% of its population living below the poverty level. Ysleta Middle School is a public school in the Ysleta Independent School District serving approximately 400 seventh- and eighth-grade students during the 2001–2002 school year who are predominately Latino of Mexican heritage. That year, 93% of the students qualified for free or reduced-price lunch, and 33% were English-language learners. The school had an open enrollment policy and, although most of the students lived near the school, a few students chose to come from other areas of the city to attend the school.

Most of the students who attended Ysleta Middle School resided in federally supported public housing communities or in small homes, apartments, or trailers. Many came from single-parent families, and a high proportion were "latchkey kids." The school had an extended-day program so that students did not have to spend their afternoons unsupervised. Despite these adversities, Ysleta Middle School forged strong partnerships with the families they served, which helped to raise expectations, performance standards, and achievement. An administrator at the school described the school's community outreach policies and practices in the following manner: "We encourage parents to participate on a daily basis. We have parent-led literacy circles, parenting programs, and parent academies monthly" (administrator survey, 8/02). According to the Academic Excellence Indicator System results (posted on the Texas Education Agency Web site at http://www.tea.state.tx.us), 88% of the students who attended Ysleta Middle School in 2001–2002 passed the state assessment test.

That school year, Ysleta Middle School employed 33 full-time teachers with an average of 11.9 years of teaching experience. Of these individuals, 4 were responsible for teaching mathematics, 3 of whom held a teaching endorsement in mathematics. The other teacher's endorsement was in special education.

SUMMARY

All of the highly effective schools selected to participate in this study are public, secondary-level schools in the United States. Table 2.1 lists which schools are middle, high, charter, and noncharter schools. The J. D. O'Bryant School of Mathematics and Science, YES College Preparatory School, and the Young Women's Leadership School (TYWLS) included both a middle school and a high school.

TABLE 2.1

Schools by Type (Middle School, High School, Charter, and Non-Charter)

Middle Schools	High Schools	Charter Schools	Non-charter Schools
Emerald MS	J. D. O'Bryant	KIPP Bronx	Emerald MS
J. D. O'Bryant	Latta HS	YES College Prep	J. D. O'Bryant
KIPP Bronx	YES College Prep		Latta HS
Rockcastle MS	TYWLS	_	Rockcastle MS
YES College Prep		_	TYWLS
TYWLS	_	_	Ysleta MS
Ysleta MS			

3

High Expectations and Sustained Support for Academic Excellence

Richard S. Kitchen

> No good tree bears bad fruit, nor does a bad tree bear good fruit. Each tree is recognized by its own fruit. People do not pick figs from thornbushes, or grapes from briers.
>
> —*Luke* (6:43–44)

This chapter is devoted to the first of the three major themes discovered at all nine participating schools. Namely, the schools placed great value on high expectations and sustained support for academic excellence. In our analysis of the research data, the three themes cut across the two research questions concerned with discovering the salient characteristics that distinguished the schools in mathematics and exploring teachers' conceptions and practices about mathematics curriculum, instruction, and assessment. The following are five areas found at the participating schools that are related to the major theme of high expectations and sustained support for academic excellence: teaching and learning as priorities, supplemental support for student learning, review of basic skills, making teaching resources available, and regular teacher access to professional development opportunities.

The research findings summarized in this chapter and the chapters to follow derive from the school- and classroom-level data collected through interviews conducted with teachers, administrators, and students; classroom observations that were carried out; classroom artifacts that were collected (e.g., teachers' lesson plans); and an administrator survey instrument. The primary research findings presented are the dominant themes that emerged from the analyses of these data sources. However, to be included, a theme had to be confirmed by two or more teachers in interviews conducted at more than 50% of the participating schools (i.e., two or more teachers from five or more schools).

TEACHING AND LEARNING ARE PRIORITIES TO SUPPORT HIGH ACADEMIC EXPECTATIONS

A strong finding across the nine participating schools was that teaching and learning were made the priority. Many of the schools had slogans that were displayed throughout their buildings, such as "Whatever It Takes," "Failure Is Not an Option," and "No Excuses." A teacher at KIPP Academy in Houston summarizes in the following passage what was found at all nine schools. Students were expected to succeed academically and the schools created an environment in which teaching and learning were the priorities:

> Yeah, you will not fail, you must learn. If there's a problem, you will find a solution. … And as a result of that, like the learning environment is so positive. … They come ready to learn. Like my class wasn't like you saw anything extraordinary. But the kids are generally quiet and on-task and focused on the lesson. … Usually everyone has the homework done, it's not even an issue. (KIPPH4, KIPP Houston, 10/02)

Another teacher at KIPP Academy Houston described how the mathematics faculty wanted to do much more than teach to minimal academic standards, and how they wanted their students to be prepared to academically "completely dominate" after leaving KIPP for high school:

> To me, it's not about [just meeting] the minimum standards. We're proud! Like okay, if these extremely wealthy kids have all these advantages coming from wealthy, educated families; if they can do it, why can't ours? There's a lot of reasons why. The environment they're in and all this other stuff. So, we have to overcome that. For me, I don't want my kids just to be above average. I want them to be not only the best, but dominating at the school that they go to [next]. … So, I want them to go in there and completely dominate. (KIPPH3, KIPP Houston, 10/02)

Undoubtedly, creating a demanding academic program that could endure was the top priority at all of the participating schools. It was quite common for students to return to the theme of how their teachers just simply would not allow them to fail. A student discussed this: "I think what makes it special to me is the teachers and the curriculum that you have. The teachers will not go home if you don't understand." It was not uncommon for the schools to also provide incentives for students to make academic achievement their most important priority. The following student talked about the rewards provided at her school for academic achievement:

I would say it [academics] was the most important thing. Athletics yes is important, but the classroom is the most important. If you do not get your work done then you don't play athletics and they give us incentives. If you do well in the classroom then you get free passes to games and other school activities so they definitely encourage academics. They push us, they make sure we get everything done; they try and cover all the standards. If you're goofing off, you don't get your work done, you don't have time, free time to sit around and dream—you're always working.

Teachers were adamant that administrators supported them as professionals, trusted them, and made it possible for them to focus on teaching. At the highly effective schools where they worked, a deal had been struck: The schools created a safe and positive place to engage in the study of challenging mathematical content and students were expected to respond by taking their learning seriously. A teacher at Latta High School summarized the high expectations at the school and the high level of teacher preparation: "When we walk in we've got a game plan and we follow it and we work at it and we work at it and work at it." A teacher at Emerald Middle School added the following: "My expectation is that they're going to learn." This teacher also added that students at the school tended to respond to such expectations.

It was clearly unacceptable for students at the participating schools to be disruptive and interrupt the learning process. Significant time was devoted to indoctrinating students to extensive behavioral norms. Students took these expectations seriously; it was not uncommon to observe students who had disrupted the learning process being rebuked by their peers at any of the nine participating schools. At Ysleta Middle School, the behavioral expectations were identical in all classrooms and teachers collaborated to uniformly uphold and enforce these expectations. At YES College Preparatory School and the two KIPP Academies, students attended summer school where they were introduced to the schools' high behavioral expectations.

Teachers came to work to practice and improve on their craft—teaching! This translated into an enthusiasm for teaching and learning that permeated the classrooms at the highly effective schools. A student at the Young Women's Leadership School (TYWLS) in East Harlem confirmed the enthusiasm of her teachers: "When they teach you, they teach you with so much enthusiasm it makes you want to learn more than they're teaching you."

At the time this study was undertaken, the Young Women's Leadership School was one of a handful of all-female, public schools in the United States. The school served students in Grades 7–12. Students at TYWLS completed 4 years of high school mathematics, although most high schools in New York City required that students complete only 3 years of mathematics. A goal at TYWLS was that every graduate of the school would attend a

4-year college. A teacher at the school told us that to accomplish this goal, "We push the kids a lot farther than the state mandates in order to get them into four-year colleges."

Teachers were treated like professionals and they responded in kind. Administrators at the schools articulated that a primary goal of theirs was to free teachers from bureaucratic responsibilities, such as non-stop paperwork, allowing them to focus on teaching. As one teacher at Latta High School in rural South Carolina put it, "We [the teachers] don't know what's going on, that may be a blessing that may be why the kids are doing so well. Because we are in the classroom teaching. ... I mean, I feel like I go in my little hole [my classroom] and that's where I stay." Teachers at Latta High School credited the administration at the school for allowing the faculty to focus on teaching: "I would say I think we can teach. I think the administration handles a lot of the problems and that we are free to go into the classroom and teach. I think we work hard at our jobs. ... We know these kids. They call us on the telephone if they need help."

Teachers at the Young Women's Leadership School praised their principal for trusting them as professionals to promote high academic expectations:

> It's true, she does leave us alone. Part of it is she can't understand the math, they're going to teach her about math; this guy coming in from City College. So a lot of it is that she trusts us. There is a lot of trust in it and she knows that we do well and she comes in and really enjoys what she sees about what's going on. (unknown teacher, TYWLS, 10/02)

A teacher at Rockcastle County Middle School in rural Kentucky talked about the administrative support in the building and how this contributed to high academic expectations for students:

> We have good administrative support in our building of what we're doing in the math department, we have had good support from our central office, our site-based management has supported whatever we needed to do as a math faculty. I think that all of that contributes to what we can achieve. I think that a lot of it too, the idea that if you can believe in yourself, you can do it. I think our students realize that we expect the best from them and that helps them in all subjects to do their best. (Rock3, Rockcastle County MS, 10/02)

A teacher at YES College Preparatory School said that the teachers could hold high expectations for students because they also worked hard and were excellent role models in this way:

> I feel like if you're trying to get at what makes this school excellent, it's a huge part of it [referring to how dedicated teachers were at school]. Our kids work so hard. I think in large part because they see models of hard work everyday. We can ask a ton of them, because we're doing hard

work as well. It would be one thing if we were getting out at 3:00, going home, not doing any work, and asking them to do the same thing. I think it's the reason that they're pushing themselves, because they see us pushing ourselves. (YES4, YES College Prep, 10/02)

The views expressed by students demonstrated that they valued the high expectations at their schools and they tended to work hard to meet these expectations. Many students indicated that they decided to attend their school because of its focus on academics. The following student at YES College Preparatory School described how much more challenging his high-achieving school was compared to his former school:

Well, I came here because I wanted like a challenge, because at most public schools, it's easy to pass and stuff and it's really easy. If you put an effort in it, you make like a B and if you put a lot you make an A. But here, you have to put a lot of effort in it in order to get a B or something. It's more challenging than most public schools.

At Emerald Middle School located in El Cajon, a suburb of San Diego, literacy had been a huge focus. The faculty spoke about how through working with their administration, mathematics had also become a priority subject area at Emerald:

I think it started with a sub-group [to give academic support to low performing students] and then it grew and it grew and grew and then the administration encouraged us. Because we were starting to fall into the trap of well, in our opinion the trap, literacy, literacy, literacy. ... Once it [mathematics] became a priority for school and staff, it all started falling into place. And then everyone used their creative ideas and juices and scores started going up. You know when scores go up and then the kids feel better, then the teachers feel better, and so it's like it just keeps going. (Emer4, Emerald MS, 10/02)

At KIPP Academy in the Bronx, the school culture demanded high expectations for student learning that were supported and reinforced by the school's administration:

It's nice, honestly. ... I feel like we have freedom, trust [from the administration], if I'm doing something. There is never any question about why I'm doing it. If I need materials, calculators, we've got them. You know the pressure is on performing. The administration gives us everything we need and is behind us because our focus is on enhancing the learning, make it fun and exciting, and it's very supportive. If there's anything, I think the administration pushed us to keep our standards up. The same way you guys ask us questions, I think their questions [the administrations] would be more pointed. "Are you keeping up to your standards?" It's the culture of the school for teachers that de-

mands that you live up to certain expectations, the quality of your lessons. I think the administration reinforces that, they're going to back
us. (unknown teacher, KIPP Bronx, 11/02)

A teacher at KIPP Academy Bronx noted that despite students coming to
school with weak backgrounds in mathematics, by the end of 8th grade,
they were expected to be very well prepared in the subject:

I expect that in high school, half of them go on to a 10th grade math
course instead of standard math. I expect the other half to be in an
honors 9th grade math or in a situation where they could get A's in
their math class. I expect them to get A's in high school in math and
that math is their stronger subject. That's what I expect! (KIPPB4, KIPP
Bronx, 3/03)

A student at KIPP Academy Bronx confirmed the quality of her classes
and described the attention she received at the school: "The biggest thing
for me is that they give you a lot of attention and they're available to help
you a lot, the classes are better than any public school that you can go to in
the Bronx, and I don't think anyone can say enough."

SUPPLEMENTAL SUPPORT IS PROVIDED
FOR STUDENT LEARNING

Many students came to the participating schools ill-prepared in mathematics. This was particularly the case at the participating middle schools. In
response, schools provided students with extensive remediation, in addition to the instruction they received in class. Administrators, teachers, and
students at the participating schools discussed how academic failure was
simply not an option because students had multiple avenues to obtain the
academic assistance needed to achieve at high levels. Frequently during interviews, faculty spoke about either tutoring students on their own time or
after school in a tutorial program.

At YES College Preparatory School and the KIPP Academies, teachers
were provided with a cell phone by the school so that students could call
them at night for academic assistance. Students at these schools also spoke
about how they sometimes called their teachers to just talk and how their
teachers helped them through personal difficulties, showing how much
they cared for them. At YES College Preparatory School, the mathematics
faculty was often available to assist students and students were expected to
call the teachers at night if they needed assistance:

I think in the middle school, the things we do are lots of tutoring, and
lots of phone calls home and we're just all available all of the time.
There's always room for every kid to go in at lunch, study hall, after

school they can stay. We have a late bus that runs at 6:30 if they want to stay. They just know we're here until all hours. They [the students] can be here until all hours and they know to get help. If not, they call friends at home, they call us, there's just lots of help available. (YES1, YES College Prep, 10/02)

It was common for students to have extended periods of time to study mathematics, particularly at the participating middle schools. At some of the middle schools, extended or "blocked" mathematics classes were part of the schedule so that students could engage in the study of mathematics for an hour and a half. For instance, at the Young Women's Leadership School, the middle school students had two long ("blocked") mathematics classes each week to supplement mathematics instruction. Because students often came to the schools ill-prepared in mathematics, the schools provided students with supplementary instructional support, not only for remediation purposes, but also to challenge them with cognitively demanding content (e.g., all of the participating middle schools made the completion of the equivalent of Algebra I a goal for the majority of its students by the completion of eighth grade). A teacher at YES College Preparatory School explained the benefits of having additional instructional time with students:

> I think one of the reasons that happened, if you think of the kids that we're serving, a lot of them, they come in 6th grade and they don't come in with the skills in order to take pre-algebra. But we try to do as much to prepare them, and slowly, even in the 7th grade and 8th grade. But a lot of it is just like reinforcement. They get double the time in math. It's better for them. ... Getting the kids in middle school with an hour and a half, it allows you to go over homework; it allows you to do a mini-lesson in-between maybe even your lesson. It allows you an opportunity to do, have a longer period for the lesson. It allows you the opportunity to give the class a chance to understand, give them class work. So having a double period is really awesome. I don't know if we could potentially teach as much as we do in a 45-minute block. I think that would be a disservice to them. (YES3, YES College Prep, 10/02)

A third teacher at YES College Preparatory School agreed with these comments and said more about the faculty's work to both remediate while preparing students to pass an end-of-algebra I examination when they finished 8th grade:

> As a 6th grade teacher, they come in on a 3rd grade reading level and on a 4.5 math level. So yeah, they come in stronger [in math], but I think it's non-negotiable. We need the double block in middle school or we just couldn't come close to getting them ready to take calculus in 12th grade or ready to pass the end of the course algebra exam at the end of the 8th

grade. It would be impossible with 45-minute blocks in middle school; on average we have two grade levels to catch up on in 3 years or a grade level and half. They come in [at a] 4.5 [grade-level], we need to get them up to 8th grade. (YES2, YES College Prep, 10/02)

At the KIPP Academy Bronx, a teacher talked about how they tried to continually do a better job and listed some of the strategies used to provide extra instructional support for their students:

There are a few students who are struggling, honestly speaking that is one of the things that we do very well is math instruction [is help these students]. What we're doing well is that we're always looking at what we can be doing better, not that we actually do anything better, but we keep looking at what we could be doing better. We never overlook the fact that kids might be struggling. Not that we always know something for those kids, but we're always aware of the fact that kids might struggle, which is at least something, we're trying. … We know what to do with the kids who are struggling. … We do a lot of pull out [of elective classes], a lot of peer stuff, a lot of one-on-one, and math club [for students who needed remediation]. (unknown teacher, KIPP Bronx, 11/02)

A student at KIPP Academy Bronx noticed the strong commitment that teachers made to students:

Yeah, we get all the help we need, definitely. The teachers are here for you around the clock, even if you need a ride home or anything. I mean like really anything, they'll give it to you, it doesn't matter. They'll go across the world if you need it. They'll really do a lot of things for you, like they'll leave their cell phone on all night even if you have to call them just to say hello, or just to see how you're doing. Or they might call you to say hello and it's like, it's a real close relationship. It's like what you'd have with your parents.

Similar to YES College Prep and KIPP Academy Bronx, students at KIPP Academy Houston were also required to attend classes on some Saturdays during the academic year to receive additional instructional time. In addition, at all three of these schools, students were expected to call teachers if they needed assistance in the evening. Teachers were provided a cell phone by the school so that they could tutor at night. A teacher at KIPP Academy Houston described the high level of commitment expected of teachers to support students' learning:

We do have cell phones [that the school pays for]. I know that if I give a homework assignment that they don't understand, that I'm going to hear from them. I may get 40 phone calls that night. Which means two things. For one, it makes me want to teach the lesson better. On the other hand, it may make you want to give easier homework, but really it makes me want to teach the lesson better. It also makes me know where my students are missing it. So, when I come in the next day, I know what to go over. ... But having that level of commitment from our teachers. ... It's almost fatalistic; all of us are going to learn. (KIPPH4, KIPP Houston, 10/02)

Another teacher at KIPP Academy Houston discussed how it was insulting to special education students if their teachers did not hold them to high academic expectations. The teachers at KIPP also provided the necessary academic support so that students could meet high standards:

Like yesterday, that little boy in special ed. We could say, "you know what, you're right. It's too hard for you. You go ahead and just do half [of the work]." If we say that, "that's your ability, doing half," we're insulting you. We're saying we don't believe that. You can do it. It may take you longer, it may take a little more effort, but you're going to do it, because you can and you will. That boy that was talking to me later, the LEP kid. Last year, he was almost in tears, saying "nobody can help me at home, so that's why I didn't do my homework" and "English is hard for me." So, [my response was] "Where's your homework? You didn't call me. You didn't come to tutoring; you didn't do any of that. I don't want to hear it, we set you up for success, you're choosing not to do it. Yeah, your parents don't support you. So what? A lot of other people won't support [you either]. So, your parents could care less if you come here. Do you want to hear my story? Have a seat." (KIPPH3, KIPP Houston, 10/02)

Ysleta Middle School served a community near the Mexican border that, at the time that study was undertaken, was the sixth poorest in the nation. Given this reality and the fact that most of their students' parents had not attended college, the mathematics faculty at the school made the preparation of their students for admittance into a 4-year college one of their principal goals. Mathematics was as important as reading at Ysleta Middle School. Teachers who taught the "KIVA" class at the school taught mathematics, even if they were not mathematics teachers. In the Ysleta School District, students learned a very specific problem-solving procedure that they were expected to follow and demonstrate in a step-by-step manner on the criteria-referenced examination used in Texas. The students became quite accustomed to what they must demonstrate on the test when solving problems:

At the beginning, every teacher has a poster in their room whether they're math or not because if they teach KIVA, they're going to be teaching the math, so they have that poster. I know I've given my kids a copy of that, so they're pretty familiar with it. Since they've been using it [the problem-solving procedure] in their elementary school, it's more the student coming in from either Juarez or other states that haven't seen it, haven't used it, and they get used to it. But here they're pretty familiar with the way it's done. (Yslt3, Ysleta MS, 9/02)

The mathematics teachers met with the teachers who taught KIVA to demonstrate the mathematics that they wanted them to teach. It was quite common that during KIVA, teachers focused on helping students learn the problem-solving procedure that students were expected to be able to demonstrate on Texas' criteria-referenced examination:

> On Friday, that's what our job is going to be is to go over that plan [the problem-solving steps] with the teachers. Because this is what we kind of want to look for in the KIVA classes and this is what we're doing in our classes, we want you to do the same thing [all teachers teach the problem-solving procedure]. A lot of them, the veterans kind of already know the system, but this is for the new teachers and some that need to have that reiteration. (Yslt2, Ysleta MS)

Another distinctive feature of Ysleta Middle School was the extensive community outreach programs. For instance, English-language courses were available for parents at the school in the evening, parents supported academic programs in multiple ways, and the school sponsored and supported community empowerment activities. Parents were regularly called on to deal with any behavioral issues, as well as to provide academic support at home:

> I think the parents' involvement here has really helped. ... It has helped, we don't have a problem with discipline. If a student needs more help, the parent tries and helps. They're here for them. Occasionally, they are just way out, but we don't have a lot of problems. (Yslt3, Ysleta MS, 9/02)

Specific courses were designed at Emerald Middle School in El Cajon, California, for students who needed remediation in mathematics. Some students enrolled in a remediation class instead of taking electives. In addition, the administration at Emerald Middle School paid the mathematics faculty to tutor students in need of additional academic assistance:

> We haven't talked about all the additional supplementary types of things that we do offer, or we try to offer. Again that changes over time. Like right now we have a student support class. So, if we have students who are really, really low in math or in English, chances are that they would be referred to that class and that's in lieu of their electives so that's a help class. The newcomer's class is another place depending, if they're brand new to the country but their math skills are high, they may ... go back for other things.

The other kind of thing that we've tried at Emerald was what we call a power class. That was a mathematics class, in addition to their regular class, that would give them that remedial time to learn things that are required. The other thing, and none of us mentioned it, every single teacher here has run some kind of an after school program. Whether it's office hours where the kids can come in for one-on-one, whether it be a tutorial. ... There's financial money that's made available to the teachers, and every teacher here has worked one day, two days, three days, what have you, per week to provide that additional instruction and make it available. (Emer4, Emerald MS, 10/02)

Teachers at J. D. O'Bryant School of Mathematics and Science in Boston indicated that students from a nearby university consistently came to provide tutoring for their students. As part of this effort, the university students pinpointed areas in which students needed additional instruction to be successful on the state test:

There are also the guys that come from Northeastern. I know every Thursday or whenever they're here, they're in the library tutoring. I know a number of my students go to the library and get tutored. ... They're graduate students at Northeastern. I think they're doing some type of research or something, but I kind of forgot. (OBry6, J. D. O'Bryant SMS, 11/02)

The Northeastern students are coming from a couple of sources. ... I don't know how it's organized, but they gave last year's MCAS to the students and that flagged certain students having difficulty. (unknown teacher, J. D. O'Bryant SMS, 11/02)

A teacher at Rockcastle County Middle School, a school that served high-poverty communities in rural Appalachia, discussed the extensive outreach and support service programs available at the school:

The 21st Century Community learning center has been a three-year federal grant that we have used for community education for adults and for student enrichment. We have a math/science part, a language arts group, and social studies for two hours after school for two days for kids. Plus, we have adult classes for French, community classes for gymnastics for any age children, computer classes, technology, quilting; to make a difference in the [poverty] factors that we've talked about at the home. We have a GEAR UP grant. The main focus [of the GEAR UP grant] is to get kids thinking about college in 6th grade and planning for college and different experiences outside of Rockcastle County to broaden their lives, to take them to college campuses. And they sponsor a lot of parent activities as well, and parent groups where they do parent education in those classes, for lack of a better term. (Rock7, Rockcastle County MS, 10/02)

Rockcastle County Middle School, Ysleta Middle School, and J. D. O'Bryant School of Mathematics and Science had GEAR UP programs.[4] This program provided the means for students to visit university campuses, an important goal at these schools given that many of the parents of the students attending these schools had not attended college. This was one of the goals of the GEAR UP programs at both Rockcastle County Middle School and Ysleta Middle School. At J. D. O'Bryant School of Mathematics and Science in Boston, teachers often referred students to the GEAR UP program for afterschool tutorial sessions:

> Kids who are performing low—all of us at the 7th–10th grade level have suggested to them to sign up for GEAR UP, which is the after school tutoring program that several of us folks are involved in. That's one of the things that I can think of to help a small group of kids that are struggling. ... Some kids will come to you when they're having trouble. ... On your own time [the teachers will tutor], everybody does their own little thing. (OBry2, J. D. O'Bryant SMS, 11/02)

Students at some of the participating schools discussed how they were not automatically promoted to the next grade level. They had to meet certain criteria to be promoted. The following student discussed the promotion policy at her school and how students could receive the assistance they needed to move on to the next grade level:

> Academics in our school are really important, grades matter on whether you're promoted or not. If you have bad grades, you're obviously not going to get promoted. They also have different after-school activities to help you with your grades, and if you still don't do good but just have enough to pass, you still have summer school.

REVIEW OF BASIC SKILLS

There was a focus on instruction of the mathematics basics at the schools (i.e., addition, subtraction, multiplication, and division of single-digit numbers), particularly at the participating middle schools. At Emerald Middle School, students regularly reviewed skills they had learned in the past:

> *Excel Math* is a published math program K–6, the publisher is actually in San Diego, but it's used in many places. It's very prescribed, self-directed, covers all of what I would call the basic skills. The nice thing about it, in every single lesson they review, the repetitive review is probably the best I've ever seen, and it covers every single strand. So,

---

[4]The GEAR UP program is "designed to increase the number of low-income students who are prepared to enter and succeed in postsecondary education" (http://www.ed.gov/programs/gearup/index.html).

every single day that they have an Excel lesson, they're exposed to geometry, addition, multiplication, measurement, nothing is left untouched. … I think that math is the kind of thing where you have to touch all the areas as often as possible. (Emer4, Emerald MS, 10/02)

Another teacher at Emerald Middle School talked about the need to review the basics because students did not study mathematics everyday in the feeder elementary schools:

We look at areas where kids score fairly low and make sure that we really concentrate more on those particular areas. … The newspaper publishes all the school results. … They published the percentage of students at each grade level at each school who were at or above the 50th percentile. I checked the 5th grade percentages of those at the 50th percentile and higher from our feeder schools, the three elementary schools that we get most of our students from. The 6th grade percentages were considerably higher than the 5th grade. We [also] bring up the number of students that are 50th percentile and higher by, it was like 12–15 percent. You know we always wonder, what are they doing in elementary school? We found, and it was verified that in the elementary school, they're not teaching math everyday. Maybe four days a week, 40 minutes a day, and when they get to us we get them for 54 minutes a day, five days a week. So the concentration, and we also spend time on things like multiplication drill, so many kids come not knowing their multiplication facts. We make that 10% of their grade and we drill every week and do a timed test every week. Most of them know their times tables really well by the time they leave 6th grade [though] they can't subtract! (Emer2, Emerald MS, 2/03)

A teacher at Ysleta Middle School identified teaching computation as a primary teaching goal because students came to the school unprepared to compute:

Computation is one. Why? Simply because our kids are really lacking in it. … We have transfer students from other districts that aren't using Sharon Wells [a state-aligned curriculum program]. They can't compute their numbers, they can't add, subtract, multiple, or divide whole numbers, fractions, decimals, integers. (Yslt4, Ysleta MS, 10/02)

A teacher at the J. D. O'Bryant School of Mathematics and Science alluded to how high school students also needed remediation work in mathematics:

I'm trying to strengthen the foundations that they have for math. For the younger kids it's adding and subtracting negatives and positives, something they've had in math for a couple of years, but some of the kids are still weak in it. So we're trying to bring in extra stuff to

strengthen that up. With the older kids same types of things, but expo-
nents maybe that they've seen before and should kind of have but
struggle with some times. Factoring and stuff like that. (OBry1, J. D.
O'Bryant SMS, 11/02)

At KIPP Academy Bronx, teachers believed that because of the high status of mathematics, success in the subject could positively impact students'
self-confidence and willingness to try and be successful in school. A strong
belief at the school was that students could be successful in mathematics,
particularly on standardized tests, if they first memorized mathematics
facts. There was great emphasis placed on students being able to recite these
facts. Teachers at KIPP Academy Bronx regularly incorporated mathematical raps in their classes in which students chanted mathematical facts (e.g.,
products of single-digit numbers):

> Just trying to make math fun. My mentor teacher, Harriet Ball, taught
> me a lot of songs, mnemonics, raps, rhymes, just a way to anchor the
> learning for kids, to make it fun for them. Harriet's a master at it, and I
> try to continue it and they like it. (KIPPB1, KIPP Bronx, 4/03)

Another teacher at KIPP Academy Bronx described how the school accul-
turated new students to the school's academic and behavioral expectations
starting the summer before they matriculated and how students needed remediation because they came to school with low skill levels. By the time the
students left the school for high school, however, they were well prepared
to compete with students from more affluent communities:

> The kids have come from private schools, public schools, from various
> levels and neighborhoods, so it's a new situation for them. Our school
> year starts in July, so in summer school we spend the first whole month
> getting them KIPP language and what it means to be a KIPPster and
> what we expect from them in terms of behavior and work and even
> things like how neat their notes should be. ... This is their first year,
> they're all over the place level [academic] wise, so it's really our job in
> the 5th grade to bring them up to [grade] level and get them all ready,
> because 6th grade is essentially a review of the 5th grade material, just
> taken up a notch. You know we get the basic skills solid in 5th grade. ...
> All of that is done so by the time they get into 7th grade, they're ready to
> start learning algebra because that's our goal. By the time they graduate
> from the 8th grade, they've taken a two-year algebra course they can
> even go ahead and take the New York State Regents Exam for algebra.
> They can be ready for geometry [and] that gets them on the road to cal-
> culus. Things like that are more likely to happen to kids in the suburbs
> than in New York City. We struggle with getting them used to going to
> KIPP and the attitude you're going to have and also getting them used
> to the hard work that lies ahead. (KIPPB3, KIPP Bronx, 4/03)

The computer-based program, *Accelerated Math*, was available to students at Rockcastle County Middle School to supplement the regular mathematics curriculum:

> If they get finished with their homework, they will work on Accelerated Math and so it's in addition to [the regular mathematics program]. They still have to master the stuff that I teach, the core curriculum that I teach for the state. But some of them are in Pre-Algebra and some of them are in Algebra I. And actually the Algebra I program that we have in Accelerated Math is actually much more difficult than the one they offer at the high school. (Rock4, Rockcastle County MS, 3/03)

TEACHING RESOURCES ARE AVAILABLE

It was common for teachers at participating schools to report that their schools had a great variety of teaching resources available to support their classroom practices. This demonstrated how teachers were trusted by their administrators who supported instruction by helping teachers obtain needed classroom materials. The following teacher from Rockcastle County Middle School discussed how there were so many materials available at Rockcastle that it was actually a bit overwhelming:

> I think I have so many materials that it's hard to find what's what; it's almost too much. I guess it's a great thing, because we have so many materials to pull from that it's almost overwhelming. We may have other materials that may be even better and you haven't got to those yet. (Rock4, Rockcastle County MS, 10/02)

Rockcastle County Middle School also had a full-time mathematics consultant whose job was to support mathematics instruction at the school:

> I think having a math consultant helps. She helps us with anything that we want or need. If we can't find the answers ourselves, we go to her and she gets right on it. She's available to help us with anything that we need help with. (Rock1, Rockcastle County MS, 10/02)

Resources were also not lacking at Ysleta Middle School. Similar to Rockcastle Middle School, the mathematics teachers had a resource person to assist them:

> Our main resource is of course the book, and then we pull from the Connected Math Program. We pull from a little NCTM workbook, we pull activities from there. We get on the Internet and look for more resources. We go to workshops, and we've gone to conferences. We also have a good resource. She's the T.A.A.S. coordinator here on campus. She comes in our department meetings and always gives us a lot of resources, from the new test that's coming in. Anything good that she

finds, she Xeroxes it for us and gives it to us. She's a big resource for us. Anytime we need something, she's there. She's here to give us new ideas, but we have plenty of resources, materials and workbooks. We've got more than enough of those to pull from. Some that the school has purchased the last couple of years that are fairly new, plus as resources we're well off. … The resources, between [the resource teacher] and the book, and the teachers that are here with us; there's plenty, more than enough. (Yslt2, Ysleta MS, 9/02)

A teacher at YES College Preparatory School talked about the value the administration placed on providing teachers with the resources they needed to be highly effective teachers to meet students' needs:

Going back to instructional supplies—the director of our school has always been a big fan—if you need something in order to get your kids where we want them to be, let's get it, there should be no excuse. So if [two other teachers] are going to be the best 7th grade teachers that they can possibly be, let's get you there. We'll do whatever it takes to get you there. (YES4, YES College Prep, 10/02)

At YES College Preparatory School, the mathematics faculty worked with students and their families so that they would prioritize spending monies that supported students' educations. For instance, they worked to convince families that purchasing graphing calculators was worthy of the expense because of its educational value. A teacher at YES College Preparatory School describes the value placed on students having access to technology at the school, and how the faculty worked with students and their families to value prioritizing educational expenses:

For the most part in the high school, all of the high school students have access to the TI-83 plus, either they purchase it themselves or one is provided for them. Actually it's the first year we were able to equip everyone in the high school and part of that is that students in the school have been here for a long time and they've used the graphing calculator for a long time. Mom and Dad are starting to know that this is as important to them as a notebook and pencil. You just need to invest in it. Although it's $100 or more, sometimes it's a long-term investment. The calculator you buy today, you're going to take to college. And we're big fans of saying, most of the kids wear shoes that cost more than $100 and six months later they need new shoes. It's a matter of really setting a few priorities. (YES4, YES College Prep, 10/02)

The teachers at Latta High School also had much to say about the availability of teaching resources at their school:

We have a number of graphing or just scientific calculators. If we need something, generally all we have to do is ask. Even though we're in a budget crunch, I guess you'd call it. (Latta2, Latta HS, 11/02)

> We have a great department chair. Every time you ask for something, most of the time she's here at 7:00 or 8:00 in the morning trying to help you. (Latta5, Latta HS, 11/02)

A teacher at KIPP Academy Houston talked about having many resources available to support the teaching of mathematics, how these learning materials excited students, and that mentoring was available from a teacher at another KIPP Academy:

> I have three cabinets full of manipulatives and any type of concrete objects for the kids. I have 10 and 11 year olds, so I think that excites them [to learn] what math really is. You can do math with different things. In terms of people [to support me], I have that everywhere. There's a math teacher at KIPP New York, he helps me. (KIPPH1, KIPP Houston, 10/02)

TEACHERS HAVE REGULAR ACCESS TO PROFESSIONAL DEVELOPMENT OPPORTUNITIES

A characteristic that strongly defined the mathematics faculty at Rockcastle County Middle School was how involved they were in a variety of initiatives. In particular, the teachers were regularly engaged in professional development activities:

> I guess by now you've probably figured out that if there's anything we can get involved in, that we think is going to help us, we do it. I'll be honest, sometimes it seems like it's overwhelming. Just listen to all of the things, and we've not even touched the surface probably of everything we do. ...
>
> I've had several people that I've taken classes with at the local university ask: "What do you all do down there?" I'm sitting here going; I don't see it as anything special. I'm just doing my job, and I try to do it the best that I can, but you know all these other schools aren't involved in RC, the Eisenhower Grant. They haven't been blessed enough to have this new computer lab that we have. They don't have the technology with the graphing calculators and stuff that we have. They do not have the resources that we have and I think that's where [the resource teacher], every so often, will come up. "Oh, we've got another opportunity to get involved in this, do you all want to do this, or are you going to shoot me?"
>
> So, we try to do whatever we think is best, and we also got ACCLAIM [a National Science Foundation funded Center for Learning and Teaching grant] and that's another big project. ... This goes back to professional development. If we want, we can actually go back and they (the district) will help us too. ... But then again, you know, every little thing is sort of building on what's already happened. (Rock4, Rockcastle County MS, 10/02)

Not only did teachers at Rockcastle County Middle School have grant monies and district-level support. In Kentucky, there were also funds available to support teachers to attend professional development workshops:

> The district supported us. In the summer, if there's anyone who wants, there's also P.D. in the summer. They're very supportive, if we think there is something that will aide us, they'll send us. Also, through Kentucky, the Teachers' Professional Growth fund has greatly assisted. Let's say it's a two million pot of money for math and science teachers. Each teacher can use up to $2,000 a year for professional development, attending conferences and they get reimbursement for registration, travel, anything that's a part of it. That has greatly added a lot of P. D. effort. (Rock3, Rockcastle County MS, 10/02)

Teachers from Ysleta Middle School were also actively involved in professional development activities:

> [An administrator] is really good about letting us know if there are any workshops. She'll let us know, she'll put a copy in our box, and writes "let me know if you want to go, we'll pay for you." ... So they do let us know if there's anything they'll want us to attend and ask "what do you think about this one?" (Yslt3, Ysleta MS, 9/02)

The trust shown teachers at YES College Preparatory School was such that teachers were allowed to design their own professional development plans that they presented to the administration for approval. After approval of the plan, generous support was provided for teachers to attend conferences and workshops that they determined to be worthwhile. A teacher at the school described the value placed on teachers engaging in professional development activities:

> Yes, I'm busily doing professional development. I mean it's something our school really pushes. The reason I'm doing it is the assistant director kind of pulled me aside last year and said, "okay, your first year is under your belt, you really need to do more professional development next year." So, she kind of led me in this way. (YES2, YES College Prep, 10/02)

The teachers at Emerald Middle School were active in a K–12 alliance that was sponsored through the state department of education in California:

> The State of California and K–12 alliance currently has members from San Francisco to here and into San Diego. It's a consortium type of organization that addressed the areas of math and science. They've been in science for years, math to the best of my knowledge, maybe for 8 years. It's a two-year commitment on our part for the school. ... Every year, Emerald's commitment to this grant was that we would bring on additional staff members. So, [two other teachers] and I were the

first to begin the program, and this year [another teacher] joined the program, and [another teacher] is going to join parts of the program. The hope is that they're there for additional support from peer coaching, for the latest models that have been developed to share and share alike. It does involve about 40 hours in the summer and then another 80 hours throughout the school year. … So it's extensive and then also, of course, is that they have another goal that is to obtain a credential in mathematics or a supplemental [credential in mathematics]. (Emer4, Emerald MS, 10/02)

At J. D. O'Bryant School of Mathematics and Science, all of the first-year teachers could receive mentoring from a veteran teacher:

In particular for the new teachers, the administration hands out a notice [to find out] who is willing to be a mentee. I guess they find the coaches. They send the coaches to the people who they think will need them, need help I guess. (OBry6, J. D. O'Bryant SMS, 11/02)

CONCLUDING REMARKS

The focus on teaching and learning, support given for student learning, professional development opportunities, and availability of teaching resources all promoted rigorous, enduring, and genuine learning environments at the schools. The nine schools that participated in the HP HAS study had created school cultures that were the exact opposite of what is often found at less effective schools. Teachers talked about being able to come to school to teach and students understood that they were expected to learn.

The majority of the schools had discipline policies that reinforced the notion that learning was the top priority and obstructing the learning of others was a serious offense. Behavioral problems were minimal at all of the schools because of the concerted focus on making learning the primary goal at the schools. Students were expected to come to school to learn and they knew it. The remarkable cultural shift achieved at the nine schools that had transformed them into places where learning was priority one was articulated best by a teacher at the Young Women's Leadership School: "It's cool to be good at math [at TYWLS]. The coolest girls [at the school], the most popular girls are also the ones who work the hardest and achieve the most." The interest that students expressed for learning at the participating schools debunks the myth that few students are interested in learning and lends credibility to the notion that when schools create exciting and challenging learning environments, students respond by actively engaging in the learning process.

Slogans at the participating schools, such as "Failure Is Not an Option" and "Whatever It Takes," that communicated high academic expectations were not merely hollow rhetoric. As an example of how this concentrated focus on academic excellence was made manifest, at Latta High School, students rarely were excused from class to attend or participate in afterschool activities such as athletic events. An administrator at the school reported working within the district to ensure that the athletic sports schedule was constructed so that student-athletes and cheer teams would not have to desert their classes early for events.

In addition to sharing a strong commitment to student learning, the schools created the necessary support structures and conditions to prioritize student learning and achievement. Extensive academic support services for students were widely available to sustain high academic expectations. Teachers spoke often about being widely available to their students. For example, at the J. D. O'Bryant School of Mathematics and Science, mathematics teachers regularly stayed after school to tutor students. Also at J. D. O'Bryant School of Mathematics and Science and Emerald Middle School, there existed strong collaborations between the schools and local universities (discussed further in chap. 7). As part of these partnerships, undergraduate and graduate students in engineering, mathematics, and the sciences regularly volunteered to tutor students at the schools. At Emerald Middle School, parents were encouraged to purchase a tutorial program that students could use on their computers at home.

At the KIPP Academies and YES College Preparatory School, students were expected to call their teachers at home if they needed help with their homework. All the participating schools had afterschool tutorial programs. At some schools, teachers were paid a stipend to tutor. Others provided students Saturday study sessions and had procedures in place to regularly assess student progress. At KIPP Academy Bronx, students could be pulled out of the one elective that was available, school orchestra, if they needed additional academic assistance in any of the core subjects.

At participating middle schools, teachers had extended class periods to teach mathematics. Teachers took advantage of this extra time to deal with students' remediation needs and challenge them with cognitively demanding mathematical content (e.g., understand and memorize their basic multiplication and division facts, while engaging them in problem-solving activities and the study of algebra). Particularly at the middle schools, there was emphasis placed on making sure that students were well versed in the traditional basics of mathematics, such as number facts. Although teachers devoted significant time to remediation of the basics, they also made sure students engaged in the study of algebra and problem solving so that they could enroll in higher level mathematics courses in high school. This two-pronged approach, instruction focused on both remediation and challenging students with a cognitively demanding mathematics curriculum, was possible because teachers had the time to do both.

Interestingly, many of the highly effective schools employed someone on a part-time or full-time basis to write grant proposals. Grants had funded some of the resource materials that were widely available at the highly effective schools. Teachers talked about how fortunate they were to have so many teaching resources. They also spoke about how when they needed something, they could simply open their closets and pull out the desired materials. In general, teachers did not feel they had to beg for materials to be effective at their jobs. The resources were available to support the primary goals at the schools: teaching and learning.

4

YES College Preparatory
School Case Study

Julie DePree

> The vision of equity in mathematics education challenges a pervasive soci-
> etal belief in North America that only some students are capable of learn-
> ing mathematics. … Low expectations are especially problematic because
> students who live in poverty, students who are not native speakers of Eng-
> lish, students with disabilities, females, and many nonwhite students have
> traditionally been far more likely than their counterparts in other demo-
> graphic groups to be victims of low expectations. Expectations must be
> raised—mathematics can and must be learned by all *students*.
>
> —*NCTM* (2000, pp. 12–13)

This chapter provides the first of three comprehensive case studies. YES
College Preparatory School in Houston was selected for this initial in-depth
case study because it is a model school for teaching mathematics to all students. YES has high expectations for all students, exemplary achievement,
and unique characteristics that distinguished it among the nine highly effective schools.

Many students who attended YES College Preparatory School were
from a poor, inner-city community where many of the public schools were
lacking in quality. Most of the students from this community rarely attended school beyond high school, so a mission of YES was to remedy this
situation. The mission of the school was to address this injustice and create a
school environment in which high expectations for student success were
coupled with the support needed to be successful.

Through a collaborative effort between faculty, students, and community, the students at YES College Preparatory School have achieved excellence in mathematics achievement. Many factors contributed to this

success, including high expectations, high-level instruction, and challenging mathematical content. Faculty support for students was also an important factor. As one student stated, "The reason I wanted to come here is I wanted a challenge" (student interview, 2002). Similar sentiments were reflected in the comments of a second student who said, "I come here because I am getting something out of it. Every little thing that we learn will help us in the future. They [the teachers] teach in a way that will help us learn" (student interview, 2002). Finally, a third student indicated, "I really like the teachers. They care about you more" (student interview, 2002).

DESCRIPTION OF YES COLLEGE PREPARATORY SCHOOL

In 2002, YES College Preparatory School was an open enrollment, state charter school for Grades 6–12. The school population of approximately 450 students came from over 40 zip codes in the Houston area and represented a variety of ethnic backgrounds, including Hispanic (88%), African American (8%), and Asian and White (4%). Eighty-eight percent of the students were classified as economically disadvantaged and qualified for the free or reduced breakfast and lunch program.

As a state charter school, YES College Preparatory had an open-enrollment policy and could not deny acceptance to anyone if space was available. As a result, in the spring 2002, 300 students were on a waiting list to attend the school. Students were selected using a lottery process. Then home visits were conducted, during which the teacher, parent(s), and student signed a Commitment to Excellence contract. The contract included items such as agreeing to adhere to school policies, attending all class sessions and meetings, checking homework, and supporting academic programs. This contract stipulated that the family and student would live up to the school motto of doing "Whatever It Takes" to pursue the school's goal of college matriculation for all graduates.

In 2002, YES College Preparatory School was the only state-chartered school in Houston providing students with a rigorous college preparatory curriculum. A unique feature of YES was that students must first be admitted to a 4-year college (not a 2-year junior college) before they could graduate from the school. Because of this requirement, faculty at YES College Preparatory School took seriously the school's mission to offer students a rigorous college preparatory curriculum. During the 2001–2002 school year, all graduating seniors were accepted to at least two 4-year colleges, with many receiving financial aid in the form of scholarships and grants. This is especially noteworthy, because 80% of these graduates were the first in their families to attend college. To achieve this rigorous goal, students at YES were required to spend additional time in school. It was reported that YES students spent 65% more time in school than the average Houston public school student, with school starting at 7:50 a.m. and ending at 5:00 p.m.

daily. In addition, students attended school on Saturdays twice a month and one extra month during the summer.

The administrators, faculty, and staff at YES focused on creating and maintaining an environment conducive to learning. In 2001–2002, the student–teacher ratio was 15 to 1, with an average class size of 25. Everyone at the school, including administrators, taught classes, a practice designed to keep them in daily instructional contact with students rather than allowing them to become isolated from students and their instructional needs.

Part of the professional expectation at YES was that teachers would work outside normal classroom hours to provide an atmosphere supportive of learning. Teachers were required to be on campus to provide one-on-one tutoring at the end of the school day and carried a school-provided cell phone to be available to help students after regular school hours. Although teachers at YES were required to spend many additional hours supporting their students' mathematics learning, they were compensated financially for this extra time.

In addition to the extended learning hours, the discipline policy at YES College Preparatory School was an important component in the promotion of learning. The discipline policy at the school was well-established and strictly enforced with the explicit goal of helping all students achieve to the best of their abilities. The discipline policy was described as harsh by the principal, who believed that strict policies were necessary to create a demanding learning environment at the school. As one student described it, "Everything here is based on academics. If you don't do very good, they don't allow you to play sports or do fun stuff until you get them [your grades] up." Another student stated, "We go to Wall Street [detention] if we're just really bad, like skip a class" (student interview, 2002). The discipline policy was communicated to teachers, staff, students, and parents and, as a result, discipline was essentially a nonexistent problem at YES.

YES College Preparatory School also offered numerous extracurricular activities for students, which the principal indicated was an important part of the school's academic success. He explained that both academic and outside experiences were crucial to the success of the school and YES was committed to providing opportunities that would not be available to students otherwise. Students participated in extracurricular activities from 4:00 p.m. to 5:00 p.m. each day. They selected from 30 clubs, including martial arts, swimming, photography, drama, and ecology, and 16 athletic teams representing 7 sports. One student said, "After study hall ... they give you a lot of opportunities to do different things and to choose a club or team" (student interview, 2002). In addition to extracurricular programs, many resources were devoted to providing students with field trips, spring trips, and college visits. For example, in the spring, each grade level participated in a weeklong, field-based learning experience that routinely took them to distant places in the country. In addition, students visited multiple university and college campuses throughout the United States to help them focus on the school's mission that every graduate attend a 4-year college.

Parents and the community actively supported the mission of YES College Preparatory School. As a condition of their child's acceptance, parents were required to sign a contract supporting the school's mission. In addition, the principal explained that formal attempts were made to involve parents in the school community and the result was that the school had an active parent group. Evidence of the involvement of YES parents was suggested by the fact that 90% attended the fall 2001 open house. Parents also worked to raise funds for the school.

According to the principal, another factor important to the success of the school was an accountability system. Teachers, students, and administrators were held accountable for academic achievement at YES. The administrator went on to say that the quality of the students, teachers, and administrators made the school successful. He also acknowledged that YES was not the right place for everyone; the success of the school depended on the faculty's willingness to put in extra time and effort to ensure learning took place for all students, and students had to be willing to work hard both in the classroom and during afterschool hours. In addition, students had to be willing to seek extra help when needed and teachers had to be willing to provide that help. In these ways, everyone at the school showed dedication and a willingness to work to achieve success.

RESEARCH METHOD

In 2002, YES College Preparatory was selected as one of nine high-achieving schools in the Hewlett-Packard High-Achieving Schools Grant Initiative. As part of the grant, mathematics faculty, students, and administrators at YES participated in interviews during the 2002–2003 school year (see appendix A for a detailed description of the research methodology used in the study). These data were examined to understand what they believed made their school highly effective in mathematics. Six faculty members participated in a group faculty interview about the mathematics curriculum, instruction, and assessment, and four of these six also participated in individual interviews conducted after a UNM researcher observed each of the four teachers teach two consecutive lessons. During the individual teacher interviews, beliefs about curriculum, instruction, and assessment were explored in relation to the observed lessons. In this chapter, a sample of one of the observed lessons is outlined and is discussed in subsequent sections. Next, findings from an analysis of the interviews are summarized. These findings are delineated under the three major themes found across the schools that participated in the study: high expectations and sustained support for academic excellence, challenging mathematical content and high-level instruction, and the importance of building relationships among teachers and students.

SAMPLE YES LESSON

This lesson on area and volume took place in a regular seventh-grade algebra class of approximately 30 students. A brief review/practice session on graphing linear equations was also included during the class session.

The teacher began the class by posing the following question to the students: "Daniel wants to build a rectangular sandbox for his little sister. He has 24 linear feet of board that is 1 foot high. What dimensions would allow for the greatest volume and what is the maximum volume?" The teacher then had students form groups of four and gave them a worksheet with tables and graph paper to support solving the problem before instructing them to complete a table of values for possible widths, lengths, and volumes. Students were also prompted to draw sketches of possible solutions and then graph the results on a coordinate grid with the x-axis representing width in feet and the y-axis representing volume in cubic feet.

Students began working in groups, however, it was not long before the teacher noticed many groups were struggling with the task, prompting the teacher to stop the group work and explain the task further. The class discussed the meaning of volume and generated formulas for finding the volume of several solids. Students then returned to the task with greater success. Students were engaged in the activity, with each group working to generate a table of values, while the teacher circulated and provided support and prompts when needed.

The class session lasted 90 minutes, so at one point the teacher stopped the class to have students do a quick stretching activity. The teacher instructed students to stand up and then, using their arms, model various linear functions as the teacher called them out. For example, the teacher said, "Model $y = 0$," then, "Model $y = -5x$," and students indicated the slopes of the lines with their arms. This activity both reviewed graphing and helped energize the students enough to resume work on the volume task.

After completing the table of values, students were instructed to study the table and look for patterns, draw conclusions, and graph their results. Then the class discussed the task as a group. During the discussion, the teacher asked high-level questions and pushed students' understanding until a collective understanding of both the task and the concept of volume and surface area was developed.

This lesson was indicative of the lessons observed in all of the mathematics classes at YES. There was a high level of participation as students were actively engaged in the lesson and class discussions.

High Expectations and Sustained Support for Academic Excellence

In both the group and individual interviews, the mathematics teachers at YES College Preparatory School expressed their views on what distinguished their school as highly effective in mathematics. One theme to emerge was the importance placed on creating a learning environment in which high expectations for student learning and support for academic excellence were the norms. The following four findings were revealed during interviews demonstrating this theme: high academic expectations for all students, coupled with academic support for student learning and achievement; a coherent, consistently implemented discipline policy; a high level of teacher commitment to student learning and achievement; and teacher access to supplementary learning materials to support student learning.

High Academic Expectations for All Students, Coupled With Academic Support for Student Learning and Achievement.   The teachers at YES had high expectations for their students. One teacher explained that teachers and students alike worked hard on a daily basis:

> I feel that if you are trying to get at what makes this school excellent … it is that our kids work so hard. I think a large part of that is because they see models of hard work everyday. We can ask a ton of them, because we're doing hard work as well. It would be one thing if we were getting out at 3:00 p.m., going home, not doing any work, and asking them to do the same thing. I think it's the reason that they're pushing themselves, because they see us pushing ourselves. (YES 4, faculty interview, 2002)

Students confirmed that high expectations existed at the school. One student stated, "I came here because I wanted a challenge. In most public schools, it's easy to pass and stuff. It's more challenging than most public schools" (student interview, 2003). Another student explained, "In the other schools you could slack off and still pass. … Here you cannot slack off" (student interview, 2002).

Teachers not only expressed high expectations, but also provided the necessary academic support to sustain students in meeting those expectations. Students took advantage of that support and worked hard to succeed. A teacher described how students worked to succeed: "They want to do well. They are doing whatever it takes. They come in for help, they call each other, and they are good at working together and supporting each other" (YES 1, teacher interview, 2002).

The teachers at YES College Preparatory School believed that regardless of socioeconomic status and ethnicity, if given good instruction, all students could learn. This was a basic premise at the school. One teacher explained:

> The principal recruits from Teach for America volunteers, but I also think the ideology of Teach for America lines up well with the ideology of YES. … The ideology for Teach for America is that any kid, regardless of socioeconomic status whether they are minority or not, can learn if

given good instruction. So that's the basic premise for Teach for America, and we believe it here. I mean even teachers that were not with Teach for America believe it. (YES 2, teacher interview, 2002)

Another teacher stated: "I think my expectations are really high, and part of that is because I've already taught a lot of them in 6th grade. So I know what kinds of things that they can do, and it's kind of like they are really strong all around" (YES 3, teacher interview, 2002).

The teachers at YES also had high expectations in terms of how they viewed their students' opportunities in the future: "Those that stick with it; I think they have a very good future. I think we instill some pretty good study skills and content material" (YES 6, teacher interview, 2003). Most of the teachers believed their students would graduate from high school and attend college in the future. As one teacher put it, "I think that our students have a good background in math and science and many are bilingual. ... I think a good number of them will likely go on to careers in engineering and the sciences" (YES 5, teacher interview, 2003).

Coherent Discipline Policy That Was Consistently Implemented.
Expectations for student learning at YES College Preparatory School were supported by a well-articulated discipline policy that all teachers and students adhered to closely. Before students began their studies at YES, they completed a 3-week summer course at the school with a strong focus on classroom behavior. By the time students began classes, they understood the discipline policy was strict and there would be consequences for their actions if they did not stick to it. One student stated, "We go to Wall Street if we are really bad. ... This is where you sit in a room for an hour and a half after school" (student interview, 2003). Students and parents also signed a contract that delineated the guidelines for acceptable behavior. One teacher explained, "I think that the contract really helps. I think the kids that come [to YES] know that they're going to work hard, and they are willing to do it" (YES 1, teacher interview, 2002).

YES College Preparatory School also enforced a policy that put students who failed on academic probation. This policy required students to attend regular classes, as well as seek additional academic support. One teacher explained how this policy worked to ensure student success:

> [Students on probation are] required to come see me during a specified time for a tutorial. It's either at lunch or during study hall. If they don't see us, then we don't sign their sheet; and that sheet goes home to Mom. That's one way of making sure we stay on them. (YES 5, teacher interview, 2003)

Another teacher discussed how once discipline issues were under control, students were given more freedom:

I need to be making sure that the students are staying in line with the discipline, but I also want to, once that's established, give them freedom to really explore in the class. I would say the amount I spend lecturing and the amount of time I spend in charge of the class will kind of go down as the year progresses. (YES 2, teacher interview, 2002)

High Level of Teacher Commitment to Student Learning and Achievement.   The high expectations and sustained support for academic excellence were enhanced by teachers' strong level of commitment to their work. One teacher explained:

Having taught in other districts, I have never seen a commitment for teaching where they put in the time and effort that they do here. They are truly interested in what the students are doing. I think it's just terrific. … I was burned out in the big schools, but it really revitalized me to see people who wanted to teach kids. … I've changed a whole lot, and I think that it has been best. I love it here. I feel like I'm doing more with the kids than I ever did in the larger schools. I think it's a great place. … Yeah, I just think this is the right way to do it. All of it. (YES 6, faculty interview, 2002)

In response, students recognized the teachers' commitment and thrived in this environment. One student said, "The reason I came here is because I really like the teachers. They care about you more. … The teachers here talk to you about anything" (student interview, 2002).

Another component of YES teachers' commitment to student learning was their willingness to make adaptations to address student needs. The mathematics teachers were willing to acknowledge the challenges they faced and devise strategies to meet students' needs. For example, some teachers discussed their belief that some students struggled in mathematics due to a lack of proficiency in English and a lack of academic support at home. The teachers saw this as a challenge they could overcome and planned to help these students: "I feel we try to make up for that by keeping them until five, by giving them phone numbers, by doing after school tutorials, in some ways we're trying to make up for the gaps that are caused by economic disadvantages" (YES 4, teacher interview, 2002).

The Teachers Had Access to Supplementary Learning Materials.   The final factor supporting high expectations and sustained support for academic excellence was teacher access to supplementary materials. The mathematics teachers were able to obtain whatever materials they needed to support their curriculum: "The director of our school has always been a big fan. If you need something in order to get your kids where we want them to be, let's get it. There should be no excuses" (YES 4, faculty interview, 2002). The teachers utilized many resources, including the National Council of

Teachers of Mathematics (NCTM, 2000) standards-based materials and other exploration-based textbooks: "I use ideas that I get out of mathematics teachers magazines. I use ideas that I get from other teachers. Anywhere I can find them. Lots of materials come in the mail. [I use] anything I can put my hands on" (YES 6, teacher interview, 2003). Another teacher explained, "NCTM, I love NCTM. We use some of their online materials and some activity books ... also we use a lot of AIMS stuff too and they're really good" (YES 5, teacher interview, 2003).

The use of standards-based learning materials was evident in a lesson observed in a seventh-grade classroom. Following a discussion on the meaning of volume, the teacher gave groups of students two sheets of construction paper and told them to make two cylinders, one tall and skinny and the other short and fat. Once students completed the cylinders, they were asked if the volumes were equal and, if not, which contained the larger volume. Students used stickers to place their votes on the board. Once the votes were cast, students filled their containers with rice to determine which had the larger capacity. Students were then told to write an explanation of their results.

The sample lesson also illustrates the high expectations and support for academic excellence that was such a critical component to the success of YES College Preparatory School. Students were expected to engage in the lesson and solve difficult problems, with the teacher pushing students to do their best. When students struggled, the teacher provided prompts and support to help all students achieve the goal of gaining a deep understanding of mathematics.

Challenging Mathematical Content and High-Level Instruction

A second theme to emerge from interviews with teachers and administrators at YES College Preparatory School was the value teachers and administrators placed on challenging mathematical content and high-level instruction. This theme incorporated five facets: demanding mathematics curriculum, focus on problem solving and making sense of mathematical ideas, a deep understanding of mathematical concepts and communication of this understanding, use of a variety of instructional practices, and use of both formal and informal assessment measures.

Demanding Mathematics Curriculum. The mathematics program at YES College Preparatory was described as rigorous by school personnel. Many students began the mathematics program with pre-algebra in the 6th grade, and then eventually moved to pre-calculus in 11th grade and advanced placement calculus as seniors. To achieve these high standards, middle school students received 90 minutes of mathematics instruction each day. This advanced curriculum required students to work with linear equations, functions, and statistical concepts in 7th grade. Teachers specialized in a particular grade level to allow them to develop a deep understanding of the mathematics to be taught in that grade. One teacher explained, "The advantage of having a 7th grade math specialist, or now two of them, is it really forces you to focus on that grade level, because we don't just think department wise, we also think grade level wise. So we meet as grade levels" (YES 4, teacher interview, 2002).

Faculty agreed on the most important mathematical ideas to include in the curriculum at each grade level and then focused on teaching those ideas. For example, in the sixth grade, problem solving, ratios and proportions, fractions, decimals, and percentages were identified as key concepts; in seventh grade, solving equations was seen as important. The teachers at these grade levels developed and implemented many activities to teach these concepts.

One lesson focusing on proportional reasoning observed in a sixth-grade classroom exemplified the advanced curriculum employed at YES. In the lesson, students measured the circumference and diameter of various circles before examining the ratio obtained to draw conclusions concerning pi. The teacher of the lesson stated, "I was really looking for them to notice that pi is not just a number some mathematician made up, but to understand that there is a proportional relationship between all circles. When you look at those ratios you can find out pi and it's the relationship between circumference and diameter" (YES 4, teacher interview, 2003).

Mathematical communication, spatial sense, and proportional reasoning were seen as crucial concepts included in the demanding mathematics curriculum at YES. One example of a lesson designed to enhance spatial sense and a sense of proportional reasoning was an activity in which students were told to draw a picture. Students were then given grid paper and used proportional reasoning to enlarge or shrink the drawing. The students enjoyed sharing their designs with their peers. Teachers also spoke of the importance of scale models, developing facility working with fractions, decimals, and percentages, and understanding the relationships among them. One teacher described several lessons used to enhance understanding of these concepts:

> We build bridges and scale them up or down depending which year it is and what I decided to be fun at the time. We actually take little cars … and we enlarge them to what it would be to be a real car. We actually go outside and draw how big it will be. And they actually sit down in their car and go, oh, this is how a car would be. It's very funny, because we put them in spots outside and when you walk out there are chalk cars everywhere. (YES 1, teacher interview, 2002)

Geometry teachers also mentioned the importance of using spatial visualization to move between two and three dimensions. In the seventh grade, linear equations and inequalities were viewed as important concepts for students to understand, as was working with graphing and with equations. The focus on these concepts contributed to a challenging mathematics curriculum.

A Focus on Problem Solving and Making Sense of Mathematical Ideas. Problem solving was recognized as a critical component of a challenging mathematics curriculum, and the entire mathematics team emphasized problem solving throughout the instruction. The teachers wanted students to be able to think logically and develop multiple problem-solving strategies. One teacher stated, "The most important thing for my students to learn in geometry is to think logically" (YES 6, teacher interview, 2003). Accordingly, teachers incorporated problem-solving strategies, such as drawing pictures and looking for patterns, in all grade levels. One teacher said, "I think one of the most important things that I stress is there is more than one way of solving anything, like getting an answer, whether it is drawing a picture, writing an equation. ... " (YES 3, teacher interview, 2002). The faculty also believed that students should become adept at finding patterns and developing ideas from those patterns to solve complex problems.

YES students were encouraged to be both persistent and to use multiple strategies when solving problems. A teacher stated, "The other thing that I try stressing with them [the students] is not giving up. If something is hard, then you break it down into easier steps. Use what you know" (YES 3, teacher interview, 2002).

The teachers at YES College Preparatory School wanted their students to see mathematics as not just something they do at school, but also something they could use in their lives outside the classroom. Hence, problem solving was an integral component of the curriculum. They also wanted their students to be independent thinkers when it came to problem solving. One teacher explained:

> Problem solving is just huge. Teaching them to be independent thinkers [is also very important]. So they don't need us. So they don't come to us to think through everything. So they really try it fully on their own. We really talk about that at our grade level meetings, so I think that's huge. (YES 1, faculty interview, 2002)

Several teachers also mentioned the importance of seeing the big picture and recognizing the connections within mathematics. One teacher stated:

> Now, I'm really interested in, do they see the big picture? I want them to know not just how do you go about solving the problem, but why do you go about doing that. What led to the development of those ideas? What I've seen over the past few years is that if they don't get the big picture in the beginning, all they're going to do is memorize their way through it. (YES 4, teacher interview, 2002)

Deep Understanding of Mathematical Concepts and Communication of This Understanding.   Another goal of the mathematics faculty at YES College Preparatory School was to help students gain a deep understanding of mathematical concepts. The extended class periods at YES contributed greatly to supporting students to develop a deep understanding of mathematics. Because the teachers at YES College Preparatory School believed their students came to them approximately one to two grade levels below where they should be in mathematics, students in the middle school grades attended 90-minute blocks of mathematics instruction. The teachers believed that with 90-minute blocks for classes, they could get students to the appropriate level of achievement by the ninth grade. One teacher explained the effectiveness of long class periods to combat students' weak backgrounds in mathematics:

> [Our sixth graders] don't come in with the skills in order to take pre-algebra, but we try to do as much to prepare them … but a lot of it is just like reinforcement. They get double the time in math. It's better for them. … It allows you to do a mini lesson in between. … It allows you an opportunity to have a longer period for your lesson. It allows you the opportunity to give a chance to understand, give them class work. So having a double period is really awesome. I don't know if we could potentially teach as much as we do in a 45-minute block. I think that would be a disservice to them. (YES 3, faculty interview, 2002)

At the high school level, mathematics courses met for 45-minute blocks 4 days a week, and for a 90-minute block 1 day a week. The 90-minute block gave teachers the opportunity to complete extended projects.

The teachers employed yet another means for helping students understand concepts by assisting them to make mathematical connections. One teacher described how students often focused on procedures and failed to see the whole picture when solving problems. To overcome this tendency, the teacher used activities designed to challenge students and take them out of their comfort zones so that they learned to look at the bigger picture. This teacher described the importance of looking at the whole picture, "It's getting [the students] to see things that they have learned aren't isolated" (YES 3, teacher interview, 2003). This teacher encouraged students to "reach out into [their] prior knowledge and apply it." One observed lesson (see Sample YES Lesson for more detail) illustrated the idea of seeing connections among mathematical topics and using this to enhance understanding. The lesson posed the following problem to students: Daniel wants to build a rectangular sandbox and has 24 feet of board that is 1 foot high. What dimensions would allow for the greatest volume and what is the maximum volume? Students were instructed to work in small groups and explore many different dimensions for the sand box in a table format before being asked to graph their results. Finally, students were instructed to write a function for the volume of the sandbox in terms of the width. This lesson illustrates how a teacher worked to have students view the problem from multiple representations and develop deep understandings by seeing the connections among concepts.

The faculty also believed in the importance of communicating mathematical understandings in both written and verbal form. Accordingly, communication played a role in the teachers' group projects designed to promote problem solving and a deeper understanding of mathematics. While students were engaged in these projects, they were routinely encouraged to communicate and clarify ideas. A teacher highlighted methods employed to promote communication:

> I let the kids come to the board and work on things so that other kids can see what they do, and I think they really enjoy it. I also have little white boards for each student, so a lot of times I use those. They just hold them up. (YES 1, teacher interview, 2002)

Another teacher (YES 2, teacher interview, 2002) stated, "Their ability to communicate the mathematics that we're learning is really important. … [I tell them to] clarify that idea so you can write it down and show it to someone else."

Use of a Variety of Instructional Practices. The teachers at YES College Preparatory School engaged students in mathematics by utilizing a variety of instructional practices. One teacher, feeling that drill and practice in the past had hindered some students' understanding, used discovery learning methods based on the assumption that such approaches capitalized on students' inherent understanding of many mathematical ideas. This individual felt it was the teacher's job to aid students' discovery so that they could make sense of mathematical ideas based on their past experiences: "I like to do a lot of discovery themes. I think today [my lesson] was much more teacher based, but with the students still actively involved. I think that is typically how it goes" (YES 1, teacher interview, 2002).

YES teachers believed it was important for students to engage in hands-on explorations designed to help them make sense of mathematics when first introducing concepts to support the development of understanding. For example, one teacher used an activity in which students made two different containers with the same surface area before being asked to determine which had the larger volume. To find the answer, students filled the containers with rice to discover the volume of each and then wrote conclusions about their findings.

Group work was another instructional practice used in mathematics classes at YES College Preparatory School, with many teachers using group activities on a regular basis. One teacher explained, "We do a lot of small group problem solving to try to promote that one person isn't going to get it and even if one person does get it, that doesn't benefit everybody" (YES 5, teacher interview, 2003). This illustrates how the teachers at YES valued the learning of all students. The teachers believed that it was important and expected that all students learn, not just a select few. Another teacher used group work as a means to provide opportunities to get around the classroom to tutor individual students in need of assistance and had competent students aid others as well:

> I try to make sure that at least once a week we do group work. ... With 22 people in the class, I can't get to all of them. ... Having key students out there who really know what's going on and can handle questions really frees me up to work with the kids who really are struggling. (YES 4, teacher interview, 2002)

Homework was assigned on a regular basis and represented another way teachers helped students develop an understanding of mathematical principles. The teachers realized assigning homework was demanding as the students were in school until 5:00 p.m. Nevertheless, students were expected to complete homework assignments. To help students with the additional burden, teachers had cell phones and were available at all hours to help with homework. One student confirmed that the support was helpful: "The system [for help on homework] at this school is really great because all the teachers have a cell phone, so you can call them any time. If you can't understand, you can get help" (student interview, 2003). The content of the homework was also important. One teacher indicated that most of the homework was "practice of what they learned in class. [The other] half of it is new things for them. There are usually two or three questions of what [the students] did yesterday and what [they] did the day before." The teacher insisted that it was important to reinforce "whatever skills [that had been taught and] led up to that day" (YES 3, teacher interview, 2002). The homework assignments and access to additional help were an invaluable part of the program.

In addition, the principal supported the use of a variety of instructional practices and explained that the mathematics faculty was valued as a group of professionals. As such, they were entrusted to continually strive to make the mathematics department better. He described how they engaged in multiple professional development activities to enhance their classroom skills, were willing to think outside of the box, and were encouraged to try new ideas as a means for developing and maintaining a stimulating learning environment.

Use of Formal and Informal Assessment Measures.   The final facet supporting the challenging mathematics content and high-level instruction was use of both formal and informal assessments. The mathematics department at YES used the Texas criterion-referenced standardized achievement test (TAAS) as one means of formal assessment. Whereas teachers at YES College Preparatory School wanted their students to do well on the TAAS, they did little extra preparation for the test beyond reviewing a few concepts and the format of the exam before the test was administered. They believed they had a strong curriculum requiring a high level of thinking every day. Due to this rigorous curriculum, the teachers believed their students would do well on any assessments they were given. One teacher explained their approach to standardized testing: "We don't worry a whole lot about our kids being prepared. We think that we are doing a good job of meeting all those requirements and basically we just teach what's in our curriculum. ... So they're pretty well prepared already" (YES 6, teacher interview, 2003). When asked if standardized testing affected instruction, another teacher supported the previous teacher's assertion:

> In the back of my mind somewhere, I'm aware we have it [standardized test] coming around soon, and I do want them to do well. I just feel like the level of thought that we ask our kids to be at everyday, I mean, I think that it is going to suit them well for the standardized test anyway. (YES 5, teacher interview, 2003)

In addition to formal assessment, YES faculty also evaluated student performance informally. One teacher revealed: "[I do] a lot of informal assessment, walking around [looking at students' work]. Talking and seeing where things are and trying to get a feeling [for students' understanding] through the year" (YES 2, teacher interview, 2002). In addition, this teacher conducted midyear conferences with students and their parents to discuss the students' progress. Another teacher described use of informal assessments: "I want to see where they're at, like who really needs the help. Then slowly ... I pretty much have it pegged. These are the kids that really struggle. These are the kids that are really good at helping. ... That's where the moving them in groups starts" (YES 3, teacher interview, 2003).

The sample lesson also depicts the challenging mathematical content and high level of instruction YES students engaged in on a regular basis. Problem solving represented a central theme of the class session, and all students were actively engaged during the lesson. Students were supported to use inquiry and pushed to develop deep understandings of mathematical concepts. The importance of being able to communicate those understandings to develop a collective understanding was also viewed as a critical component of the class session. Challenging mathematical content and high-level instruction were important components in the high mathematical achievement of the students at YES College Preparatory School.

The Importance of Building Relationships Among Teachers and Students

A third theme to emerge from the faculty, administrator, and student interviews concerned the importance of building relationships among teachers and students. This theme was reflected in three findings: the mathematics faculty collaborated on a curriculum that was a work in progress, teachers developed a comfortable classroom environment in which student participation was encouraged, and teachers modified instruction to meet the needs of students.

The Mathematics Faculty Collaborated on a Curriculum That Was a Work in Progress.   Through regular meetings, the YES mathematics faculty wrote and continually revised their mathematics curriculum. These meetings began during the summer and continued throughout the academic year. The seventh-grade mathematics teachers even met on weekends to plan lessons. A teacher described this process by saying, "At the beginning of the year, actually during the summer, every teacher here revises their curriculum to make sure it changes from the year before" (YES 2, teacher interview, 2003). Another teacher cited some of the crucial questions that were asked to make curricular decisions: "Is our curriculum age appropriate for our kids? Is it challenging? Is it too easy?" (YES 3, teacher interview, 2003).

The faculty worked together as a department to ensure that each teacher's curriculum supported curricular goals that had been established at each grade level. A teacher explained:

> This summer we actually got together and helped [another teacher] write his [curriculum], and they helped me write mine. They helped [second teacher] write hers. Although they stay very similar, just little adjustments. ... We try to make sure that my curriculum will build on [the other two teachers' curriculum] and [a third teacher's] will build on mine. (YES 1, teacher interview, 2002)

In this way, faculty members worked closely together to share and develop lessons to meet the needs of their students. They often asked each other for new ideas for conveying concepts, employing the same methods of communication they tried to achieve with their students. They questioned one another about what worked best for students. One teacher highlighted the benefits of collaboration: "I know what I want the students to experience in class, and [another faculty member] and I talk about it. I feel much more confident when we work together. We work ... and we work on the weekends" (YES 5, teacher interview, 2003).

As teachers were regularly evaluating their mathematics curriculum, it was an eternal work in progress: "There is definitely a lot that we do [with our curriculum] we feel are the needs of the students. We ask what are their strengths; what are their weaknesses? If something is a weakness, then we'll try to place it in key places throughout the curriculum to really build on those skills" (YES 4, teacher interview, 2002). This same teacher provided an example concerning the high school students' lack of proficiency working with fractions. This deficit was brought up for discussion at a mathematics faculty meeting where the faculty decided to emphasize various representations of fractions in the mathematics curriculum in the middle school to ensure proficiency by the time they reached high school. One lesson observed in a sixth-grade classroom demonstrated how concepts relating to fractions were reinforced as a means for preparing students for the curriculum they would face in the seventh grade. Students played a "Factoring Game" from the National Council of Teachers of Mathematics Web site in which they worked on the prime factorization of numbers, a skill they could later apply when working with fractions. Another teacher explained:

> A lot of times we'll do [an activity called] "Fractions of the Day." We'll change fractions to decimals and percents, multiply and divide, just things they know. They've learned at some point, but it's easy to forget. ... So making them remember those skills and making them do it every single day is really good. (YES1, faculty interview, 2002)

This consistent monitoring of the curriculum to identify strengths and weaknesses allowed teachers to adapt the curriculum when necessary. They also worked closely to ensure that the curriculum covered the Texas Essential Knowledge and Skills (TEKS) for their grade level and part of the next grade level.

Because the YES teachers created their mathematics curriculum, they did not rely solely on one mathematics textbook. In fact, many of the teachers stated they did not use a textbook often, choosing instead to supplement their curriculum extensively with group projects and activities. To support this teaching style, YES teachers often had extensive self-generated resources to draw on for innovative lessons to help their students gain a deeper understanding of the mathematical concepts being taught. One teacher explained, "I would say the majority of my stuff, I make on my own. ... I have over 200 files on my computer that I've made up on my own over the years" (YES 2, teacher interview, 2002).

Teachers Developed a Comfortable Classroom Environment in Which Student Participation Was Encouraged. The importance of building relationships among teachers and students was exemplified by the YES teachers' efforts to provide a comfortable learning environment for their students, one critical element of which was having a good rapport with students. The teachers felt this rapport supported students in mastering the challenging curriculum. "[My] basic premise is if you make it fun, kids learn better; if they're excited and interested" (YES 2, teacher interview, 2002). This teacher went on to say: "I'm always surprised how naturally kids are learning, like they want to learn." Experience teaching mathematics helped this teacher discover that students were naturally "good learners." One way to create rapport is through praise. One teacher remarked that it is important to praise students when they do well to promote a sense of accomplishment. Such praise lets students know teachers care and appreciate their efforts.

Another aspect of the comfortable learning environment created and maintained by YES teachers was the expectation that students would discuss mathematics with their peers as well as the teacher. This discussion was intended to reduce stress on individual students while developing a sense of community. However, counterbalancing this practice was the teacher belief that it was important for students to discover concepts on their own. This was encouraged by eliciting individual student responses whenever possible. This practice was evident during an observation of a sixth-grade lesson on volume during which the teacher carefully led the discussion by eliciting responses from many students. Students actively engaged in the discussion and, after multiple interactions, one student explained that volume was like the stuffing in a turkey. Many of the students liked this response and it appeared to help them develop a deeper understanding of the concept of volume.

One teacher described a proactive approach used to encourage all students to participate in a nonthreatening learning environment: "I definitely try to engage the students as much as possible in a dialogue as we go back and forth about homework or whatever questions are at hand. So I kind of lead that, but I want them to take over" (YES 5, teacher interview, 2003). This teacher represented the faculty's conviction that active participation was an essential element of the mathematics classroom. Another teacher discussed encouraging students to participate: "I think there are a few kids that I would like to participate more. I tease them a lot. I say, 'You owe me two hand raises today,' and they'll do it" (YES 1, teacher interview, 2002). In describing a lesson in which students measured the diameters and circumferences of various circles to discover the meaning of pi, the teacher expressed the opinion that discussion was critical to students' success. Students had to develop and communicate the ideas on their own and not just memorize ideas communicated by the teacher.

Teachers Modified Instruction to Meet the Needs of Their Students. The last of the findings supporting the importance of student–teacher relationships was reflected in the sensitivity of teachers to student needs. Mathematics teachers at YES adapted instruction in their classes when necessary.

One teacher explained that one class might have a harder time understanding concepts than another class. If this happened, then the pace of the class was slowed down a little and more repetition was provided for the students who needed it. Another teacher agreed that differences from class to class had to be addressed, stating that, "I think any good instruction needs to [be adjusted]. ... There's core things that should probably stay the same, but there's also ways to tweak things to meet the needs of the kids" (YES 2, teacher interview, 2003). Another teacher explained in detail how instruction changed, noting that, "It changes from one class period to the next depending on what I see in the kids. I try to adapt to whatever I see or sense from the kids—all the time, day to day, week to week, throughout the year" (YES 6, teacher interview, 2003).

Teachers also worked to make lessons relevant to students. The teachers described their belief in the importance of having their students see that mathematics is applicable in real-life situations: "It is important for students to see that mathematics is everywhere, and we use it to describe what's going on in the world as we see it and to interpret or predict what might happen based on what we see" (YES 5, teacher interview, 2003). To make mathematics relevant, YES teachers believed it was important to consider their students' lives when planning lessons while respecting the cultural diversity of their students and attempting to address and affirm this diversity in the mathematics classroom: "I feel like a math lesson has to be relevant to their real lives or it's not interesting and ultimately it's not effective. ... [For example], I like to connect to food [in my lessons]. Food is always a good way to connect culture" (YES 4, teacher interview, 2002). Students also needed to be encouraged to apply the mathematical skills they had learned in the past to new situations. Furthermore, the teachers believed that students should be able to explain why they were doing something and understand what led to the development of those ideas.

The sample lesson also represents the supportive relationship among teachers and students. Both the teacher and students had a well-defined sense of purpose focused on the learning of mathematics even when it seemed difficult. Students were supported in this endeavor through the careful and supportive prompting of the teacher. The classroom atmosphere was one in which students were expected to take risks to enhance learning. Students were required to push their understanding, but were supported throughout so as not to become too frustrated. The atmosphere permeating the classroom was one of high expectations and the knowledge that everyone could learn mathematics with the support of peers and the teacher.

FINAL REMARKS

YES College Preparatory School is truly an exemplary school. Many factors contributed to this school's success in teaching mathematics. Similar to other researchers' findings, we found that excellence in mathematics education requires high expectations (Ball & Cohen, 1999; Ladson-Billings, 1995; NCTM, 2000). Teacher expectations influence students' learning (Brophy & Good, 1986), and the teachers at YES upheld high expectations for their students. They expected all of their students to work hard and to do well. Students were expected to turn in all assignments and teachers accepted no excuses for missing work. Teachers believed that if they maintained high expectations, then students would strive to meet those expectations both during their tenure at YES and into the future.

Apple (1990) believes improving teaching requires enacting democratic conceptions of equity in which social, economic, and political inequalities are overcome to provide all students access to a rigorous curriculum. Such conceptions of equity were evident at YES College Preparatory School. The faculty at YES was continually striving to empower all of the students to learn. They provided support for students to learn challenging mathematical content through extra tutoring before school, at lunch time, and after school. In addition, all teachers carried cell phones provided by the school, so students could contact them at night to ask questions on homework.

In the *Principals and Standards of School Mathematics* document (NCTM, 2000), the notion that the mathematics curriculum should be well articulated across grade levels is advanced. At YES College Preparatory School, the teachers placed great emphasis on articulating the mathematics curriculum across the middle and high school grades. They had a challenging curriculum that the faculty reviewed and evaluated yearly. This curriculum placed great value on mathematical problem solving and was aligned with both state and national mathematics standards. The students at YES were well prepared for college after graduation because of the rigorous curriculum.

Clewell, Anderson, and Thorpe (1992) found that it was important to use a variety of instructional approaches to improve academic performance, and this was also evident at YES College Preparatory School. The teachers at YES used a variety of instructional methods and encouraged high levels of student participation. They reviewed skills when needed, had students work in small groups, focused on problem-solving skills, and required students to communicate their ideas both orally and in writing. Boaler (2002) found that teachers that used reform-oriented mathematics materials achieved a reduction of class inequalities in their schools, and this was also the case at YES. We found, as did Boaler (2002b), that teachers set a goal of conceptual understanding for all students, and then provided mediation of different approaches to ensure that all students attained this goal.

Similar to the findings of other researchers (see, e.g., Clewell et al., 1992; Ladson-Billings, 1995), we also found that a critical component of the challenging curriculum at YES was the worthwhile mathematical tasks that were regularly implemented during class on a regular basis. Henningsen and Stein (1997) found that "not only must the teacher select and appropriately set up worthwhile mathematical tasks, but the teacher must also proactively and consistently support students' cognitive activity without reducing the complexity and cognitive demands of the task" (p. 546). The teachers at YES College Preparatory School had an extensive collection of worthwhile mathematical tasks and were very skilled at using these tasks and challenging students to increase their understanding of mathematics. We found the students at YES were actively engaged in learning and making sense of challenging mathematical content on a consistent basis.

Another factor that contributed to the success of the mathematics program at YES was the importance the teachers placed on connecting to their students (Ball & Cohen, 1999). The teachers respected the cultural diversity of their students and considered their students' lives when developing lessons. The mathematics teachers also stimulated students' imaginations by using a variety of innovative and thought-provoking instructional materials gleaned from multiple sources rather than basing their instruction solely on a textbook. Teachers shared materials freely and they used these materials to extend their students' experience beyond simple memorization of facts to a higher level of understanding of mathematical concepts. The teachers also had good rapport with students and frequently offered praise and encouragement. The teachers endeavored to provide a comfortable, yet challenging, learning environment in which all students could learn.

Lastly, as other researchers have found (e.g., V. E. Lee & Smith, 2001), in highly effective schools a collective responsibility for learning is shared among all faculty, and this was apparent at YES. The faculty had a shared sense of purpose, and the majority of the faculty engaged students in interactive learning where developing a deep understanding of mathematics was the norm.

5

Challenging Mathematical
Content and High-Level Instruction

Richard S. Kitchen

This chapter is devoted to the second of the three major themes discovered at all nine participating schools: Challenging mathematical content and high-level instruction were of great importance at all of these schools. It explores the five areas related to this theme: (a) Problem solving is prioritized. (b) At middle schools, students completed the equivalent of algebra I by eighth grade. (c) Students communicate mathematically and engage in inquiry. (d) Mathematics curriculum is a work in progress. (e) Teachers prepare students to be successful on standardized tests, but they teach beyond the test.

CHALLENGING MATHEMATICAL CONTENT
AND HIGH-LEVEL INSTRUCTION

Focus on Problem Solving

During both the fall 2002 and spring 2003 visits, teachers were asked to identify the three most important mathematical ideas for their students to learn. It was common for teachers to discuss the value they placed on mathematical problem solving and students' capacities to communicate mathematically. Teachers often spoke directly about the importance of their students learning how to think, and this was accomplished through engaging in challenging problem-solving activities. In the following, a teacher from YES College Preparatory School identified the importance of students developing critical thinking skills through problem solving:

> Now I'm really interested in, do they have the big picture? You know, why do you study these things? So whether it's my Algebra II class,

we're doing augment, inverse matrixes, I want them to know not just
how do you go about solving the problem but why do you go about doing that. What led to the development of those ideas? Obviously I want
them to be able to solve those problems. What I've seen over the last few
years is that if they don't get the big picture in the beginning, all they're
going to do is memorize their way through it. And that's not the kind of
teacher I want to be. I had too many of those teachers in high school,
and I really resented them for trying to train me like a monkey to just
memorize and solve. If you look at the AP calculus curriculum and
other higher level math classes, they're really now trying to focus more
on what you've learned and being able to ask critical questions. What
would happen if I changed this about the problem? So, that's one thing
that's really important to me. (YES4, YES College Prep, 10/02)

Another teacher at YES College Preparatory School highlighted the importance of preparing students to be good problem solvers and independent thinkers:

I think we have a shared purpose. … Besides I guess the academic part,
problem solving, there is a huge emphasis. We have one thing we want
to start, we're still debating on how we want it to happen; having a
problem that the middle school kids and the high school kids can all
work on but at different levels, maybe cokes in the cafeteria, something
they could do. So the problem solving is just huge. Teaching them to be
independent thinkers so they don't need us, so they don't come to us to
think through everything, so they don't come to us immediately. They
really do try it fully on their own. We talk a lot about that at our grade
level meetings. So I think that's huge. (YES1, YES College Prep, 10/02)

At Ysleta Middle School, teachers taught a very specific problem-solving
strategy that students were expected to demonstrate on the TAAS, which is
the standardized test administered in Texas at the time this study was undertaken. In El Paso, students were expected to explicitly demonstrate their
competence to use all four steps of this problem-solving process on the
TAAS. Clearly, this impacted teachers' conceptions and practices at the
three participating Texas schools, and it was particularly evident at Ysleta
Middle School, where teachers had attended workshops conducted by
Sharon Wells and used her instructional materials in their classes. These materials were aligned specifically to the Texas Essential Knowledge and Skills
(TEKS), which at the time this study was undertaken, was the state curriculum framework. The TAAS was designed to align with the TEKS. A teacher
from Ysleta Middle School talks about students learning the four steps that
they were required to demonstrate on the TAAS, but also pointed out the
value of students understanding these steps:

Also problem solving strategies [are important to teach]. [They] not
only do have to write a real life problem, hopefully something that they

really do, [but they have] to show the process of coming up with the op-
eration to justify it. [They also learn] UPSE, Understand, Plan, Solve,
and Evaluate or justify. I want them to know the steps; why they came
up with that solution. (Yslt4, Ysleta MS, 10/02)

While addressing the three most important mathematical ideas to teach,
a veteran teacher at Latta High School selected the development of students' thinking and problem-solving skills as top priorities:

I think my number one thing is I like to get the kids thinking. And I
know that there are situations that rote memorization is important, but
unless they are able to think through things, analyze, that is just so important. So, thinking is number one and if you're able to think, you become a better problem solver. It doesn't matter if it's a math class but
wherever you are, if you're a good problem solver you can go so much
farther with whatever it is that you're pursuing. (Latta1, Latta HS, 3/03)

A teacher at the J. D. O'Bryant School of Mathematics and Science valued
the development of students' critical thinking and problem-solving skills:

Mathematically, I would say that I want my students to be able to think,
to problem solve. I like to run a classroom where it's inquiry based,
where students are asking a lot of questions. I'll do problems where I
want them to problem solve. It might not be a problem that they've
seen before, but they learn how to problem solve and try to figure out
an answer even if it's not something I've exposed them to. And doing
group work leads to students trying to figure out how to do something.
So, that's another thing I want them to do mathematically speaking is
problem solve. (OBry3, J. D. O'Bryant SMS, 11/02)

A teacher at the J. D. O'Bryant School of Mathematics and Science
wanted students to be able to solve problems in more than one way:

I like them to know that there is always more than one way to get the
answer. They're always constantly trying to get the answer rather than
the process, but there is always more than one process and that really
shows up. ... So I try and stress that with all of the classes. That's one
thing, trying to get the kids to think. (OBry1, J. D. O'Bryant SMS, 11/02)

Although a goal at most of the participating schools was to structure the
mathematics curriculum to prepare students to be successful on state and
national tests, it was commonly the case that teachers did not solely use
skills-based curricula and instruction. Even at schools that had a
skills-based mathematics curriculum, the development of students' problem-solving capacities and critical thinking skills were highly valued. At
both Ysleta Middle School and the KIPP Academy Bronx, time was allotted
during the day for students to solve mathematics problems in classes other

than their mathematics classes. At Ysleta Middle School, this problem- solving time occurred during the KIVA classes. One of the goals of these KIVA classes at Ysleta was to explicitly teach problem-solving approaches that were tested on the Texas, criteria-referenced test, the TAAS. At KIPP Academy Bronx, these "thinking skills" activities in mathematics were carried out by teachers throughout the school in the morning, but the students' work on these activities was reviewed during mathematics class. As the following teacher at the school describes, a primary goal of these activities was to regularly engage students in mathematical problem solving: "Everyone does thinking skills in the morning [in addition to their mathematics class]. … And we spend half an hour during the class, about 20 minutes, going over that, where they discuss the problem solving. That's what they do" (KIPPB4, KIPP Bronx, 4/03).

In Middle School, Focus on Number and Algebra

Teachers at the participating highly effective middle schools identified the importance of their students having both strong number and number sense skills. For instance, teachers said they devoted significant time to helping students understand and be able to convert between fractions, decimals, and percentages. In addition, at all of the participating middle schools, students began learning algebra in middle school.

A teacher at KIPP Academy Bronx spoke about the importance of middle school students developing their understanding of number and basic operations: "So I think my job is to help [the students] have a good understanding of number sense, and numbers, basic operations, and most specifically changing from different types of number. That, I think is very true, especially in 7th grade" (KIPPB2, KIPP Bronx, 10/02).

A teacher at Rockcastle County Middle School valued the development of students' skills in number, particularly making connections among fractions, decimals, and percentages. Students also began studying algebra in 7th grade:

> Well, the major focus in 7th grade is the fractions, decimals, and percents, where they can look at something and get equivalent fractions and know what the decimal and what the percent are. We spend a lot of time working with those, where they can interchange them. So, that's a big focus in 7th grade. Algebra, we start working on that [too]. (Rock2, Rockcastle County MS, 3/03)

As discussed in an earlier chapter, substantial academic support was provided at the participating middle schools to both help students with their remedial needs in mathematics and to prepare them to be successful in Algebra. At YES College Preparatory School, students studied pre-algebra for 2 years in the middle school:

> We kind of think with them, pre-algebra as a two year commitment, which given that they're in 6th grade, I don't think is that unrealistic. I have really high expectations for them, [another teacher] actually will come in sometimes and call them his pre-, pre-, pre- pre-, pre-calculus class. (YES2, YES College Prep, 4/03)

The mathematics faculty at KIPP Academy Houston believed that they had been successful teaching their middle school students algebra and had begun to pay more attention to integrating geometry with algebra:

> KIPP has been traditionally weak in geometry. They're [the students] rocking in algebra when they graduate from here. They pass out of algebra in high school and they go straight into honors geometry and they have a really hard time. So I mean, I'm just a believer in that we teach both geometry and algebra and how we can integrate the two very easily. And it's not like your taking away from algebra in a geometrical context. I think that they strengthen each other and support each other. (KIPPH2, KIPP Houston, 10/02)

Students Communicate Mathematically and Engage in Inquiry

Many of the teachers discussed how much they valued students communicating their mathematical ideas in class. Others described how they used instructional strategies in class that engaged students in mathematical inquiry. One of the classroom strategies the teachers incorporated to achieve these goals was to have students work in collaborative groups.

A teacher at the J. D. O'Bryant School of Mathematics and Science believed students learned better when they had to communicate mathematical ideas: "The group work; I would like students to work in a group in order for them to be able to communicate their ideas a little bit better. I find that if they do that they tend to remember things a little bit better especially in geometry" (OBry4, J. D. O'Bryant SMS, 11/02).

A goal of a teacher at Emerald Middle School was to engage multiple student voices in class. She also discussed using groups as a means to assist English-language learners:

> I don't use [students' raising] hands as much as I use cards, to call on students. I, at some point, ask everyone in the class something as we go around the room. "I would like you to respond." If I use hands, then I'm calling on the same people all of the time. ... I don't put them together, all Hispanics in one group or anything. I try and get a mixed group so they're hearing the language; that they are participating in the discussion that the students in these classes for the most part are able to at least participate in discussions with peers. (Emer3, Emerald MS, 10/02)

A teacher at YES College Preparatory School believed students learned for understanding when they were allowed to discuss and discover mathematical ideas:

> My class is very much discussion oriented and I try as often as possible. It gets difficult sometimes, but I try as often as possible to let them come up with what I'm trying to teach instead of me just telling them what I'm trying to teach. (YES2, YES College Prep, 4/03)

As presented in detail in chapter 8, teachers at the Young Women's Leadership School worked to create and foster an active, cooperative, inquiry-based learning environment:

> In terms of the volume of the class and the talking among the kids, it's almost always like that. In terms of activity level and movement and stuff, it's always like that. I would say that on a normal day, usually we start off with an activity that's a little bit longer and start with a problem that I'll kind of do on the board. If it's a new activity, I'll introduce it or new information and then come up with an activity for them to do. If it's just a practice day, then they'll do an activity to practice. If it's a new activity, we'll do something that's a discovery activity and then they'll just do that right away. There is always some interaction [among students], not very often is it teacher directed. (TYWLS3, TYWLS, 4/03)

A teacher at Rockcastle County Middle School allowed students to engage in more inquiry-based projects as the school year progressed:

> I guess I start small, and then work way up to the larger things that make sense. I still have the most control, I guess over most of it in September, and then turn it basically over to them. That goes back to the inquiry-based learning, you know, giving the students more responsibility to learn on their own. (Rock4, Rockcastle County MS, 3/03)

Mathematics Curriculum as a Work in Progress

Teachers at participating schools talked about how the mathematics curriculum was continually evolving. A teacher at Rockcastle County Middle School believed that for this to occur, the mathematics faculty at the school needed to move "beyond" the perspective that the textbook defines the mathematics curriculum:

> I think one challenge for us, the math staff, is getting beyond the textbook. I think we've made some progress in that and the realization that our textbook is not our curriculum. We are constantly looking for the materials that will supplement and develop what we need; we're very supported by our administration in that. (Rock3, Rockcastle County MS, 10/02)

Another teacher at Rockcastle County Middle School used the analogy of the mathematics curriculum as a block of ice that needed to be sculpted over time. According to this teacher, curriculum design and implementation is an ongoing, dynamic process that should sustain high student expectations:

> I think our goal is to meet every year and revise to make it (the curriculum) better. … It's just a constant, kind of like a sculpture, like an ice sculpture. You take a block of ice and you chip away and you chip away until you get something that's really good. You find out you have to do a little bit more, a little bit more to make it perfect. … It is just that constant growth and the striving to improve across the levels, not only in math but school wide. And it is difficult. I was part of the textbook adoption committee six years ago when we chose and I thought, "this is a good textbook." I very seldom use it because what we want now is very different. … What we want five years from now should be different than what we want now. Our expectations of our student achievement should be higher than what it is now. If not, we're not doing a very good job. (Rock5, Rockcastle County MS, 10/02)

A teacher at Emerald Middle School also alluded to how the school's mathematics curriculum was dynamic and about the need to supplement the textbook. This teacher had strong opinions about the importance of teachers critically evaluating their curriculum materials to positively impact both student learning and motivation:

> We've found in the last few years, that our math approach is certainly not static, it's dynamic. … I don't use the textbook. I am using it, but I don't use it every single day. I supplement the course with Excel Mathematics at the 6th grade level because I think it's extremely effective, it's got proven results behind it. … If you want the child to love mathematics and have success, you cannot rely on that text, if you do you're going to destroy a lot kids and parents. I think that what we find that maybe we haven't addressed a whole lot is that every single person here that I know, supplements, supplements, supplements. … I don't think we focus on any one text to do the job, because we don't. My experience tells me, I've never found a textbook that can teach children mathematics effectively and as the standards have increased. … That is where we, as teachers, have needed to be much more creative and supplement that curriculum with some understanding and motivation and fun. (Emer4, Emerald MS, 10/02)

Another teacher at Emerald Middle School believed that it was more important that students made meaning of what they were learning than it was for them to cover the material in the textbook: "The whole thing is trying to bring meaning; everything that we do has got to bring meaning. Even sometimes when it seems so abstract and they'll never use it; 'like when will

I ever use it?' ... But most of the stuff I'll relate to what's going on in the real world, what I'm doing is meaningful" (Emer1, Emerald MS, 2/03).

A teacher at Ysleta Middle School also alluded to how teachers at the school tended to avoid the use of mathematics textbooks: "I use textbooks if I feel there is a need, but we don't use a lot of textbooks. I don't even use textbooks much in my language arts classes" (Yslt1, Ysleta MS, 9/02). Another teacher at Ysleta Middle School referred to the materials used to teach the seventh-grade curriculum as "Heinz 57" because it was drawn from multiple sources:

> Since we don't use textbooks, we had to find everything from the manual, the workbook, teacher's manual. So we pull from CMP, NCTM workbooks, every little thing that you can find that we have. So the 7th grade math one [curriculum], is like Heinz 57, it's from everywhere and anywhere. We compile those into our little module binder and from there we pull [other materials]. ... The 7th grade one, we have a book as a resource, but I haven't opened it in two years. (Yslt2, Ysleta MS, 2/03)

At KIPP Academy Bronx, one of the teachers was writing a textbook for use in 5th grade that could be used at KIPP Academies throughout the United States:

> The kids don't have a math book; we create all of that stuff on our own. That comes from looking at various textbooks and also at things that we've seen work in the past and recreating materials that we've used before. One of the nice things of working with [another teacher] is that this is his 11 years of teaching, so he brings 11 years of experience of teaching 5th grade math. ... He knows what's there [on the standardized test] and he's figured the best way to teach kids solid math concepts that are really math skills that they're going to need for the rest of their lives. It's also aligned with the expectations that the state has for 5th grade. So, he's worked out things that work that way and we've actually put together binders of lessons that we do with the kids, whether it's solving two-step word problems or how to teach rounding numbers. (KIPPB3, KIPP Bronx, 4/03)

At Latta High School, the teachers were more concerned about teaching the South Carolina mathematics standards than they were about following a particular textbook:

> We do have a textbook, but I follow a course outline that I got off the South Carolina state [department of education] web site. I have probably used that textbook about 20% of the time, and I pull from another Algebra I textbook and I pull from other Algebra I textbooks. I pull from supplemental materials. You almost have to develop your own curriculum. (Latta4, Latta HS, 3/03)

At the Young Women's Leadership School, a middle school teacher described drawing from multiple sources to teach mathematics:

> I don't have a textbook that we use. I think the school has the CMP, Connected Math Program. I use the activities in Connected Math, but I don't use the book. I also use stuff from Prentice Hall. They make a series of six little books that they have. ... So, I use those and I make a lot of their worksheets up and I think that over the years I've collected things I like from various books. (TYWLS3, TYWLS, 4/03)

A teacher at YES College Preparatory School rarely used a textbook and preferred having the students complete problems more than worksheets:

> We do have a math book; I think it's the Heath Integrated Algebra book. We use it probably, I don't know within a month, I would say probably twice. It's more of a resource book for them. I tend to do my own worksheets most of the time. I like giving them problems where they're focusing on different things, like two or three parts of the problem. I hate worksheets that are already made or book problems. ... One of the other things that we use a lot is AIMS; they always have really cool stuff. (YES3, YES College Prep, 4/03)

Teachers Prepare Their Students to Be Successful on Standardized Tests, but Teach Beyond the Test

The final feature contributing to the delivery of challenging mathematical content and high-level instruction was the belief shared by teachers at the study schools that they needed to prepare students to be successful on standardized tests, but that they should also teach beyond the test. At all of the schools, teachers were mindful that they were being evaluated on their students' academic achievement, often based on their students' performance on standardized tests. For instance, at Ysleta Middle School, teachers were well aware that they were held directly accountable for their students' test scores in mathematics. Many mathematics teachers had left the school in recent years as a result of this pressure for student success on tests:

> In the last four years, we've had four different math teachers. They were here one year and they were gone, here one year and gone. You're accountable for doing their curriculum and everything else the school demands from you, and the GT (gifted and talented) stuff, the KIVA stuff, anything on the side you have to do to support the language arts. ... They [the administration] look at your kids, my kids, [another teacher's] class and how many of mine passed [the test]. How many of her students passed? What percentage? And they compare it like that and the growth. What growth they have from last year's test to this year's test? Did they go up in score? Did they go down in score? Is it a

pattern? How do you compare to the other teachers? She does that in all curriculum areas; language arts, to the science teachers. Okay, she breaks up the kids and let's see who's been doing the job?

So it's pressure that comes from the top, pressure that I put on myself. … I pressured the kids and it trickles down. It comes from the principal to you and you pressure the kids. It's basically, "look guy, we got to produce if you want that optional high school credit [for passing the algebra test]." … And so they compare your scores with the district exit scores, compare them with the state scores. They take your scores and compare them to other middle schools in your area, or economically [comparable schools] around Texas, and they see what you are doing. (Yslt2, Ysleta MS, 9/02)

Motivating and preparing students at Ysleta for success on the Texas, criteria-referenced test—the TAAS—was hard work, as described by the following teacher:

I have all of the students who come up in the 8th grade that are working on a 4th grade level and some even, it's sad to say, they can't even add and subtract without the little tap. And I'm supposed to catch them up and my purpose is to catch those kids up where they can function as regular math students in the 8th grade and that is a huge challenge. Oh, and it is hard because those are the kids that have quit. You know, three or four years ago, they just flat quit. Our job is to get those kids and to embrace them and somehow motivate them, get in their face, whatever it takes! A lot of after school hours and one-on-one tutoring and finding out what the problem is. … But I have to reach them; I have to get cooperation from home. And if I can't … maybe a coach [can help]. [Names a coach] is fabulous! And no pass, no play is a benefit. With a good coach and a good math teacher, we do marvelous. (Yslt4, 9/02)

Although one of the teachers at Ysleta Middle School taught with the standards-based curriculum, Connected Mathematics, another teacher expressed the tension between using this text and preparing students to be successful on the TAAS:

But you cannot fulfill the whole curriculum [Connected Math] and do it because the things are really. … If you had math for an hour every day, you could do it and most middle schools even do have math everyday, and those people can work on those projects [that are part of the Connected Math program] and take them and then get all of the curriculum in. We have every other day [to teach our math classes], and it's just 20 lessons. … You've got to fit pair and order and add and subtract decimals, and compare and order and simplify lowest terms, fractions … in one day! (Yslt4, Ysleta MS, 9/02)

This Ysleta Middle School teacher continued by discussing the satisfaction of teaching students and helping them be successful on the test:

> I'm prideful. Because I take pride in my job and student achievement, I want them [the students] to pass. This is my 32nd year of teaching. ... I want them to know what I've done; I can get the most accomplishment in the shortest time with the clearest understanding. That is the perfect situation, if I can get that done and get to every kid, and then I feel good about me and my job. ... I'm a survivor. I may not survive this year, but I'm a survivor because I'm one of the few that taught over 20 years and hasn't been run out of town. Why? Because of my T.A.A.S. scores, because I teach math, because I don't have too many discipline problems, not a lot of parent complaints. (Yslt4, Ysleta MS, 9/02)

Teachers at Emerald Middle School talked often about mathematics curriculum and teaching and received release time to analyze their students' scores on the standardized examination that they were administering, the STAT 9 test:

> Many of the other things, I think we're always talking about math. I know we're always talking about math, in the hallway, at lunch, what have you. But we've also been provided release time to develop [curriculum], [and] we've analyzed STAT 9 scores. We'll analyze a weak area such as measurement and statistics and then we'll have release time to develop a supplemental unit to enhance those skills that will be taught in addition, not in substitution but in addition, to what our regular curriculum is. So I think we've been really lucky to have the amount of release time that we've been given as well because all we have to do is go to [the principal] or our former principal and say that our math department needs to meet. We want to meet and these are the things we need to do. (Emer4, Emerald MS, 10/02)

Another teacher at Emerald Middle School believed that through analyzing test scores, teachers had developed instructional units that had directly improved test scores at the school:

> She [former school principal] asked us to meet and identify the weak scores, STAT 9 scores in each grade level. As [another teacher] said, we've developed our units to enhance our scores and to make sure we've taught them wherever they were appropriate and that was a part of it. That brought up our scores because we focused on them. (Emer3, Emerald MS, 10/02)

The process of writing these supplementary units afforded the mathematics teachers at Emerald Middle School a meaningful forum to be connected and have ongoing conversations:

I was here the first year with [former principal] when we did that. I think it laid down a good foundation for us to continue to do that even after she [the former principal] left. We found that it was so useful that we still continued to have afternoon meetings to work with those supplemental units. I thought it was a pretty powerful way to stay focused and stay connected and to have conversations with each other, to keep us on the same line or in the same direction. (Emer5, Emerald MS, 10/02)

Like teachers at Emerald Middle School, teachers at Rockcastle County Middle School involved students directly in identifying the areas in mathematics in which they needed further study based on their performance on a standardized test. Teachers at Rockcastle County Middle School also analyzed test scores to identify the mathematical content in which students needed additional instruction: "We also look at last year's scores, what they're [the students] doing, what the lowest [areas are] and what we can do to improve our scores for next year. Looking at the areas of the most needs" (Rock1, Rockcastle County MS, 10/02). Engaging in an item analysis of the standardized test used at Rockcastle County Middle School informed the teachers' instruction:

I think we let the data drive a lot of what we're going to do. For instance, last weekend I was looking at the test scores of 6th graders from last year, from my students, an item analysis. There are some things that they did not do well on. ... I've got to change what I'm doing this year to make it better. I think all of us, we do that, we use that data constantly to drive what we do, making changes and revisions when necessary. (Rock3, Rockcastle County MS, 10/02)

Teachers at Latta High School believed that teaching to the state standards prepared students to be successful on South Carolina's high school exit examination:

Along with what [another teacher] said, our main purpose is to get these kids ready for the high school exit exam. ... That's the biggie that we have to do. ... [Another teacher] kind of covered it with the standards and we talk to one another an awful lot about what needs to be covered in this class. If you don't get there, we hope we can pick it up in this class and we hope to get all the standards covered. (Latta3, Latta HS, 11/02)

At the Young Women's Leadership School, the majority of the teachers identified preparing students to be successful on the New York state high school graduation test, the Regents Exam, as one of their primary goals. This test was initially administered to students when they were in 10th grade: "Our number one purpose is getting kids through the Regents Exams. I think that is very [important], it seems to be what we talk about most of the time. So, I would say that's a shared sense of purpose" (TYWLS4, TYWLS, 10/02). To ensure that students were successful on the Regents Exam, the teachers at the Young Women's Leadership School devoted time to "work backwards" to vertically align their mathematics curriculum through Grades 7–12:

> Eventually, our goal would be to sit down to figure out in order to get them to the top to pass all the Regents. We work backwards in order to be able to figure out where to start in 7th grade, what they need to get down in the 8th grade in order to get them ready for high school, so we can move them to calculus and pre-calculus. (unknown teacher, TYWLS, 10/02)

Like the mathematics faculty at the Young Women's Leadership School, the teachers at KIPP Academy Bronx engaged in backward curriculum planning, except that their goal was to prepare students to be successful in high school algebra. There was also a focus at KIPP Academy Bronx on pre-paring students to be successful on standardized examinations, which the following teacher did not believe was an unreasonable goal to accomplish:

> The test does drive [the curriculum]. The reality is you [the research team] wouldn't be here; we wouldn't have won the award [for being a high-achieving school] if it wasn't for the [exemplary] test scores. The fact is it's very much in the back of our minds. However far above [the mathematics benchmarks] we're going, we have to make sure we're go-ing to meet those benchmarks. The other thing is, it's not like those benchmarks are unreasonable. If you look at those math tests, it's like basic stuff that kids should know how to do. (unknown teacher, KIPP Bronx, 11/02)

Although teachers at KIPP Academy Bronx were mindful of the impor-tance of standardized tests, they were more concerned about preparing stu-dents well for success in their next mathematics course: "It's not a waste, because they're always going to have to take tests. But in terms of my gen-eral lesson, I'm not thinking of the test really. I'm thinking of what I have to get done before algebra" (KIPPB4, KIPP Bronx, 4/03).

Similar to his counterpart at KIPP Bronx, the following teacher at YES College Preparatory School believed that by teaching beyond minimal stan-dards, students would be well prepared for standardized examinations:

> Definitely [my teaching is influenced by the test, but also] it's influ-enced by standards quite a bit. … But the ways in which they are as-sessed [on the test] I think is a lot lower level thinking than what I was doing today. So I try in my class in general to meet the standards, but not use those as a kind of minimum level of what I should be doing. So I feel like you know, if I didn't have the standards I might not be teaching

this at all, but since I have those it's something I focus on. I definitely use those as kind of a guideline for what I should be doing. (YES2, YES College Prep, 4/03)

CONCLUDING REMARKS

The analysis of teacher narratives made evident that across the highly effective schools problem solving and the instruction of algebra and higher level mathematics were very much valued. In addition, teachers valued students communicating mathematically in the classroom, considered the mathematics curriculum as a work in progress, and the teachers' instruction was strongly influenced by standardized testing. The case study of Emerald Middle School in the following chapter offers in-depth insights into the value the teachers at Emerald place on a challenging mathematical curriculum and high-level instruction.

Interestingly, although only Rockcastle County Middle School, Ysleta Middle School, and the Young Women's Leadership School used standards-based curriculum materials (specifically the Connected Mathematics Program), problem solving was highly valued across the school sites. At all the participating schools, but particularly at the charter schools, teachers highly valued problem solving (A. Thompson, 1992) and challenging students to think and reason. Teachers frequently discussed the importance they placed on problem solving and how they viewed problem solving as a means to develop their students' thinking skills. Also, across the nine participating schools, teachers often talked about the importance of developing students' problem-solving abilities in addition to mastering the basics of mathematics. In other words, teachers did not sacrifice engaging students in problem solving to focus solely on the basics.

In the analysis of the classroom observation ratings (see appendix D for the full summary of these ratings), the charter school ratings were higher than the non-charter school ratings for all of the subscales (intellectual support, depth of knowledge and student understanding, mathematical analysis, discourse and communication, and student engagement). The differences in the means between charter and non-charter schools were statistically significant for all the subscales except intellectual support. At the participating charter schools, YES College Preparatory School and the KIPP Academies, teachers adamantly described how their primary goal was to develop students' problem-solving skills and taught challenging mathematical content with the objective of positively impacting their students' abilities to think critically. This may help explain why we found higher levels of mathematical analysis in the charter school classrooms observed, instruction that focused on depth over coverage, and higher levels of mathematical discourse. This finding lends strong support to the notion that at schools where the development of students' mathematical problem-solving skills is prioritized, exceptional learning and high achievement take place. It also demonstrates that teachers at highly effective schools greatly valued engaging students in mathematical problem solving, a primary recommendation of documents that advocate for standards-based reforms (see NCTM, 1989, 2000; NSF, 1996).

The analysis of the classroom observation ratings also established that participating middle schools[5] outperformed high schools for all of the sub-scales, although the middle school lessons observed were only statistically significantly higher in the engagement subscale. This means that in the middle school classes observed, students tended to be more actively engaged in learning mathematics than their counterparts in the high school classroom. This finding lends support to the notion that the highly effective middle schools provided more engaging instruction than was found in the high schools.

Another finding at participating middle schools was of the importance that teachers placed in developing students' skills with numbers and number sense. For instance, teachers at Rockcastle County Middle School and the Young Women's Leadership School worked hard to help their students make connections among fractions, decimals, and percentages. In the middle schools, the teaching of algebra was also a priority. Generally, students were expected to complete the equivalent of an algebra I course by the completion of eighth grade, although some schools taught the course over 2 years (e.g., YES College Preparatory School).

Faculty at KIPP Academy Houston discussed how they had been so successful teaching algebra to their middle school students that they had decided to place greater emphasis on the instruction of geometry, a subject in which their students were not as successful. At J. D. O'Bryant School of Mathematics and Science, students were expected to successfully complete pre-calculus before graduation. At the Young Women's Leadership School, students were required to complete 4 years of coursework in mathematics, but only 3 years were required in New York City.

Given how teachers were continually collaborating to create challenging, well-articulated mathematics curricula from grade-to-grade, the mathematics curriculum was a work in progress at the participating schools. Teachers at the schools did not make use of solely one mathematics textbook and frequently supplemented the curriculum. The teachers often talked about pulling from various sources to create their mathematics curricula. A teacher at Emerald Middle School summarized why no one textbook was adequate, given how the state standards in California had expanded: "I've never found a textbook that can teach children mathematics effectively as the standards have increased."

---

[5]J. D. O'Bryant School of Mathematics and Science, YES College Preparatory School, and the Young Women's Leadership School included both a middle school and high school.

Standardized testing had a powerful influence on mathematics curriculum and instruction at all the participating schools. When this study was undertaken, the No Child Left Behind (NCLB) legislation had been approved and schools across the United States were shifting their resources and foci to prepare students for success on "the test." Given the accountability measures of NCLB, this shift was certainly understandable. The schools that participated in this study would not have been selected for inclusion if their students had not been successful on standardized tests. Clearly, teachers at the participating schools placed a huge emphasis on preparing their students to be successful on standardized tests. Structures were in place at the schools so that students could be successful on the test. For instance, at the Young Women's Leadership School, special test preparation sessions were offered on Saturdays. At Ysleta Middle School, Rockcastle County Middle School, and Emerald Middle School, teachers engaged in test item analysis to decipher areas in which their students needed additional instruction and wrote instructional units to address their students' mathematical deficiencies.

Nonetheless, teachers spoke about teaching beyond the test. Participating teachers often alluded to how, by teaching mathematical content that went beyond state standards, they were preparing their students for success on standardized tests. At Latta High School, the focus was on aligning curriculum and instruction with the state standards. The teachers at Latta High School believed that by teaching to the state standards, their students would have success on the test. In addition, teachers were also more interested at some schools in preparing students for success in a particular mathematical subject than on standardized tests. For example, the focus of the middle school mathematics curriculum at KIPP Academy Bronx was for students to complete a rigorous algebra course before high school.

As schools attempt to deal with the mandates of NCLB, the pressure to teach solely to the test will mount. The schools that participated in this study worked to help their students be successful on standardized tests, but the test did not necessarily dictate mathematics curricula and instruction. Instead, the focus on high expectations for student learning coupled with the support mechanisms for students to thrive academically led to high achievement at the participating schools. This finding is an important one for schools given the high-stakes testing climate that currently exists in the United States.

6

Emerald Middle School Case Study

Julie DePree
Jonathan Brinkerhoff

> The teachers here are really great. When I came to Emerald, I learned a lot more than I did in elementary school. Everything seemed more challenging but I could do it because I was taught how to do it by teachers; the teachers would teach me. I think the method of teaching is very unique. The teacher I had last year would take a question that someone had and really explain it and make sure you understood it.
>
> —*student interview* (2003)

In this chapter, the second of three comprehensive case studies is provided. Emerald Middle School was selected for an in-depth study because it had a diverse student body and some of the highest ratings in the area of challenging mathematical content among the non-charter schools. Emerald serves as a model for non-charter public schools, because it was not high achieving in mathematics until the faculty made this a priority. When the faculty decided to focus on mathematics and make deliberate changes in the program, the result was higher student achievement. High expectations, challenging mathematical content, supportive relationships among students and teachers, and high-level instruction are some of the components that made Emerald an exceptional school in the teaching of mathematics.

DESCRIPTION OF EMERALD MIDDLE SCHOOL

Emerald Middle School, a Title I public school located in an urban neighborhood in eastern San Diego County, served approximately 1,050 sixth, seventh, and eighth graders during the 2002–2003 school year. The ethnically diverse student body represented 14 different nationalities and spoke 16 different languages, with 44 % identifying themselves as Caucasian, 31% as Hispanic, 10% as African American, 10% as Chalean/Arabic, 2% as Asian, and 1% each of American Indian/Alaskan Native, Filipino, and Pacific Islander. Seventy-eight percent of the students at Emerald Middle School qualified for the free or reduced lunch program.

A clear mission statement defined the charge of the school, stating that Emerald Middle School should "enable Emerald staff, students, and families to enjoy working and learning together" (Emerald Middle School Web site, 2003). To achieve this mission, students will:

> Master basic skills and new concepts through a quality program which includes technology, projects, and enrichment activities; show respect and acceptance toward others; contribute to a safe, orderly, caring school environment; take pride in themselves and their school; benefit from a positive partnership between home and school; experience success at Emerald, in high school, and in future careers. (Emerald Middle School Web site, 2003)

The Emerald Middle School staff charged with meeting this mission statement consisted of 45 regular and special education teachers with an average of 9 years teaching experience. Sixteen teachers taught at least one section of mathematics. None of these teachers held a degree or minor in mathematics, however, 3 individuals had supplemental mathematics credentials. Each of the 16 teachers taught five classes and had 1 hour of preparation time. Many of the teachers opted to relinquish their prep period to teach an extra class, for which they received extra compensation.

The principal had worked at Emerald Middle School for 2 years. He described his leadership style as collegial and often solicited advice from staff, although he retained sole responsibility for final decisions. The principal provided leadership for the school through active involvement in curriculum development and the supervision of teachers. He viewed his role in the supervision of instruction as one of monitoring student assessment and instruction, implementing the California State Curriculum Standards, and evaluating teacher effectiveness. In his role as leader, the principal supported staff and involved teachers in decision making relevant to meeting state standards. Staff members also held leadership positions at Emerald, with teachers acting as team leaders and department chairpersons.

To promote a sense of community, Emerald Middle School was organized into instructional teams consisting of 4 teachers and approximately 160 students. All instruction for the team's students was provided by the same 4 teachers. The team structure afforded frequent opportunities for collaboration among teachers while permitting greater student support through increased communication between students and faculty. Within the team structure, students were provided a minimum of 54 minutes of mathematics instruction each day; however, teachers reported that, on many occasions, students received more than this because the team structure promoted the integration of standards-based curriculum across the four core subject areas.

Emerald's mathematics curriculum was split into two tracks. In the regular track, students took general mathematics in sixth grade, pre-algebra in seventh grade, and algebra in eighth grade. In the advanced track, students took pre-algebra in sixth grade, algebra in seventh grade, and geometry in eighth grade. The algebra and geometry classes were equivalent to those in high school.

To support both the mathematics and other curricula, Emerald had a schoolwide homework policy consistent with district school board requirements specifying the amount of time students should spend doing homework at each grade level. The mathematics department supported the practice of giving homework on a regular basis, and homework was typically incorporated into the grading system for each course.

In addition to the homework policy, support for the school's curricula also came from the school's discipline policies. The school had a well-established discipline plan that was disseminated in written communications to staff, students, parents, and teachers, and was also posted in each classroom. Students had the opportunity to provide input on the discipline policy through a student representative who served on the school site committee responsible for the discipline plan. Based on the discipline policy, expectations for student behavior were established early in the year and were consistently maintained throughout the year.

Another important component of Emerald's discipline policy was the staff-developed, award-winning character education program that permeated the school. The program, called *The Emerald Way*, emphasized desirable character traits on a regular basis, and was considered an integral part of the school. One example showcasing the integration of *The Emerald Way* into the school's culture was a daily student broadcast addressing issues involving character education and academics. As the technology magnet school for the district, the school had its own broadcasting system through which student teams presented a live broadcast each morning. Through the broadcast, content supportive of the character education program and the rigorous academic standards was presented.

Another way in which Emerald strove to limit behavior problems was through positive student engagement coupled with rewards for achievement. According to Emerald's principal, teachers at the school established and maintained classroom environments that engaged students through participation in purposeful learning activities promoting positive interactions among students. Student achievement was acknowledged by teacher praise, placement on the school's honor roll, awards, medals, trips, letters of commendation, and public recognition at school meetings and functions. During the student group interview, many students voiced an appreciation for these rewards and said the additional incentives inspired them to try their hardest. One student stated, "This school is special because it recognizes the kids" (student interview, 2003).

The net result of the schoolwide discipline policy, character education program, emphasis on positive student engagement, and the recognition and rewarding of student achievement was a low incidence of discipline problems at Emerald. During the 2001–2002 school year, there were approximately 70 cases of student suspension out of 1,050 students, a rate of approximately 6.7%.

Extracurricular activities offered at Emerald represented another positive aspect of the school environment. Teachers encouraged student participation in extracurricular activities as a means for developing skills in making decisions and working collaboratively as well as independently. Students had the opportunity to participate in a variety of clubs, including Spanish, computer, morning broadcast, discovery, and cheerleading. Additionally, an afterschool homework club was available to students wanting assistance on assignments. Finally, students could opt to engage in both intramural and extramural sports programs. The principal reported that between 11% and 20% of Emerald Middle School students participated in these afterschool activities.

All these various programs and activities were supported by the community in a number of ways. These included the tutoring of Emerald students on a regular basis by students enrolled in local colleges, as well as the provision of musical instruments by local music stores to support the school band program.

In addition, parents were encouraged to become active within the school community. The school had a parent–teacher association that occasionally conducted workshops for parents. There was also an active group of parent volunteers representing approximately 15% of Emerald's parents. The school held regular Meet and Eat Days where parents joined students for lunch, as well as Parent Tag Along Days. The school had also recently received a GEAR UP grant for development of an outreach program to increase parent and community involvement. With the support of the GEAR UP grant, administrators, faculty, and community members intended to meet on a regular basis to develop and implement a plan to further increase community and parent involvement, because many of the teachers expressed a need for more support from a greater percentage of parents on a daily basis.

METHOD

Researchers visited the school site twice, once in the fall and once during the spring 2002–2003 school year. In the fall, eight mathematics faculty members participated in a group interview. Four of the eight teachers were selected to participate in classroom observations and focused individual interviews. These four teachers were observed for two consecutive class-room lessons before participating in a follow-up interview in both the fall and the spring. During the spring visit, the principal was interviewed and completed a survey instrument. Additionally, a group of students repre-senting different grade levels was interviewed.

Findings concerning Emerald's success in teaching mathematics based on these data are summarized in the remainder of the chapter. First, a sam-ple lesson observed during one of the classroom observations is presented. This sample lesson exemplifies the following three major themes that emerged from the data collected at Emerald: high expectations and sus-tained support for academic excellence, challenging mathematical content and high-level instruction, and the importance of building relationships among teachers and students.

SAMPLE LESSON

This mathematics lesson was conducted in a regular sixth-grade classroom with approximately 30 students. The topics covered included drill and re-view of adding integers; mental math with basic operations; mixed practice with whole numbers, fractions, and decimals; and the concept of volume.

The class began with three activities focused on basic mathematics skills. The students began the class with a 5-minute warm-up activity in which they used mental math skills to solve various problems. For example, the teacher would say, "2 cubed times 3 minus 2 divided by 11 plus one," after which students would raise their hand with the answer.

Next, students moved to a timed drill of adding integers. A timer was dis-played on an overhead projector and students had 4 minutes to solve 50 problems. Students completed timed drills on a daily basis and made a bar graph of their scores to show their progress over time. Students seemed to enjoy seeing evidence of progress in their graphs.

Next, students moved to a review of basic skills with fractions and deci-mals. In response to teacher questions, they wrote answers on individual white boards and held them up so the teacher could quickly check for accu-racy. The teacher would randomly select one student to share results by drawing cards with students' names. Throughout all three of these activi-ties, students were actively engaged by the fast pace and active participa-tion. This review of basic skills lasted about 20 minutes each day before the teacher moved on to the lesson's new topic.

The new topic during the observed lesson was volume. First, students were placed in groups and were given dictionaries. They were told to de-velop "working" definitions for solid, cubic, cube, volume, proof, and jus-tify. Once they had written definitions, groups shared results and the class discussed the new terms. The class talked about filling up a coffee cup with coffee and how that related to volume. The last activity of the day involved working with manipulatives to better understand the concept of volume. Students were given cubes and told to build rectangular solids and record dimensions on a handout. The handout required students to record the length, width, height, shape, number of cubes, and total volume of their rectangular solid. After completing the handout, students were asked to examine their results and draw conclusions about the relationship between length, width, height, and interior volume. The handout included an inquiry-based question asking students to determine the possible exterior dimensions of a rectangular solid given its volume.

This sample lesson demonstrated the first major theme to emerge from the data: high expectations and a deliberate focus on teaching and learning. The content and structure of the lesson made it evident that the teacher exhibited high expectations for student learning. Each lesson component was well planned and focused. The teacher used multiple methods to reach all students and appealed to students' different learning styles by using visual aids, mental math, oral communication, white boards, and manipulatives. She had students work individually, in pairs, and in small groups. This variety of instructional strategies combined with quick lesson pacing served to keep students actively engaged throughout.

This sample lesson also illustrated the second theme because challenging mathematical content and high level of instruction were apparent during this lesson at Emerald Middle School. The content of the lesson included a combination of skills development and review coupled with mathematical inquiry. All of these concepts were taught at an advanced level for sixth grade. Test preparation seemed to be key to some of the review of basic skills, but the lesson went well beyond teaching for the test. A focus of the lesson was developing a deep understanding of the concept of volume. Emerald Middle School mathematics teachers endeavored to provide a challenging mathematics curriculum for all of their students.

Finally, the sample lesson also illustrated the third major theme. The importance of building relationships among teachers and students was evident in this lesson. The teachers and students at Emerald had a well-defined sense of purpose. All students were expected to learn the mathematics concepts, an expectation of which students were well aware. Additionally, all students were required to participate, not just the few that raised their hands. If a student had trouble answering a question, then the teacher artfully provided guidance and prompts to help the student; she did not just let the student off the hook. All of the students and the teacher seemed comfortable with this process; it was what was expected. Also, the team structure of the school allowed the mathematics teacher to extend the volume lesson into the science class. The students and teachers had a well-defined sense of purpose and that purpose was to have students gain a deep understanding of mathematical concepts.

High Expectation and Sustained Support for Academic Excellence

The first major contributor to Emerald Middle School's success in teaching mathematics was the culture of high expectations and sustained support for academic excellence. In both the group and individual faculty interviews, teachers addressed questions related to their views about high expectations. Themes that emerged from these interviews included a focus on teaching and learning, use of supplementary support for student learning, the availability of teaching resources and supplementary materials, and access to professional development opportunities.

Focus on Teaching and Learning. Emerald Middle School teachers emphasized instructional design focused on promoting students' high achievement in mathematics. This emphasis included a deliberate, sustained concentration on curriculum and instruction designed to provide a challenging mathematics curriculum. One teacher explained:

> We offer 6th grade pre-algebra, 7th grade algebra, and 8th grade geometry. We're the first ones in our district to do that. … It originated with a couple of kids who excelled higher than what we were offering and the principal at the time said that we should be offering a class to accommodate these students. We got approval from and support from the superintendent and so it's gone from 5 students to now 26 students. (Emerald 7, faculty interview, 2002)

This emphasis on teaching and learning at a high level was identified as important by another teacher, who explained, "We have a commitment to raise our standards a little higher. … We as a department have committed to that" (Emerald 7, faculty interview, 2002). Another teacher (Emerald 2, teacher interview, 2002) stated, "I see great things for my students." Although the teachers recognized that many of the students' basic skills were weak, they did not let this deter them from their goals. As one teacher explained:

> I have high expectations for the kids even though they come in lower than I would like. My expectation is that they're going to learn if I give them enough opportunities and try a lot of different approaches. They deserve the chance to learn, and sometimes I think that the kids aren't expected to excel to the point where they're able to; they're not challenged. I think all of us here expect a lot in math. We expect them to make leaps and bounds. We expect them [to do this] if we provide the foundation for them to do that and having good expectations for them helps a lot. (Emerald 8, faculty interview, 2002)

Students also recognized the high teacher expectations for academics. As one student (student interview, 2003) indicated, "One reason I came to this school is that I think the academics here are really important."

Teachers' deliberate focus on teaching and learning resulted in the use of a variety of instructional strategies. The mathematics teachers routinely varied instructional practices and design to address the diverse needs of Emerald's students. One teacher portrayed their instructional process by saying:

> I try to change strategies; I plan a lot with different kinds of things. I differentiate instruction. Some students love talking time; others hate it. I try to make visual components by drawing because I'm not sure if we're all abstract thinkers and a lot of math is abstract. I try to guide it and relate it to real life. … So I think it is more an individual basis depending on the child. (Emerald 1, teacher interview, 2003)

The incorporation of a variety of instructional approaches was used by many of Emerald's mathematics teachers. Another teacher (Emerald 2, teacher interview, 2002) stated, "I like trying new things. I like working in groups. I like the kids communicating with each other where I am not always at the center. I like doing lots of activities."

Another instructional practice representative of Emerald teachers' utilization of varied instructional strategies as a means for promoting learning was the use of visualization in mathematics and the frequent use of manipulatives to help students grasp abstract concepts. One teacher (Emerald 4, teacher interview, 2003) stated, "I do various things with manipulatives … and a certain amount of hands on things." Another teacher described the difficulties students initially had in grasping the idea of a variable and believed that manipulatives helped students understand abstract algebraic concepts more clearly. This teacher (Emerald 2, teacher interview, 2003) stated, "I think the students really understand those concepts [variables, combining like terms] better because of hands on equations."

This incorporation of a variety of instructional practices was also observed in classroom visitations such as the sixth-grade lesson described earlier in the chapter. In that lesson, the teacher moved seamlessly from one activity to another while continually engaging students. The teacher "warmed-up" by challenging students with mental math, then moved on to a 5-minute timed integer test reviewing integer operations. Next, the teacher had students review basic skills using white boards. Finally, students engaged in several discovery activities relating to the concept of volume in small groups. During the lesson, there was no wasted time and all students were engaged throughout the entire class period.

A final way teachers emphasized teaching and learning was through the use of meaningful mathematical tasks. The mathematics faculty at Emerald emphasized the importance of mathematics in real-life situations. One teacher (Emerald 2, teacher interview, 2003) explained, "Everything that we do has got to bring meaning, even sometimes when it seems so abstract, and they'll never use it. … I'll relate what's going on in the real world." Accordingly, real-world mathematics was introduced through the use of supplemental units and math games. A teacher described some of these activities used to make math meaningful:

> I have an extreme football game. It's football and it's with dice and a little map that looks like a football field. They have a little football that moves up and down so it looks like ... it talks about the scale. ... We're also doing fantasy baseball. ... They get a packet of cards. ... It is like the draft. ... They're in groups, they're a team. ... They have to open up their cards and come up with a statistical analysis [to determine which players to select]. (Emerald 2, teacher interview, 2003)

Another teacher explained:

> I try to make up a problem to help them understand something. ... If I'm introducing direct variation, it's easy to say you're buying a 6 pack of coke and it costs $2.00 ... using the money situation. ... I try and use those kinds of real-life situations that I make up. (Emerald 3, teacher interview, 2003)

The teachers at Emerald also commented on the diversity of the student body and how this was drawn on to make mathematics more meaningful for students. One teacher (Emerald 3, teacher interview, 2002) stated, "If I know something about a student, or group of students, and somehow it can fit in and make them understand better, then I do [incorporate culture, language, and gender in my teaching]." Many teachers mentioned that their students had a wide variety of life experiences that they capitalized on when teaching mathematics. One teacher described how the students shared their beliefs and interests, which the teacher then incorporated into lessons. This teacher (Emerald 4, teacher interview, 2003) stated, "I try to use examples and things that make sense to them; their life ... I draw from them. They educate me on their culture. ... We're very culturally diverse." The teachers also created examples using money, shopping, food, the stock market, and famous performers to relate mathematics to their students. One teacher described a specific example where the class discussed different money systems when students talked about visiting other countries. Through such lessons, the mathematics teachers at Emerald tried to convey meaning in the mathematics students were learning.

Supplemental Support Provided for Student Learning. The second theme supporting academic excellence included the variety of supplemental learning opportunities made available to students, including homework assignments, tutoring sessions, and the use of technology. Most teachers gave homework assignments to reinforce learning taking place in the classroom. One teacher described a homework contract that was often used: "The contract will say they have to have certain requirements. They have to do their homework, and the parents sign it, too. It's them and their parents saying that this is a class that requires you to complete your homework" (Emerald 2, teacher interview, 2003).

To support students in successfully completing their homework, some teachers organized a system of study buddies. Pairs of students exchanged phone numbers in the event they might need additional help when doing their homework. One teacher described the study buddy idea:

> Say, I give a homework assignment. ... For some I may adapt the lesson, and some of them I meet after school. ... Some of them I may pair up. ... They have study buddies and so we taught them reliance on that person to call and think about [the homework assignment] together. (Emerald 1, teacher interview, 2003)

An additional means for supporting student learning was an afterschool homework club staffed with volunteer tutors from the community. One teacher (Emerald 4, teacher interview, 2002) explained, "The school ... offers a homework club that runs Monday through Friday." Finally, most teachers were available every day after school for additional support. One teacher (Emerald 3, teacher interview, 2002) stated:

> We try to get support at home, and I have tutorial after school on Tuesdays that they can come to get help. There is also a computer disk that the parents can buy that's a tutorial. We also will put that on all of our computers. ... The teacher can monitor several students at once, at different levels, so we will put those on the computer and encourage them to come in and use those.

With access to these various support structures, students' ability to successfully learn mathematics was enhanced. One student (student interview, 2003) stated, "In algebra when I first started, I didn't understand something like writing equations, so I would go in after school. I got help everyday until I understood."

Another supplemental form of support used by teachers was technology. Most teachers recognized that technology could play an important role in the teaching and learning of mathematics. Teachers described how calculators were readily available and used in mathematics classes. One teacher (Emerald 3, faculty interview, 2002) stated, "The district provides classroom sets of calculators, and we also encourage students to have their own scientific calculator." Computers were also used in many lessons to enhance mathematics learning. One instructor described how students participated in an extended project using stock market information. Students used the Internet to select a stock and track its price for a period of time. The teacher (Emerald 2, teacher interview, 2003) went on to say, "We can actually bring the computers in and the kids can check their stocks. In addition to that, this year I'm going to do Excel. They're going to do their own spreadsheets."

Teaching Resources Were Highly Available. The third emergent theme concerned the availability of teaching resources. Many teaching resources and supplemental materials were available for Emerald Middle School's teachers to use in supporting academic excellence. Whereas textbooks were used to varying degrees in Emerald's mathematics classrooms, all faculty supplemented these textbooks with materials such as manipulatives. One teacher (Emerald 1, teacher interview, 2002) explained, "The curriculum that I use changes. One day we were doing mental math. ... And today we were more into the text with concepts. The next day we'll change to literature where I'll share a book with them related to math. So every day is different." Another teacher (Emerald 3, teacher interview, 2002) explained, "I do mostly a lot of textbook, but I supplement it." Another teacher (Emerald 4, teacher interview, 2003) stated, "I think we each have our collection of supplemental materials, and we share any time we find something that is really good. ... We have a pretty decent budget, so when we find something we want, we generally can get it."

Supplemental materials included algebra blocks, hands-on equations, and the AIMS Education Foundation materials. One teacher explained, "I have AIMS. I love AIMS. It's just great, and the kids love them too. ... I also use these tile activities that are all problem solving working in groups. ... I have tiles for equations. I have tiles for order of operations. They go all the way up into the algebra standards" (Emerald 2, teacher interview, 2002).

The sixth-grade mathematics teachers also described their use of a supplemental program called Excel Mathematics:

> Excel Math is a published math program, K–6. It's very prescribed, self-directed, and covers all of, what I would call, the basic skills. The nice thing about it is in every single lesson the review; the repetitive review is probably the best I've ever seen. It covers every single strand so every single day that they have an Excel lesson, they're exposed to geometry, addition, multiplication, measurement. ... Nothing is left untouched. (Emerald 1, teacher interview, 2002)

Another teacher indicated that she inserts additional lessons into her curriculum if students do not fully understand a concept. The teacher explained:

> We did a metric unit ... and they only had one lesson with metrics and I said, "Oh, we need more time with that. ... " I have a little metric Olympics that I do. They [the students] have to measure. They throw little cotton balls for the shot put and a straw for the javelin. (Emerald 2, teacher interview, 2003)

Faculty also developed their own supplemental lessons to reinforce concepts identified as needing additional reinforcement. During an observed lesson, the teacher gave students cards with metric units and standard units of measurements. The students worked in pairs to determine which cards cited metric units and which cited standard units before separating them accordingly. Then students were instructed to separate the metric units into meters, liters, and grams and place them in descending order. The teacher (Emerald 4, teacher interview, 2003) explained, "The students had a lot of trouble with knowing what's bigger."

Teachers also communicated on a regular basis to develop additional resources focused on enhancing the curriculum to address the unique needs of Emerald students. One teacher (Emerald 3, teacher interview, 2002) explained, "We get together and say, these are areas of weakness that we need to work on and where is it in the textbooks. These are addressed and [we ask] how can we expand … add to it to make sure that it is covered." Several teachers described that at one point, measurement and statistics were identified as weak areas for the sixth-grade students, so teachers met frequently to work together to develop supplemental units of instruction to reinforce these concepts. One teacher explained:

> We have a supplemental unit in measurement and statistics. We met with all of the teachers at the grade level and had them combine the very best lessons in that particular area that are hopefully in line with the standards. And we teach those in 30 days along with whatever our other curriculum is and we try to embed it. … [These lessons are] activities, lots of activities, some are writing down and I would say lots of constructing and manipulating paper. … So it is collection of different things. (Emerald 1, teacher interview, 2003)

Access to Professional Development Opportunities.   The final theme to emerge concerning support for academic excellence was teacher access to professional development. Mathematics teachers at Emerald Middle School participated in a variety of professional development activities. One teacher (Emerald 2, faculty interview, 2002) said, "We've attended a lot of workshops, and we like to share. When we get excited about something, we share; we do that as much as possible. We're also involved in the K–12 Alliance Group." Teachers were provided with release time and some financial support to attend professional meetings and conferences covering such topics as mathematics content, reform, and standards, as well as seminars on cross-cultural communication. Most of the mathematics faculty attended the annual state mathematics conference each year as well as county- and district-sponsored workshops. Emerald teachers also participated in a mentoring program for beginning teachers, and several of Emerald's teachers served as mentor teachers (administrator survey, 2002). The final professional development activity that several of Emerald's mathematics teachers participated in was the K–12 Alliance of the State of California in which teachers devoted many hours during the summer and throughout the school year to improve mathematics instruction.

Challenging Mathematical Content and High-Level Instruction

Information gathered from the site visits led to insights about teachers' perspectives on curriculum and instruction. A second theme to emerge was the emphasis teachers and administrators placed on delivering challenging mathematical content and high-level instruction. The major factors supporting this theme were a demanding, standards-based curriculum; a focus on making sense of mathematical ideas; a focus on communication of understanding of mathematical concepts; and the use of formal and informal assessment measures.

Demanding, Standards-Based Curriculum.   The mathematics curriculum at Emerald Middle School was based on the California Standards for mathematics. When asked what determined the mathematical content covered during the year, one teacher (Emerald 1, teacher interview, 2002) responded, "First off, I'm familiar with the standards and I know that in El Cajon Valley, you need to be teaching to the standards. I also know that for this particular group of students, I know what it is they need to know by the end of the year to pass the algebra one test." Another teacher (Emerald 3, teacher interview, 2002) explained, "My primary guidance is the state standards that we're given. ... When I first started teaching, there were not [standards], everybody did their own thing. I'm a strong proponent that there are standards and expectations that everybody should go along with."

Whereas the curriculum at Emerald was primarily based on California State Standards, it was adapted to meet the distinctive needs of Emerald Middle School students. One teacher (Emerald 4, faculty interview, 2002) explained, "Everything is really based on what do they [the students] know and where can we go from there." Another teacher (Emerald 2, faculty interview, 2002) went on to say, "So every year we have to modify always to ensure that they're getting those previous standards."

The challenging curriculum at Emerald was also modified each year to address specific mathematics content identified as weak student performance areas by standardized tests scores. One teacher (Emerald 4, faculty interview, 2002) said, "We meet to identify weak test scores and then develop units to enhance our scores and to make sure we've taught them." Another teacher explained:

> We've analyzed STAT NINE scores, and we'll analyze a weak area such as measurement and statistics. Then we will have release time to develop a supplemental unit to enhance those skills that will be taught in addition, not in substitution, but in addition to what our regular curriculum is. (Emerald 1, faculty interview, 2002)

A third teacher continued:

> The first year that I was here, we had afternoon meetings to work on supplemental units [to enhance test scores]. I think that it laid down a good foundation for us to continue to do that. … We found that it was useful. I thought that it was a pretty powerful way to stay focused and stay connected. (Emerald 7, faculty interview, 2002)

One teacher pointed out, "I don't consider this teaching to the test, because the concepts being taught are concepts that students need to know. The focus is on understanding the concepts, not test questions" (Emerald 3, faculty interview, 2002).

Emerald teachers showed creativity in enhancing the curriculum with fun, motivational activities designed to increase understanding of mathematical concepts. One teacher (Emerald 1, faculty interview, 2002) explained, "Our math approach is certainly not static. It's dynamic; we're doing a multitude of different kinds of things." The teacher (Emerald 1, faculty interview, 2002) continued, "We as teachers have needed to be much more creative and supplement that curriculum with some understanding, motivation and fun."

Focus on Making Sense of Mathematical Ideas.

The mathematics teachers at Emerald emphasized the importance of having students construct their own meaning of the mathematics they were learning. One teacher (Emerald 1, teacher interview, 2003) described how she has students "show, tell and explain concepts so that they personalize them and understand." The sample lesson described previously, which taught the concept of volume, illustrated the focus teachers maintained on helping students construct an understanding of mathematics. First, students were asked to look up the word volume in the dictionary and were told to come up with a "working definition" (one that helped them understand the concept) of volume. Students then worked with a spreadsheet and determined the volume of various objects when given the appropriate dimensions. During this exercise, students were encouraged to show, tell, and explain as they worked in groups. After this activity, the teacher challenged students to explain the various ways they could prove the volume of a given solid based on the total number of cubes used in its construction. Again, the focus was to show, tell, and explain. Mathematics at Emerald was often taught in a context where students were able to see meaning and gain a deeper understanding.

Emerald Middle School mathematics teachers also implemented projects designed to help students see the usefulness of mathematics in the real world. One teacher (Emerald 2, teacher interview, 2002) stated, "A lot of kids at this age don't think that math is meaningful." To help students make connections between mathematics and the real world, the teacher had students conduct interviews with professionals concerning how they used mathematics in their careers. After their interviews, students presented their findings to the class. The teacher (Emerald 2, teacher interview, 2002) explained, "It was really kind of an enlightening experience. It's just meaningful, how math is applied in the real world, and kids at this age really need that."

Focus on Communication of Understanding of Mathematical Concepts. The mathematics faculty at Emerald Middle School recognized the importance of communication in mathematics and required students to explain mathematical concepts. One teacher (Emerald 2, teacher interview, 2002) stated, "The students have to work together. They have to communicate and help each other. ... I situate the kids accordingly ... so they can explain it to someone, and they'll listen to their peers." The teacher went on to describe how students often worked in pairs or groups and were encouraged to present ideas both orally and in written form. Another teacher emphasized the importance of communication by requiring students to justify ideas in written and oral form. The teacher explained: "I think it is wonderful if the kids can explain concepts, because I think then they personalize it and it helps them understand. Perhaps you internalize it [concepts] because you can repeat it and re-express it" (Emerald 1, teacher interview, 2003).

Another teacher described a process of using communication to help students clarify their understanding of concepts by telling the students:

> You need to think about it. If you can't, let's talk about it. Let's talk about it with the person across the aisle before you answer. ... Talk to the person next to you, behind you, in front of you, but I want to hear something from you. (Emerald 3, teacher interview, 2003)

This teacher (Emerald 3, teacher interview, 2002) summarized the importance of communication in the mathematics classroom by saying, "Students are going to need to be able to not only solve problems but be able to communicate because it is all communication."

Students Were Assessed in Formal and Informal Settings. Emerald teachers assessed students through both formal and informal means. Although standardized test results were used to guide curriculum and instruction to ensure that students were mastering concepts, teachers stated their belief that standardized test scores, however important, were not the driving force of instruction. One teacher (Emerald 3, teacher interview, 2002) explained:

> As far as standardized tests are concerned, we get together and say these are areas of weakness that we need to work on. ... We make sure we cover it in the textbook and add to it to make sure that it is covered, but it is not our day to day thinking. I don't get out the standardized tests every day and say, so have I done this?

The results of standardized tests did, however, play a role in determining the mathematics content taught at Emerald Middle School. Teachers described how they examined the results of standardized testing by grade level to determine areas of weakness. One teacher explained:

> Well, the lesson I did on Monday, the measurement thing, geometry and measurement, are consistently areas on the standardized tests where our students need to improve. So yes, we do focus a lot on measurement and geometry. And the other section that they're always low on is statistics, so we always do a lot of supplemental stuff on that. (Emerald 4, teacher interview, 2003)

The teachers described how they worked together to develop the group's best ideas for supplemental units to address weaknesses identified by standardized tests. One teacher explained:

> At the grade level, in order to address standardized testing in areas where we felt weaknesses, that we felt we needed to improve upon, we do supplemental units. … We met with all of the teachers at the grade level and had them combine the very best of the lessons in that particular area. (Emerald 1, teacher interview, 2003)

In these ways, the mathematics teachers at Emerald used the results of standardized testing to enhance curriculum and instruction.

The results of informal assessment measures were used to ensure proper placement in the various levels of mathematics classes and help individual students. Several teachers mentioned they were constantly doing informal assessments of individual students and the class as a whole. One teacher (Emerald 2, teacher interview, 2002) explained, "You know, I do an assessment of the kids and if I see certain needs, then I will throw in different activities … if they are having problems with fractions. … So I do different things like that for kids' special needs." Another teacher said:

> When they first come in I assess them to get a general feel to where it is they're at, and very often they still don't know multiplication; they still don't know measurement. … These are big factors and I think it has to be. Attention has to be paid to all facets, not just straight curriculum. (Emerald 2, teacher interview, 2003)

Another teacher (Emerald 4, teacher interview, 2003) explained, "If I see something that isn't working, I'll alter that. I try to get around the class and see what each student is doing." If students lacked understanding of a particular concept, the teacher adapted and kept working with that concept as necessary. One student (student interview, 2003) stated, "If the class doesn't get something right away, they'll [the teachers] go over it again until we do get it." Students explained that if some kids needed more work, the teacher helped them after school. One student (student interview, 2003) explained, "The teachers also make sure that we're getting good grades. If we're starting to slip a little, they'll tell us and ask if we can come in and get help."

Another aspect of informal assessment contributing to Emerald's characterization as high achieving in mathematics was the use of ongoing informal assessment to ensure proper placement in advanced courses. One teacher explained:

> If students are not doing as well as they should [in the honors courses], then we weed them out. We take them out of there because this particular class is not a requirement. They are there because they want to be and because they're willing to put forth the effort. (Emerald 3, teacher interview, 2002)

A third component of informal assessment that contributed to the success of Emerald students was the incorporation of homework in the assessment process. Teachers stated their belief that homework was essential in learning mathematics because students needed additional practice to master basic skills and to understand concepts more deeply. One teacher described how homework used as a form of informal assessment benefited student learning:

> For the student I'm thinking of particularly that's struggling, he needs more time. He's given opportunities, because I understand that he's trying to master a concept instead of moving over it. He needs me to be more generous in the way I grade it. That he's assessed on that, but I also need to stay in contact with the parent and with the student. How is it coming? Are you doing this at home? Because that particular concept needs to have it enriched at home. ... I rely a lot on the buddy system, and I teach two heads are better than one. I teach the parents that as well. It's okay, you know, you're going to college and the only way to make it through is with a study buddy. (Emerald 1, teacher interview, 2002)

The teachers used homework grades as a way of monitoring to ensure students completed assignments. One teacher stated, "They [students in the honors algebra course] can have no homework not turned in. They've got to do it" (Emerald 2, teacher interview, 2002).

The Importance of Building Relationships

The third major contributor to Emerald's success in promoting high mathematics achievement was reflected in the relationships between fellow teachers as well as between students and teachers. Several major themes emerged: strong and well-defined sense of purpose, relationships among teachers, and relationships between faculty and students.

Strong and Well-Defined Sense of Purpose.   Relationships between the mathematics faculty at Emerald were characterized by a strong and well-defined sense of purpose. When asked why Emerald was high achieving in mathematics, one teacher (Emerald 1, faculty interview, 2002) responded, "I think it's because it's a priority here; I mean it wasn't going to happen until mathematics became a priority." The teachers explained that whereas mathematics hadn't always been a top priority at Emerald Middle School, they began to see improvements once both the administration and teachers made it a priority.

This shared sense of purpose in fostering high achievement was further supported through relationships between teachers and students emphasizing high expectations for both behavior and learning. During interviews, the teachers described their high expectations for student behavior and explained how their team structure and character education program aided in classroom management, something they considered a foundation for educational achievement. One teacher explained:

> So you work in a team with your English, math, science, and social studies, so we deal with behaviors and classroom management. … If you don't have good management skills, the kids aren't going to get it. … So the fact that I have a team that I work with helps me with that part; allows more freedom to have math, to work in the math, so I'm not always dealing with behaviors. (Emerald 2, faculty interview, 2002)

Another teacher discussed the focus on character education:

> We try and award kids that are showing good character and responsibility for their education initiative, so we focus on a different character trait. So we hope to demonstrate all the characters at all times, but we focus on one every month. Then we end in June with success, so we all want to be very successful. And they might not get those character traits at home, and then if they don't, we're the only role models that they have. (Emerald 2, faculty interview, 2002)

A student (student interview, 2003) went on to give his perception of the character program: "The 'Emerald Way' is posted in every classroom. It's courtesy, respect, responsibility, honesty, initiative, commitment, appreciation, self-discipline, cooperation and success. We have one 'Emerald Way' trait every month." Both students and teachers recognized the importance of good character traits and their impact on achievement. These high expectations for behavior and character contributed to the success of Emerald's students.

Relationships Among Teachers.   Emerald's mathematics faculty supported each other in their common goal of achieving excellence in mathematics. When the principal was asked what made Emerald Middle School high achieving in mathematics, he answered (administrator interview, 2003), "The quality of the teachers is outstanding." He went on to say that the school had a critical mass of very dedicated professionals that drove excellence. Another teacher explained:

> If I was not working with a team of such strong math teachers who have great ideas, I would be floundering. I think the fact that we have a team, and we actually support each other and share ideas (is critical). I can go over to Emerald 1's room and say, I'm just not getting this, do you have any ideas; what are you doing? That makes such a big difference. (Emerald 7, faculty interview, 2002)

This dedication was reinforced by congenial, cooperative relationships among faculty members. One teacher (Emerald 1, faculty interview, 2002) explained, "I think that we [math faculty members] are always talking about math; I know we're always talking about math." Another teacher explained that the faculty members worked within and across grade levels to ensure student learning. This teacher stated, "The eighth grade teachers are planning this year. We meet about every three weeks" (Emerald 6, faculty interview, 2002). The teachers were also willing to share ideas and materials. Another teacher (Emerald 4, faculty interview, 2002) explained, "We've always been a group that shared everything. We e-mail each other and ask if anyone has such and such so we can locate materials."

In summary, the mathematics faculty was dedicated and hard working. They met on a regular basis, worked well together, and supported each other in their efforts to teach all students.

Relationships Between Faculty and Students. The faculty also communicated across grade levels to address students' curricular needs. One teacher (Emerald 2, teacher interview, 2002) explained, "I talk a lot with the 6th grade teachers in the transition [from 6th to 7th grade], so when they come to us we know where the kids are. ... If they have some weaknesses, I have no problem reviewing it."

Emerald faculty knew their students and focused on meeting their needs. One teacher explained:

> As we were told yesterday in a staff meeting, a large number of your kids are not passing. Instead of saying, what are the kids doing; they are not doing their homework, or they're not picking up their pencils when they walk in the room. Instead [we, the teachers] ask what we are doing to see that they do pass. (Emerald 3, teacher interview, 2003)

FINAL REMARKS

There are many factors that contributed to the success of Emerald Middle School, but it is evident that the school became highly effective in mathematics when the entire mathematics faculty, with the support of the administration, placed a deliberate focus on teaching and learning mathematics. V. E. Lee and Smith (2001) found that in highly effective schools the faculty, as a group, focuses on student learning, and this is what the mathematics faculty at Emerald successfully accomplished. With this new focus on mathematics, changes occurred in curriculum, instruction, student expectations, and interactions among faculty members.

V. E. Lee and Smith (2001) also found that highly effective schools have a more demanding curriculum and encourage all students to work hard. This was evident in how the faculty members at Emerald deliberately focused on improving the mathematics curriculum at each grade level and then saw improvements in achievement. The curriculum was adapted to address state standards and assessment measures were analyzed to identify areas of weak performance so that these areas could be addressed by supplementing the curriculum. The faculty made a concerted effort to adapt the curriculum to meet the unique needs of Emerald's student body.

In the *Principals and Standards of School Mathematics* document (NCTM, 2000), the case is made that effective teaching requires reflection and continual efforts to seek improvement. This was evident in the manner that Emerald's mathematics teachers focused on instruction. Teachers attended professional development sessions to enhance their instructional strategies and then shared ideas to help all the mathematics teachers improve instruction. The teachers at Emerald often shared teaching successes and failures with each other so that they could improve instruction for their students.

Similar to the findings of V. E. Lee and Smith (2001), we found that the mathematics instruction in the majority of the classrooms was interactive and teachers taught for understanding. The teachers used a variety of instructional strategies that engaged students. Students were involved in learning of mathematics through active participation in group projects, through communication with classmates and the teacher, and by developing and seeing meaning in mathematics.

High expectations for academic success in mathematics resulted when the school placed a greater emphasis on mathematics instruction. The teachers had high expectations for their students and communicated these expectations to their students. The teachers also believed that the students could meet these expectations and teachers were held accountable for student success. The students also were committed to these high expectations and sought additional help when needed to meet these expectations. As other researchers have found (see, e.g., Ball & Cohen, 1999; Brophy & Good, 1986), the teachers' high expectations contributed to student success in learning mathematics.

The mathematics faculty at Emerald was very dedicated and committed to their goals of excellence. The team structure of the school supported their collaborative efforts. In the *Principals and Standards of School Mathematics*

(NCTM, 2000), the argument is made that mathematics curricula should be well articulated across grade levels, and the faculty at Emerald accomplished this through collaboration among all mathematics teachers on a regular basis. Teachers communicated often and were always willing to help each other with supplemental materials and new ideas for lessons. The mathematics teachers had the common goal of helping all of their students learn mathematics.

Emerald Middle School has found a way to successfully meet the needs of a very diverse group of students by providing a challenging, yet comfortable, environment in which students can learn. The efforts of Emerald Middle School should serve as a model for other public schools that wish to become highly effective in the teaching of mathematics.

7

The Importance
of Building Relationships

Richard S. Kitchen

This chapter is devoted to examining the third of the three major themes discovered at the participating schools: Relationship building among the teachers with one another and among teachers with students was highly valued. The following four areas are explored in this chapter related to this theme: a strong and well-defined sense of purpose among mathematics faculty, faculty that collaborates and supports each other, a focus on student disposition toward mathematics, and teachers that understand and care for their students.

THE IMPORTANCE OF BUILDING RELATIONSHIPS
AMONG TEACHERS AND STUDENTS

Strong and Well-Defined Sense of Purpose
Among Mathematics Faculty

Mathematics teachers at participating schools had a strong sense of purpose. One feature that all nine participating schools had in common was high academic expectations in mathematics. Support was provided for students to meet these expectations in the form of additional mathematics instruction. A teacher at YES College Preparatory School spoke about how the faculty worked together to create a program that prepared students well in mathematics:

> There's definitely that shared sense of responsibility, but that is no way unique to the math department, but it's across the school. The vertical teaming happens, the sharing of best practices happens, and there are a lot of really good models out there for us to look at. ... Success in mathe-

matics means this sort of fluency in number and you can see mathematics in the real world and you cannot just solve a quadratic equation faster than anyone else, but you can see why you would want to do that. And you can see why things develop and apply them in the real world. Although we may not generate a lot of math majors coming out of the program, I think we generate kids who are very willing and able to go into careers that involve a lot of mathematics and they don't have to be afraid that they're not prepared for that. (YES4, 10/02)

Another teacher talked about how student team building, and vertical and horizontal planning were also important at YES College Preparatory School:

I think that student team building is also a focus with students and the teachers. We meet as a department twice a month in the high school and the middle school separate, but we also meet with each other pretty frequently too; between high school and middle school and in the classroom we promote that as well. Problem solving in groups, a lot of things I've done in group activities, but it's not an independent sport, we've always come up with cooperation. I think we've done a pretty good job with that. (YES5, YES College Prep, 10/02)

One of the faculty's well-defined purposes at KIPP Academy Bronx was to positively impact their students' attitudes toward mathematics. The mathematics teachers spoke about teaching mathematics as a means to develop their students' attitudes to be willing to try and be successful. A teacher also spoke about students learning mathematics as a means to "transcend" societal expectations the students faced in the South Bronx:

It's no different than what we're trying to do in orchestra. We're not training musicians; we're trying to train people with the attitude of trying to be successful. So, even if our students don't become mathematicians, they still need to learn the algebra and the steps they have to take from the 5th to 8th grade to get there. That's what we're all about.

Whether or not they have to grasp sine, cosine, and tangent is again secondary to [developing] the attitudes to be successful. This isn't easy compared to the challenge they face to try and transcend the societal expectations for kids growing up in the south Bronx. (KIPPB1, KIPP Bronx, 11/02)

A philosophy at KIPP Academy Bronx that clearly distinguished the school from the other participating schools was the belief that the mathematics classroom was where students were socialized into the school's strict behavioral expectations and rigorous academic program:

Our general view in the grade level is that math is life, you know, everything we see in math is a reflection in their attitude. ... I think that

50% of our classes [in fifth grade] is preaching [about the behavioral expectations at the school]. I think 50% of our class is math culture that's going to permeate the rest of the four years. (unknown teacher, KIPP Bronx, 11/02)

The mathematics faculty also described the mathematics classroom as the location where students had to initially experience academic success. They believed that because students could clearly see their academic progress while studying mathematics, their sense of accomplishment would build. High achievement in mathematics would then transfer to other subjects and students would have academic success in other classes.

There is no debating the right answer, you know, and … you can break it down so clearly and easy in progression, an obvious progression. I think it makes it easier for us as teachers to gauge where we are and also it makes it easy for the kids to see how far they've come. They get a sense in 5th grade, we did this much where as in Social Studies, we just studied the different subject in the same way, or read a different book in reading. But in math, you're just climbing up a hill and you're seeing actually how far you've come and it's like visible progress. (unknown teacher, KIPP Bronx, 11/02)

At Rockcastle County Middle School, the teachers' clearly articulated focus was on the students' education. One teacher outlined some of the many activities the teachers were engaged in to accomplish their goal:

I think we have a shared sense of purpose and that is the education of the children here. We have content area meetings where we sit down and we discuss our goals for improvement.

We're trying to get our curriculum aligned where we know what we're supposed to be teaching and what's being taught for 6th grade, 7th grade, and 8th grade and I think we all work at the purpose of promoting that education at the middle school here. So I think the primary purpose is to improve the math instruction. (Rock5, Rockcastle County MS, 10/02)

This teacher continued by discussing how the mathematics faculty at Rockcastle County Middle School worked to instill a joy for learning in their students:

We not only work hard, but we're hungry, we're hungry to learn more, for better ways. I think we try to instill that hunger into the children to try to get them to desire to go that next step through the use of manipulatives or activities or projects or whatever. We're really trying to set those kids up and make them want to learn because without that desire to gain that knowledge, we have a much more difficult task. (Rock5, Rockcastle County MS, 10/02)

At the Young Women's Leadership School, an important aspect of the school's mission statement was to foster a collaborative learning environment in which all students could academically thrive. The mathematics teachers at TYWLS clearly supported this mission in this work and the following teacher explained how students at the school were socialized to a cooperative, noncompetitive learning environment (see chap. 8 for more about this):

> We spend a huge amount of time getting them [the students] to change the way they think about going to school and being in the classroom. When they [the students] start here they are so competitive, and they won't answer questions if they feel embarrassed or they think they might not know. ... We spend so much time in 7th grade talking about that. And talking to them or just demonstrating and making them be cooperative, even setting up the room where they have tables instead of desks. In lots of math classes, we do cooperative work and try to do things that are non-competitive in order for us to live in an all-women's world. (TYWLS3, TYWLS, 10/02)

The J. D. O'Bryant School of Mathematics and Science was the only exam school among the nine schools that participated in the study. As one of three exam schools in the Boston Public School district, students had to do well on an entrance examination to be able to enroll in the school. Two teachers at J. D. O'Bryant School of Mathematics and Science discussed their shared purpose as preparing students to be successful in college, and more immediately, to be successful on the Massachusetts Comprehensive Assessment Standard exam (MCAS):

> I think we do have a shared sense of purpose. It came from our mission statement that we developed in preparing students for college and their careers following that. (OBry8, J. D. O'Bryant SMS, 11/02)

> I think the other purpose we all share is to get the kids to pass the MCAS exam. We all know it's real and it's here and it's here to stay. I think all of us to some capacity are working on getting to be comfortable with the types of questions to expect and the content involved on the MCAS. (OBry9, J. D. O'Bryant SMS, 11/02)

Another teacher at J. D. O'Bryant School of Mathematics and Science described the shared sense of purpose that the mathematics faculty shared regarding high academic expectations for students:

> We have students who like math, I think the faculty, all of us; we push the kids. I look around at everybody here, you don't see any free periods, or the same old things as last year. We all push the kids ... a lot of notes, a lot of homework, projects. By the time I get them, they get a

pretty good background in Algebra I and arithmetic and everything else, so it's a group effort. (OBry7, J. D. O'Bryant SMS, 11/02)

At Latta High School, the teachers collaborated to develop a shared sense of purpose focused on teaching to their state's mathematics standards:

I'm constantly talking to [two teachers named] since they've been here a long time and [another teacher]. I'm constantly getting input from them and I'm trying to find out what I need to do and we get together and find out what I need to do. And we get together and talk about the classes we teach because a lot of them are pre-requisites to the others. And there are standards that need to be covered and that's our main goal is to cover all the standards. ... So we can count on helping each other and make sure we cover the standards in each individual class. I think for all of us, our main goal is to cover the state standards and as much of them as we can and I think we do a good job as a whole. (Latta2, Latta HS, 11/02)

Another teacher at Latta High School responded to a question about why Latta was such a high achiever by stressing how the teachers worked hard to ensure there were high academic expectations for students at the school:

I think it's because we push, push, push! We emphasize it day in and day out [students improving academically] and it's hard because we try to change attitudes. I may have one or two [students] who may not have made progress, but I don't think there are any who are going in the opposite direction. I have one or two that are about the same. The majority of them are coming around, but now this has been sort of a long time coming. Every day I'm in there ranting and raving, saying you've got to learn, got to learn it, and we don't have days that we do nothing. When we walk in we've got a game plan and we follow it and we work at it and we work at it and work at it. I do think, it's sort of what you said earlier today, I think success breeds success. (Latta4, Latta HS, 3/03)

At the KIPP Academy Houston, a teacher discussed how the faculty's purpose had shifted from preparing students to be good at the "mechanics" of mathematics to focus more on teaching mathematics for understanding:

I think we're also enriching it [the curriculum] too from the standpoint of trying, as a whole school, to move to teaching for understandings, as opposed to teaching just mechanics. In the past, our students have been very good at mechanics and can pass all of the tests, even the end of the course algebra exam, which is relatively difficult. They almost always pass that. (KIPPH4, KIPP Houston, 10/02)

A teacher at Emerald Middle School spoke about the faculty's focus at Emerald was raising the mathematics standards to teach algebra and geometry at the middle school level:

> We also have a commitment to raise our standards a little higher. We offer at 6th grade pre- algebra, the 7th grade algebra, and the 8th grade geometry. We're the first ones to in our school district to do that. We all as a department have communicated to commit to that. (Emer5, Emerald MS, 10/02)

Faculty Collaborate and Support Each Other. It was quite common for mathematics faculty across the sites to express how they felt supported by their colleagues. A teacher at Emerald Middle School pointed out that the faculty worked in interdisciplinary teams at the school. The teacher also believed that the collaborative approach at Emerald allowed for a focus on teaching rather than a focus on students with behavioral issues:

> Yeah, so you work in a team with your English, math, science and social studies [teachers]. So, we deal with behaviors and classroom management. ... I don't care how great of a teacher you are, if you don't have good management skills the kids aren't going to get it. You can have the best person, the person who knows everything about mathematics come into the classroom. Most likely they won't succeed because they don't know how to relate to the kids. So, the fact that I have a team, that I work with people ... it allows me more freedom to teach the math, to work in the math area, so I'm not always dealing with behaviors. Behaviors, people help me with that so I'm able to focus on my actual subject area. That's been beneficial, too. (Emer1, Emerald MS, 10/02)

Another teacher at Emerald Middle School who had taught physical education and health before teaching at Emerald was very grateful for the team approach in mathematics at the school:

> That's something that I was going to add when you asked why we've excelled in math. If I was not working with a team of such strong math teachers who have great ideas, I'd be floundering. I think the fact that we have a team, and we really support each other and share ideas. I can go over to [another teacher's] room and say, "I'm just not getting this, do you have any ideas, what are you doing?" That makes such a big difference, because I didn't teach math before I came here. (Emer5, Emerald MS, 10/02)

At the Young Women's Leadership School, a teacher described how both the faculty and administration worked well together, classes were small, how friendly things were at the school, and how students were looked after in the building:

I was going to say the classes are small and the school is small and the faculty is very close and the administration is very close, so like it's all on a first name basis and it's all friendly. So, I think fewer of the kids get lost. I was at a bigger high school before, and if you [a student] were in the wrong class, you were basically in the wrong class all year. No one would look out for you. No one would notice. You went through the program and all of a sudden you would start to change and they wouldn't know and no one would know. The teachers didn't talk to each other. [Here], the teachers talk, the principal knows basically everyone. You know, we all know almost all the kids, or you know them pretty much even if they're not in your grade. Kids can't get lost ... we keep track of them. (unknown teacher, TYWLS, 10/02)

At Ysleta Middle School, mathematics faculty at the school made sure to identify time to collaborate:

I think we do have time to plan together, which really helps especially when it was my first year. So I had the time to actually really work with both of them. It helped me to continue, to know what was expected of me in 7th grade, what was expected of me to teach the 8th grade. So, that really helped at times, and it helped me along. We are working a lot more together this year. What are we doing? What are we going to do differently? How are we going to help our kids? So that's been a good thing we have. (Yslt3, Ysleta MS, 9/02)

Besides collaborating on a consistent basis, the mathematics teachers at Ysleta Middle School engaged in vertical teaming, examined their students' scores on the state's criteria-referenced test (the TAAS), and enlisted faculty across the school to teach mathematics during a class called KIVA:

We have our curriculum and the scope and sequence. We try and align the 7th grade math stuff to go with the 8th grade math stuff, but as 8th graders they'll be at a little bit higher level. But we plan almost every other day. When we meet, we plan our curriculum, things that we're doing in class. We look at scores from T.A.A.S., weak kids, strong kids, but we're constantly planning, talking to each other about materials that we're using, methodology that we use in the classroom. ... We also have the teachers; in the school all the teachers teach math. We also have KIVA. (Yslt2, Ysleta MS, 9/02)

The resource teacher at Rockcastle County Middle School spoke about the cohesiveness of the mathematics faculty. The faculty collaborated often to identify and address "gaps" in students' learning, continually worked to improve the mathematics curriculum, and engaged in vertical teaming:

I do think that since the middle school has been here we have tried to work at grade levels and tried to make sure that gaps [in student learning] are identified from grade level to grade level. It's a work in progress and we're still working on that. It's hard today and I think that's a hallmark for this faculty that we're not finished with anything, but it's always a work in progress. It can be refined and improved and this year we have set as a goal to meet once a week, as grade level math teachers. Part of it will be to make sure that we are teaching the same in each team, grade level by grade level and we work with our curriculum. As a resource teacher, I am available most of the time to assist in the classroom, to assist during planning, to help find resources, just whatever the needs are. … We're a hard working faculty that works hard together and supports one another and that's the key. (Rock7, Rockcastle County MS, 10/02)

A teacher at Rockcastle County Middle School described how the faculty regularly collaborated to improve mathematics curricula, how well they got along, how they motivated and held each other accountable, and how they had resources to teach:

It changes from year to year, the curriculum does and we try to refine everything, every year, try to … to see what's working, what's not working. But we do that a lot of times and have meetings and stuff that we all attend after school and I think the math department here is sort of unique. We all get along really well and we are all here for a common purpose. It's not only for the education of the kids but I think we all support each other really well, also. I also believe that most of us work really hard and I think because we each push one another, from grade level to grade level, besides already having the curriculum aligned and working on that, I think we challenge one another. We have a resource teacher, we have so many manipulatives, so many resources that we all have, and that helps us out as well. I don't know of any other [school]; I've talked to several other people from other counties and schools and they just don't have [resources like we do]. They just don't work together and [do] things like we do. (Rock4, Rockcastle County MS, 10/02)

At the KIPP Academy Bronx, teachers indicated that they met daily to discuss the curriculum. Having time to lesson plan and collaborate were highly valued at the school: "If you want for people to come in with a really good lesson, and you want people to be on all the time, which is really how we got to be here [as a high-achieving school], you have to have the time to figure out exactly what it [a good lesson] is" (KIPPB3, KIPP Bronx, 11/02). A teacher at KIPP Academy Bronx also emphasized the responsibility the teachers felt to one another to prepare students for their next mathematics class: "I feel a strong sense of obligation to [names two teachers] that they've got to be ready so when [another teacher] gets them in 6th grade, he doesn't have to re-teach them, and when [another teacher] gets them in 8th grade they know what a fraction is. I really feel guilty if I don't do a good job" (unknown teacher, KIPP Bronx, 11/02).

Another teacher at KIPP Academy Bronx also spoke about the expectation for excellence at the school and how the extended academic day allowed teachers time to tutor students, collaboratively plan, and communicate with each other:

> [The extra planning periods allow us] to grade papers and to meet with kids who need help. I think the flip side is a lot of small schools and even larger more traditional schools, they don't build that in [the school day]. ... There is an expectation here for excellence, and it's not, it's stated in a lot of respects. But as [another teacher] said we're small, and it's like, being a pack of gazelles. ... We're looking at people who are going to run, and we'll help people who are going to run. I think the explicit expectation is if we're building this schedule like this [with extra planning time], you should be able to run for our students. So, from an administration's point of view, while we recognize it's still hard work, I'm not aware of another school that provides a schedule like this. Your basic day is 9½ or 10 hour days, but you're really only directly providing services for 4½ hours to 5 of those hours. You have a good [amount of] time to plan, now whether it's used effectively or not is another story, but it certainly allows for the conversation to be had. (KIPPB1, KIPP Bronx, 11/02)

At YES College Preparatory School, the teachers had frequent conversations about mathematics curriculum and lessons:

> One of the things that we're very good in doing is going to each other for help. When teaching certain subjects and topics, and even saying, "I know you taught this last year, what is this that they know"? "Where is it that you left off?" We do that a lot at the beginning of the year and even as the year progresses. We get to know the kids better and it's really easy to go to the 7th grade or 6th grade teachers. "What worked?" "What didn't work?" Even for me, [another teacher] saved me. I said, "I really want to do this, I don't know how else to extend," then [the teacher] said you know, with the Algebra II kids, I'm going to do something ... or whatever. I think that's been very helpful this year. (unknown teacher, YES College Prep, 10/02)

Focus on Student Disposition Toward Mathematics.   Not only did teachers value building strong working relationships with each other at the participating schools, but they also shared similar values across sites regarding what they wanted to accomplish with their mathematics students. For example, teachers across sites expressed a concern for their students' affect in general, and wanted to develop their students' confidence in mathematics while still challenging them mathematically. A teacher at the J. D.

O'Bryant School of Mathematics and Science believed mathematics could be both challenging and fun to study:

> Oh man, I think math should be fun. I think that if you ask students how they have done in math historically and ask them if they had fun, they would say no! So, then you ask yourself if they didn't have fun, what emotions did they go through? So, math should be fun. I think a lot of people think that if it's fun, it means it's easy. But no, it doesn't have to be easy, but they should enjoy it. They should look back on it and not say it was the worst time of my life. … The way we teach math, drill and kill, that's what it [the problem] is. … I have to teach this curriculum but psychologically, I'm trying to get them to see that they can do it and that they can feel good about it [mathematics]. … Hopefully, even if they struggle, they can say, "I learned a lot in [OBry3's] class and I also had fun doing it." I hope. (OBry3, J. D. O'Bryant SMS, 11/02)

Many of the students entered KIPP Academy Bronx with low skill levels in mathematics. A goal at KIPP was that by the time they finished eighth grade, students would be well prepared and confident in their knowledge of and abilities in mathematics:

> What we're really trying to do is get the kids to be successful in the subject area and at the same time we're trying to make them feel like it's fun, exciting, and that they can go to high school confident. No matter who gets them next, or where they end up next, they're going to know that whatever they're doing is the same skills that they've done and have been successful in the junior high school setting. (unknown teacher, KIPP Bronx, 11/02)

The teachers at KIPP Academy Bronx believed that success in mathematics could build students' general level of confidence in their academic abilities:

> I guess the third [instructional goal] would be, I maybe should have said it first, is the level of confidence with math. … It's so easy to teach but it's really also so easy to mess it up if you don't build that number sense. The understanding of the words and numbers go together. If you don't find a way to foster that understanding … that's where the whole "I hate math" thing comes from, that's sort of the American phobia of hating mathematics. So, just creating confidence in a lot of them that they can do the work. … [If they] find that math, especially at the beginning, is very basic and really fun and easy to learn, they do really well on the math test across the board. … We slowly get harder and more complex and it's one of those things that builds their confidence in school in general and then they want to come to school. … So, using math as a confidence builder for the entire curriculum, it's an attitude booster. (KIPPB3, KIPP Bronx, 4/03)

A teacher at Emerald Middle School discussed how students needed to see that mathematics is relevant to their lives, while developing confidence in their mathematical abilities and preparing students for algebra:

> The first one is that math is real; it's not a fictional set of numbers and symbols out there, but it's real and that it has a predictable pattern they see. ... Two, a goal I would have is that they become confident, that they're not just sitting there crossing their fingers and going I hope, I hope, I hope [I can do mathematics]. ... So, to make them confident in the math that they're doing. Three, another goal that I would have, aside from the material that I have to introduce at this particular grade level for the 6th grade in pre-algebra, you have to catch up on multiple years in one year in order to get them ready for that algebra. So, there's a lot to do there. But I also need to make it exciting, fun, motivating and they want to do it. (Emer4, Emerald MS, 10/02)

Another teacher at Emerald Middle School wanted students to persevere in mathematics, communicate their mathematical ideas, and apply those ideas in problem-solving situations:

> Perseverance ... if the first thing doesn't work, it doesn't mean that you're wrong, it just means that you need to try something else. You have to continue trying until you can show that there is no other way. After that, it depends on the level of the student that I'm working with. ... I'm concerned that they'll be able to solve problems using their algebra, that they learn the terminology that they are going to need to be able not only to solve problems, but to be able to communicate because it's all communication. So, perseverance, communication, and application or problem solving and none of those are specifically math. (Emer3, Emerald MS, 10/02)

Teachers Understand and Care for Their Students. Lastly, it was quite common for teachers across the participating schools to express a sincere interest in developing strong and authentic relationships with their students. This was made manifest by how teachers spoke about their students' socioeconomic backgrounds and how they genuinely cared about students.

Teachers were well aware of the difficult circumstances in which many of their students' lived. A teacher at Ysleta Middle School believed it was important to consider students' home circumstances, but held all students to high academic expectations:

> I know the students who live in the projects, I know the kids that are transfers, and their two worlds are totally different. But, I want these guys to be successful no matter what type of living environment they're in. If they're living with a single mom and five other kids that doesn't mean that you can't do this [succeed in school]. (Yslt2, Ysleta MS, 2/03)

A teacher at YES College Preparatory School in Houston talked about being able to relate to the students, having come from a similar cultural and socioeconomic background as the students at the school: "I think I'm at a good advantage in a sense that I can relate to their lives a lot. I mean I pretty much came from the same type of environment that they did. You know, I know what it's like for a lot of them, like their home life" (YES3, YES College Prep, 4/03).

Many of the students who attended YES College Preparatory School were from a poor, inner-city community where the school originated. According to a school administrator, few students from this community ever went on to attend a 2-year junior college, much less a university, if they finished the equivalent of a high school education. This fact was primarily attributable to the shameful quality of public schools in the community. A driving impetus for the school's original mission was to address this historical injustice by honestly acknowledging the challenges students faced, while creating conditions at the school that would allow students to overcome these hardships. A teacher at YES discussed the socioeconomic disadvantages of the students who attended the school and the extra work they did to make up for these disadvantages:

> There's some, I would say that some of our students who have parents who work at night and they don't have the benefits of going home and having parents who can help them. ... So, there's that as a barrier, which you know is probably tied to the socioeconomic aspect of it. But I feel like we try to make up for that by keeping them until five [at night], by giving them our phone numbers, by doing after school tutorials. In some ways, we're trying to make up for the gaps that are caused by those economic disadvantages. (YES2, YES College Prep, 4/03)

In addition to expressing how they understood and were empathetic with their students' home situations, teachers at the nine participating schools often spoke about how much they cared for their students. A teacher at Latta High School believed that the personal relationships developed with students were as important as teaching mathematics:

> Yeah, I do consider who I'm talking to and where they're from. I guess my relationship with the kids is a little different than most teachers here. ... If it takes five minutes at the end of class to talk to them about what they're going through as far as home and their lives, I do it. I think that's just as important as anything else we're doing here. If you can talk about it, the better chance of them paying attention the rest of the day. If they've got something on their mind and they don't get a chance to talk about it, they're not listening to anything I've got to say. That's one thing that I pride myself in is communicating with the kids. I thing that's one of my strongest things about being a teacher is that they can, they can communicate with me about anything. (Latta2, Latta HS, 3/03)

Latta High School is located in a small community in South Carolina that takes tremendous pride in the accomplishments of its high school. One of the mathematics teachers spoke about how she was from the community and about her parental devotion to the success of the school: "I think we're committed to it from not only a professional level but at a personal level. We have children in this school, our personal children. I think that makes a difference. I think that drives us a little bit differently knowing that we have children coming through. I think a lot of it is the small town community" (Latta4, Latta HS, 11/02). A student at Latta High School noticed the value that teachers at her school placed on her success and how they communicated their availability to help her attain her academic goals: "Teachers are always encouraging you. They tell you the minute you walk in that they are available if we need help before and after school."

A teacher at Rockcastle County Middle School also thought it was important to be more than a teacher to the students: "I think it's nice for them to be able to see me as a person not necessarily just a teacher, even though we still have to have that student–teacher relationship. But they need to see that I'm human and I think that helps a lot" (Rock4, Rockcastle County MS, 3/03).

There was much value placed at the Young Women's Leadership School on advising and supporting students, in general. All the students at TYWLS were part of the Advisory Council Program where they could receive advisement and assistance from a faculty member. A faculty member in mathematics spoke about how this program helped to create a sense among the students that the faculty cared about them:

> We also have an Advisory Council Program so they [the students] just don't come into homeroom. They come in and we have by grade level, we have specific lessons, like self-esteem, we stress issues, we talk about a lot of things that they're going through, and help each other out, counsel each other. But students support each other. These schools with homerooms [and no advisory program like ours], they [the students] have nobody that cares. I think that has a lot to do with them wanting to be here and feeling good about being here. People care for them [at TYWLS], that they are important and what they do is important. (TYWLS2, TYWLS, 10/02)

The teachers at the Young Women's Leadership School were also adamant that they cared for their students and that this created an environment at the school where faculty and students cared for and trusted each other:

> I see it, that we do have relationships with students, person to person, I don't mean inappropriate [relationships]. I just mean we care about their feelings. … If you care about somebody like that, then they care about you and they trust you and they want you to like them and they want you to accept them. You can only ask for more [in a school like ours]. (unknown teacher, TYWLS, 10/02)

Students at the Young Women's Leadership School confirmed the sense of caring that existed at the school and had many positive things to say about their teachers. The following TYWLS student described the dedication and enthusiasm of her teachers:

> When they teach you, they teach you with so much enthusiasm it makes you want to learn more than they're teaching you. You might get upset that you're leaving [the school] and it might feel early because the teachers are getting so enthusiastic with you and they're getting to a point that they're feeling like family. They're really like going for the gold and it's like their sole purpose is to teach you and to make you have fun.

CONCLUDING REMARKS

For teachers searching for one magic bullet in this study that they could implement to impact their students' learning and achievement, the collaborations that existed among participating faculties may be it. In interview after interview, teachers across the highly effective schools spoke about how they worked with their colleagues to horizontally and vertically align curriculum, shared teaching ideas, discussed their students' mathematical strengths and weaknesses, and even modified and wrote curriculum together. At the charter schools, time was built into the daily schedule for the mathematics teachers to meet. At Ysleta Middle School, Emerald Middle School, and Rockcastle County Middle School, teachers were paid stipends from funded grants to meet after school and during summers to do curriculum work. At Rockcastle County Middle School, teachers credited their extensive and long-term collaborations as key to the school's dramatic academic turnaround over the course of a decade. Novice teachers at both Emerald Middle School and Ysleta Middle School said that the support and mentoring they were provided allowed them to focus on teaching, not only behavioral problems.

At the nine participating schools, teacher meetings often revolved around standardized testing, reviewing students' performance on "the test," and designing instructional units to prepare students for testing. At Latta High School and Emerald Middle School, teachers devoted significant time to preparing instructional units aligned with state mathematics standards. Clearly, the conversations that the teachers had with one another were important and of great value to them. In general, the focus on curriculum, testing, and standards motivated strong collaborations among mathematics faculties at the participating schools and there is little doubt these collaborations were among the primary reason why these schools were highly effective.

Teachers valued making mathematics both challenging and fun for their students. A teacher at the J. D. O'Bryant School of Mathematics and Science spoke about how having fun in mathematics does not need to equate with mathematics being easy. Teachers at Emerald Middle School wanted mathematics to be relevant to their students. One of these teachers valued students developing the ability to persevere in the subject. Teachers at Ysleta Middle School and YES College Preparatory empathized with their students' difficult home condition, but believed that all of their students could succeed and needed to be held to high academic expectations.

A strong sense of caring was evident at the participating schools. For instance, at the Young Women's Leadership School, every student was in an "advisory" group with a teacher who kept track of the student's academic performance. The advisory groups also promoted the development of strong personal relationships among teachers and students at the school. A teacher at Latta High School talked about how seriously they took their work since their own children attended the school. At Ysleta Middle School, there existed a very strong community outreach program that actively engaged parents in their students' educations. A student at KIPP Academy Bronx summarized the feeling of being cared for by teachers, a sentiment shared by many students at the participating schools: "They'll really do a lot of things for you, like they'll leave their cell phone on all night even if you have to call them just to say hello, or just to see how you're doing. Or they might call you to say hello and it's like, it's a real close relationship. It's like what you'd have with your parents."

The case study of the Young Women's Leadership School in the following chapter provides more in-depth insight into the particular characteristics of one highly effective school that was particular distinctive for its highly collaborative learning environment. At TYWLS, teachers worked to create a culture of success, constructed a collaborative and supportive learning environment, expected girls to become leaders, and established a sense of belonging for the girls.

8

The Young Women's Leadership School Case Study

Sylvia Celedón-Pattichis

> The vision of equity in mathematics education challenges a pervasive societal belief in North America that only some students are capable of learning mathematics. … Low expectations are especially problematic because students who live in poverty, students who are not native speakers of English, students with disabilities, females, and many non-white students have traditionally been far more likely than their counterparts in other demographic groups to be the victims of low expectations. Expectations must be raised—mathematics can and must be learned by all *students*.
>
> —*NCTM* (2000, pp. 12–13)

The *Principles and Standards for School Mathematics* places equity as the first of its six core principles (NCTM, 2000), calling attention to the need to raise expectations for all students in mathematics, to make accommodations for non-English speakers and special education students, and to provide high-quality mathematics programs that support student learning for all students. Given the increased attention to the No Child Left Behind Act, there is a need to understand what makes schools highly effective with students from culturally and linguistically diverse backgrounds.

The purpose of this 1-year case study is to investigate factors that contribute to the success of a single-sex school, the Young Women's Leadership School (TYWLS), particularly in mathematics. The school enrolled 7th-through 12th-grade girls from low-income backgrounds.

First, I discuss the literature review on gender issues and single-sex classrooms. Second, the methodology that was used to conduct this study is described. Third, the research findings are presented using relevant themes that emerged from the data. The chapter ends with conclusions, implications, significance, and limitations of this study.

BACKGROUND

This study is based on two bodies of literature. One includes the work of Sadker and Sadker (M. Sadker & D. Sadker, 1994; D. Sadker & M. Sadker, 2001) regarding single-sex classrooms and gender bias in the classroom and reports published by the American Association of University Women (AAUW) in the 1990s. The second includes environmental variables that influence women's choices in pursuing mathematics-related careers.

AAUW Reports on Single-Sex Classrooms

During the past 15 years, there have been several research reports that have added to the national debate on the use of single-sex schools as part of educating children. In the 1990s, the AAUW played a major role in highlighting findings that showed a disadvantage for girls in co-ed schools. For example, a 1991 national poll, *Shortchanging Girls, Shortchanging America*, emphasized that girls from age 9 to15 suffered from low self-esteem, had lower interest in mathematics and science, and were less willing to stand up for their views with teachers. Another report, *How Schools Shortchange Girls* (1992), found that girls were being called on less frequently in the classroom and were being encouraged less than males. M. Sadker and D. Sadker (1994) asserted these findings in their publication, *Failing at Fairness: How America's Schools Cheat Girls*. In this 3-year study, the researchers visited more than 100 classrooms in several states and conducted structured observations. Their findings indicate that, compared to girls, boys were called on more frequently by their teachers, teachers elaborated more on their responses to boys' questions, boys were praised more often, and boys received more encouragement when working through problems.

In 1995, AAUW endorsed single-sex schooling as a response, simultaneously asking for changes in existing co-ed schools to address inequity issues. At the higher education level, V. E. Lee and Marks (1990) found that smaller colleges produced a "disproportionate share of women leaders" (p. 579). Similarly, V. E. Lee and Bryk (1986) found at the high school level that single-sex schools, especially girls' schools, "appear to deliver specific advantages to their students" (p. 394). These advantages included "academic achievement gains ... future educational plans ... affective measures of self-image ... attitudes and behaviors related to academics" (p. 394). To follow up on this research, Lee and Marks found that these results were sustained upon entry into college, regardless of whether students enrolled in co-ed or single-sex colleges. V. E. Lee and Marks (1990) explained that, compared to girls in co-ed schools, girls in single-sex schools tend to focus more on homework, to hold less stereotypic beliefs about roles of women in the workplace, and to be more academically oriented. In addition, Haag (1998) concluded that compared to girls in co-ed schools, girls in single-sex schools tend to view mathematics and physics as " less 'masculine' and may have stronger preferences for them " (p. 18).

More importantly, Riordan (1990) found that the impact of single-sex schools is even more positive for African American and Hispanic students, male and female, who are low- and working-class minorities. His findings indicate that the performance of African American and Hispanic students who attended single-sex schools is, on average, almost 1 year higher on all exams compared to that of similar students in co-ed schools. He also found that for students from middle-class backgrounds or advantaged students, the consequences of attending co-ed or single-sex schools are virtually zero.

Based on the aforementioned research findings, the U. S. Department of Education (1994) recognized that single-sex classrooms may have positive outcomes, especially for young girls. Collectively, these findings point to the need to continue research of single-sex classrooms, particularly for low-income minority students.

GENDER DIFFERENCES IN MATHEMATICS EDUCATION

Some of the issues that have been raised in the literature regarding differences in mathematics include participation rates for women in mathematics, performance, and differential coursework hypothesis. A brief explanation of these issues follows.

Participation rates consider the number of females and males enrolled in advanced mathematics courses. Armstrong (1981) uses the results of two national surveys (National Assessment of Educational Progress, NAEP) to indicate that more American males than females take the more advanced high school mathematics courses. Algebra II seems to be the cutoff level because this is the point where most courses become optional. These results are supported by the AAUW (1999) report, which confirms that most girls tend to end their high school mathematics courses with algebra II.

There is much overlap in the performance in mathematics of males and females. Few consistent differences in performance are reported at the early primary school level. However, substantial evidence suggests that by the beginning of secondary schooling males frequently, although not invariably, outperform females on standardized tests of mathematics (Brandon, Newton, & Hammond, 1987). More recent data from an NAEP report by Perie, Moran, Lutkus, and Tirre (2005) indicate that gender differences in average scale scores have been quite small between 1990 and 2003, with males slightly outperforming females in mathematics in the 4th, 8th, and

12th grades. In addition, in their longitudinal study from 1st through 3rd grade, Fennema, Carpenter, Jacobs, Franke, and Levi (1998) found that there were no significant differences between boys and girls in the number of correct solutions for number facts (addition/subtraction or nonroutine problems). However, what was striking in their findings was the fact that boys consistently used abstract strategies or invented algorithms at each grade level more than girls, who tended to use modeling or counting strategies.

The differential coursework hypothesis reflects some of the NAEP findings. Ethington and Wolfe (1984) indicate that many of the differences in mathematics achievement between women and men can be explained by differences in ability, background, grades, attitudes, and formal exposure to mathematics in the classroom. Of these variables, they found exposure to be the most important in explaining variation in mathematics achievement. In a report on the National Center for Education Statistics, Freeman (2004) found that girls and boys take almost the same number of mathematics courses; however, they caution that the same patterns may not be true when the data are analyzed by race and ethnicity. In a report by AAUW, *Gender Gaps: Where Schools Still Fail Our Children*, the authors note that the gap in courses taken by girls and boys is diminishing, with more girls enrolling in algebra, geometry, pre-calculus, trigonometry, and calculus than in 1990. However, algebra II is most likely the last course girls will take in high school.

Oakes's (1990b) findings indicate that tracking has a detrimental effect on females' participation in mathematics. Furthermore, students in lower tracks learn less mathematics and take fewer advanced courses. Also, her findings show that teachers recommend high-ability girls less often than high-ability males for advanced placement in mathematics courses. Next, environmental factors that contribute to girls' choices in pursuing mathematics are discussed.

ENVIRONMENTAL VARIABLES THAT INFLUENCE WOMEN'S CHOICE IN PURSUING MATHEMATICS-RELATED CAREERS

The choice women make to pursue a mathematics- or science-based field is strongly influenced by environmental variables. Boaler (2002c) emphasizes that researchers tend to focus on variables that place the blame on the students (i.e., "girls lack confidence, develop anxiety, and attribute failure to themselves," p. 139). Furthermore, Boaler states that "these tendencies have generally been presented as properties of girls rather than as responses that are co-produced by particular working environments" (p. 139). Thus, it is important to consider the broader environment. Leder (1992) identifies the following as possible environmental variables: school variables, teacher variables, the peer group, the wider society, and parents.

School Variables

Single-Sex Classrooms.   Gender-segregated education has come to be an alternative to coeducational classrooms (D. Sadker & M. Sadker, 1985). Various school- and system-level interventions aimed at improving the learning climate for girls have experimented with single-sex classrooms (Fox & Cohn, 1980; Jackson, 2002; V. E. Lee & Bryk, 1986; Lockheed, 1985; Stage, Kreinberg, Eccles, & Becker, 1985). Collectively, these studies show that carefully timed, organized, and implemented programs may indeed lead to qualitative (attitudinal), if not quantitative (achievement), benefits in the learning of mathematics for at least some females. In addition, these studies point to subtle factors that may disadvantage female students in a coeducational setting, for example, choice of curriculum (the hidden curriculum), time-tabling of courses, textbook selection and content, availability of equipment, counselor's advice, methods of assessment, and administrator's implementation of certain instructional policies, as well as student's own perception of the learning climate.

In short, the way that the school system is structured creates inequity in the mathematics classroom. The next section addresses teacher behaviors and their impact on student achievement.

Teacher Variables.   Teachers play an important role in implementing school policies, whatever the setting in which mathematics is taught. The ways in which teachers interact with students is crucial in any setting. Believing that participation is an indicator of learning, teachers are likely to ignore females because they participate less than males. Furthermore, teachers are often unaware that they are concentrating on teaching males because the process of classroom interaction is unconscious, and they respond automatically to student demands for attention (D. Sadker & M. Sadker, 1986).

Brophy and Good (1974) examined patterns of teacher interactions with male and female students. They found that indeed there were differences in the ways teachers behaved toward the two groups of students. They reported that males tended to receive more criticisms, were praised more frequently for correct answers, had their work monitored more frequently, and had more contact with their teachers. The gender of the teacher did not seem to affect these conclusions.

Other research studies have replicated these findings (Becker, 1981; Leder, 1987; D. Sadker & M. Sadker, 1986). Analyses of classroom discourse involving children between age 9 and 11 in different settings found that boys took three times as many turns speaking (Redpath & Claire, as cited in Schwartz & Hanson, 1992), and a study of college-age students showed that men dominate discussions even more as they get older, in some classes speaking as much as 12 times longer than women (Krupnick, 1985). Similarly, Klan (as cited in Clark, 2004) shared Silber's findings from the teachers she observed for gender bias in co-educational classrooms. The teachers who were observed tended to ask questions of boys 92% of the time as a form of punishment for keeping them on task.

Peterson and Fennema (1985) conducted a study in which they observed teacher behavior on small-group instruction. They found that girls excel in a cooperative learning environment, whereas boys excel in a competitive environment.

The Peer Group.   In the previous section, teacher–student interactions were examined. This section considers peer groups. The peer groups that are established in schools tend to play a part in the way attitudes and beliefs about gender-typed roles are shaped. According to Leder (1992), "The peer group acts as an important reference for childhood and adolescent socialization and further perpetuates gender-role differentiation through gender-typed leisure activities, friendship patterns, subject preferences, educational and career intentions" (p. 611). What this implies is that whatever the peers value will reflect, reinforce, and shape differences in the attitudes, beliefs, and behaviors of the individuals that make up the group.

Huston and Carpenter (1985) observed that males prefer active games and pastimes that focus on skills and mastery of objects, whereas girls prefer play concerned with interpersonal relationships. This observation is important because the learning of mathematics and science involves understanding concepts (at the concrete level) through the manipulation of objects.

Another aspect that is important in peer groups is "peer pressure." Girls are sometimes pressured to conform to the "expected" role of women by their own peers. This suggests that females aim for excellence in careers congruent to their expected roles, that is, areas that require social skills, and males favor achievement in the traditionally highly valued areas of intellectual expertise and leadership skills (Boswell, 1985). Such attributions are reflected in the course choices of individual students. Moreover, the beliefs and attitudes attributed to the peer group reflect not only the general views of the individuals in that group but also those of the broader society.

The Broader Society.   There are many factors that shape community attitudes against which students often measure their beliefs, expectations, and aspirations. The media plays an important role in molding these attitudes and beliefs as well as reinforcing popular beliefs.

Jacobs and Eccles (1985) studied the impact of media reports about gender differences in mathematics achievement. They examined parents' general (i.e., stereotyped) and specific (i.e., for their own children) beliefs about gender differences in mathematics learning before and after coverage of a controversial article on this topic. Their findings showed that parents became more gender-stereotyped in their beliefs after reading media excerpts of the original work and of other relevant research reports. Similarly, Leedy, LaLonde, and Runk (2003) found that gender-based differences in the beliefs regarding mathematics persist even in mathematically talented students.

The media frequently portrays the difficulties encountered by successful professional women in balancing job demands with interpersonal needs. These accounts, as well as stereotyped portrayals in films and television (Kellner, 1990), reinforce and perpetuate the idea that females achieve success at a price (they may have to pay for later) and that they need to work hard to attain success. The media is also very likely to reproduce collective ideas about gender-appropriate roles for males and females, as was shown in the previous section.

Parents. The role of parents in their daughter's education is another factor that deserves attention. Eccles and Jacobs (1986) identified parents as a critical factor. In fact, they argued that parents have a much more direct and powerful effect than teachers on children's attitudes toward mathematics.

Furthermore, Armstrong and Price (1982) found that students' attitudes toward mathematics and their decisions to continue with mathematics were linked to their parent's conceptions of the educational goals of mathematics. Because parents are believed to be more supportive of their sons' than their daughters' mathematical studies (Fennema & Sherman, 1977), this is particularly disadvantageous for girls. Similarly, Boswell (1985) found that female attitudes about mathematics were significantly related to their mothers' attitudes about mathematics, whereas male attitudes about mathematics were related to their fathers' attitudes.

As already pointed out, environmental variables influence girls' decisions to pursue mathematics. The next section describes the methodology used to study the factors that contributed to the success of a single-sex school, the Young Women's Leadership School (TYWLS).

METHODOLOGY

Research Design

The data for this case study were collected over the 2002–2003 academic year as part of the Hewlett-Packard High-Achieving Schools Initiative. The case study design used was selected because it "becomes particularly useful where one needs to understand some special people, particular problem, or unique situation in great depth, and where one can identify cases rich in information" (Patton, 1990, p. 54; Merriam, 1998). According to Patton, the case study seeks to describe a particular situation in great detail, in context, and holistically.

Participants

The participants of this study included 1 administrator, 4 mathematics teachers, and 10–15 students. The sample of students who participated in a focus group interview represented students from Grades 7 through 12.

Site

At the time this study was undertaken, TYWLS was one of the 10 public single-sex schools in the country. It is located in East Harlem, but it serves girls from across New York City. With an enrollment of 360 students in Grades 7 through 12, the school consists of 63% Latina (primarily Domini-can and Puerto Rican, but also some Mexican, Honduran, and Guatemalan) and 37% African American females. The school also enrolled a small number of students from East Africa. Over 86% of students qualified for free or reduced lunch.

Data Collection

The data collected for this case study came from five sources: a group inter-view conducted with TYWLS mathematics faculty in the fall 2002, individ-ual interviews conducted with mathematics faculty members in the spring 2003, a group interview conducted with a randomly selected group of TYWLS students in the spring 2003, school-level and classroom-level arti-facts collected during school visits in the fall 2002 and spring 2003, and an in-terview and survey conducted with a school administrator. The goals of the data collection and analysis were twofold: to identify the salient characteris-tics that distinguished TYWLS as a highly effective school and to learn about teachers' conceptions about curriculum, instruction, and assessment. In this case study, the focus is solely on reporting the characteristics that were identified by teachers, students, and the administration that distin-guish the school as highly effective. This is because classroom observations and individual teacher interviews were not conducted at TYWLS in the fall 2002, and there was insufficient data to address teachers' conceptions about curriculum, instruction, and assessment.

DATA ANALYSIS

By doing a microanalysis of the data, I analyzed the factors that contributed to the school's success. The interviews, observations (field notes), docu-ments, and the survey were coded using a constant comparison analysis (Glaser & Strauss, as cited in Lincoln & Guba, 1985, p. 339). These data analy-ses involve unitizing, categorizing, chunking, and coding by choosing words, phrases, or sentences that specifically address the research questions. As categories were coded inductively, I documented recurring themes or patterns in the data. These themes were compared across classifications, and categories were collapsed, merged, or redefined. I developed working hypotheses accordingly by noticing similar patterns across data from all participants.

RESEARCH FINDINGS

The preliminary findings of this case study indicate four relevant themes regarding the factors that contribute to the success of this single-sex school. These areas include creating a culture of success, constructing a collaborative and supportive learning environment, expecting girls to become leaders, and establishing a sense of belonging.

Creating a Culture of Success

One of the themes that emerged was setting a culture of success. What made TYWLS special were the girls and the dedicated faculty who were committed to fulfilling the school's mission, which included preparing young women for college and careers in mathematics, science, and technology. The teachers played a crucial role in developing this culture of success by not only preparing students academically, but also in preparing students to be successful in general. The culture set by the school and the girls themselves was one of "it's cool to be good at math. The coolest girls, the most popular girls are also the ones who work the hardest and achieve the most" (teacher interview, 2003). All girls were expected to complete up to pre-calculus as a minimum requirement for graduation. To present an example of the mathematics content covered at the TYWLS, a discovery lesson observed during the fall 2002 in pre-calculus is presented in the following vignette:

> *Vignette*
>
> The teacher greets all students. He explains that today they will work on an activity in groups to find out what conditions cause a vertical or a horizontal shift in a function. The teacher tells all students to work on Parts A and B first, then they will discuss the solutions as a class. Parts A and B deal with vertical shift, whereas Parts C and D address horizontal shift. All students are actively engaged in the activity. I include Parts A and B here to illustrate what mathematics the students were learning in the early part of the fall semester.
>
> *Part A:*
>
> 1. Enter into your graphing calculator $y = x^2$. Observe what this function looks like. What is the y-intercept? What is the vertex?

2. Enter the graph $y = x^2 + 1$. Graph this function. What happened to the vertex? What is the y intercept?

3. Enter $y = x^2 + 2$. Graph this. Where is the vertex now?

4. If the next equation to be graphed is $y = x^2 + 7$, predict what this graph will look like. Where will the vertex be?

5. Graph $y = x^2 + 7$. Was your prediction correct?

6. Summarize what happens when you keep adding a number to this function.

Part B:

1. Clear all of your graphs.

2. Graph $y = x^2$.

3. Predict what the graph of $y = x^2 -1$ will look like. Where will the vertex be?

4. Graph $y = x^2 -1$. Was your prediction correct?

5. Predict what would happen if you were to graph $y = x^2 -6$. Where do you think the vertex will be?

6. Graph $y = x^2 -6$ and check your prediction.

Using your observations from Parts A and B, write in your own words what happens when constants are added or subtracted from a function.

Students are given enough time to complete the activity, then the teacher asks students to go over the solutions with the entire class. After they check all solutions, the teacher then tells students to continue with Parts C and D, in which students have to graph and explore what happens with horizontal shift. Similar questions are discussed within groups, and the teacher covers the solutions using whole class discussions. When students have explored and conjectured about the vertical and horizontal shifts on graphs, they practice predicting the vertex of each graph. For example, one function used was

$g(x) = (x -4)^2 -2$. Students solved similar problems and the teacher discussed the solutions with students. As part of the homework, the teacher asks students to think about how this mathematics might be used. Students respond with architecture, weather, and video animation. The teacher explains that they will have a problem on weather. The homework problem is shown next.

Tracking a Hurricane

It is hurricane season! Hurricane Joe has just made land fall. Joe has been declared a Category 5 hurricane—he is a catastrophic mess. Joe is very erratic and seems to be moving with an unpredictable path. Hurricane Joe looks like the graph $y = x^3$. His "eye" is located at (0,0).

Your job is to track Joe by writing equations for the location of his eye. After you write your equations be sure to check each of your answers with the graphing calculator.

Position 1: The "eye" is located at (5, 0).

Position 2: The "eye" is located at (4, –1).

Position 3: The "eye" is located at (–2, –3).

Position 4: The "eye" is located at (–6, 0).

Position 5: The "eye" is located at (–1, 5).

This vignette is used to illustrate that the mathematics the students were doing in pre-calculus supported the NCTM Standards (2000). Students were engaged in making observations, predictions, and conjectures about the mathematics content. Furthermore, to help meet the academic needs of girls at TYWLS, the school made a sizable budgetary commitment to extra academic support by offering Extended Day small group tutoring, Saturday New York State Regents Examination prep, Academic Intervention Services, and standardized test preparation.

In addition to helping girls achieve academically, the school also helped girls deal with real-life issues. In its daily schedule, the school included an advisory period in which students met with their homeroom teachers. During this time, the teacher interacted with girls openly on any issues they were dealing with personally; otherwise, the teacher followed the curriculum provided on issues involving AIDS, dating, and similar topics. As one teacher commented,

> We also have an advisory council program so they just don't come into homeroom. They come in and we have by grade level … we have specific lessons, like self-esteem, stress issues. We talk about a lot of things that they're going through, help each other out, council each other, but students support each other. Like these schools (referring to other schools) with homerooms they have nobody that care, and I think that has a lot to do with them wanting to be here and feeling good about being here. People care for them, that they are important and what they do is important. (mathematics faculty interview, fall 2002)

According to Ladson-Billings (1995), the culture of success must address both academic and life success. These two pieces were important components of the culture of success at the Young Women's Leadership School.

Constructing a Collaborative and Supportive Learning Environment

A second theme that was evident in all of the teacher interviews and the student interview included a focus at the Young Women's Leadership School on the construction of a collaborative and supportive learning environment. This culture established by the school and by the girls allowed them the freedom to work at the board in the middle of instruction, to debate with one another and their teacher about a particular solution, and to help one another. As one teacher stated, "The students sit in small desks, or tables so they are always helping each other. They're used to helping each other, so I try to get them to work together as much as possible. … Just put up a problem and let them work through it" (teacher interview, spring 2003). Cooperative learning was evident in each mathematics class visited and throughout the school. In this way, the school set a "friendly mathematics" culture. As one teacher noted in a faculty interview:

> I think too because we're an all girls school they come in 7th grade … we spend a huge amount of time getting them to change the way they think about going to school and being in the classroom. When they start here, they are so competitive, and they won't answer questions—if they feel embarrassed or they think they might not know and they think they might be dumb at stuff and really the way they treat each other. We spend so much time in 7th grade talking about that. And talking to them or just demonstrating and making them be cooperative even setting up the room where they have tables instead of desks, and lots of lots of math classes we do cooperative work and trying to do things that is non competitive in order for us to live in an all women's world. All that kind of stuff just so that kids will try, because I feel a lot of times they get to 7th grade math and they have never tried to answer a question in class. In the beginning of the year, I never call on kids to answer, and in the beginning of the year kids don't raise their hands and I walk behind to see if they have the right answer, and then I'll call on them by now they're feeling we can do it or they can actually, I socialize them in the classes. (math faculty interview, fall 2002)

The previous quote represents the mathematics faculty's sense of purpose for the students at TYWLS. These teachers felt this component of helping students become familiar with the school culture was unique to the school. This finding supports previous research findings (Peterson & Fennema, 1985) about girls excelling in cooperative learning environments. This two-way dialogue and opportunity to debate between the girls and the teacher also points to the need to empower minority students. Cummins's (2001) framework for empowering minority students includes pedagogy that allows interactions to occur freely between the students and the teacher. Pedagogy should not follow a transmission model, where students are seen as empty receptacles to be filled with facts (see banking model in Freire, 1993). At TYWLS, students were encouraged to interact with the teacher and their peers. The students were also asked to help their peers whenever someone could not understand a problem.

Expecting Girls to Become Leaders

A third theme involves the expectation that all girls would be leaders in their own communities. In fact, 100% of the first (2001) and second (2002) graduating classes were accepted to college. About 90% of the graduates were the first in their families to attend college. Among the factors that contributed to this high success rate included the extracurricular activities and tutoring beyond regular school hours that also helped the students experience success on the Regent's exam. The students' involvement in extracurricular activities helped them to remain active within their own schools and beyond. As part of the school requirements for graduation, the girls had to serve the community for about 60 hours. For example, some girls served at a local nursing home; others volunteered work in other community projects. In addition, at TYWLS, there was an onsite college counselor who was provided by the Young Women's Leadership Foundation and who made students aware of the expectations of different colleges and/or universities. The college counselor also arranged trips to colleges for girls at all grade levels. As one student stated, " It's like we're all here to be leaders so we try our best to move up in society to move up in the world, it's not like we're just there, it's a really important school" (student interview, spring 2003). This statement echoes V. E. Lee and Marks's (1990) findings of how colleges produce women leaders, except that this study included 7th through 12th graders who viewed their emerging leadership roles as important not only in school but in society. Another student added,

> There is always something for you to do at this school, and they're always trying to make sure that you're intellectual with the people around you. You just have something called Seven-Eleven. The 11th graders help out the 7th graders, you're supposed to be like big sisters for those who don't have any, so there is always something for us to do. (student interview, spring 2003)

This quote shows how girls at higher grades served as mentors to girls in lower grades, particularly those who were new to the school at the 7th grade. Thus, this experience allowed the 11th-grade girls to experience leadership roles. At the same time, the 7th-grade girls had mentors and derived great benefit from the experience.

Establishing a Sense of Belonging

A fourth theme was a sense of belonging and community. The following statements were representative of how the girls thought of school as a home and viewed their teachers as their parents, as a family.

> So after I came to this school, it was like no distraction and it's like a better way for me to learn because I don't have to be worrying about

whether the boys are going to bother me or how do I look, because we all have the same uniforms so it's like a second home, it's exciting. (student interview, spring 2003)

Another student added, "Yes, I think it's like one big family, it's like one person, in one grade you try and help out, it's like a sister relationship and like the teachers are like our parents and we're all sisters trying to help each other if we can" (student interview, spring 2003). The first student mentioned that there were no distractions once she entered this single-sex school. This finding is consistent with that of V. E. Lee and Marks (1990), who found that students focus more on academics when they do not have to worry about "male–female socialization issues" (p. 589). In addition, both students thought of school as a second home and as part of their extended family. They compared other female students as their sisters and their teachers as their parents. This finding contributes to the notion that teachers' roles need to be as co-parents, especially with students who come from culturally and linguistically diverse backgrounds (Knight, 2003; Ladson-Billings, 1995).

The following two students also discussed their views on their single-sex school. They also saw TYWLS as a home where they were constantly being challenged.

S4: I think that the fact, that we're all at home, and the fact that we have good things to think about, we don't think about negative stuff, so there are things to think about that we're going to be something good. (student interview, spring 2003)

This student echoed what the first students said about leadership roles, that the students would be "something good." The statement also affirmed the previous students' comments about their views of school as a home. Another student added the following to the conversation:

For me, I get bored fast. I don't like getting bored, so to me this school is always challenging. I'm never bored in this school, and for me, if I have a bad day at my house, I can come here and I have my friends, and like she said, you can take your mind off of it, in this school and you don't have to think about it if you leave, and sometimes you don't want to leave the school. (student interview, spring 2003)

Collectively, these statements point to the need to consider caring and co-parenting roles involving Hispanic and African American children and that extend to other student populations (Knight, 2003).

CONCLUSIONS AND IMPLICATIONS

The purpose of this case study is to document the factors that contributed to the success of a single-sex school, the Young Women's Leadership School. Reports that have been published in the past by the American Association of

University Women (AAUW) and studies by Sadker and Sadker were discussed, as were studies focusing on environmental variables that influence girls' choices in pursuing mathematics. The case study findings include the importance of setting a culture of success for these girls, both academically and in their daily life experiences; establishing a cooperative and supportive learning environment at the school; holding high expectations for all girls, including that all girls be leaders in their communities; and viewing the school as a home and as a family. These findings have important implications for educators.

One implication includes having the resources to help students meet high expectations. For example, at TYWLS, high expectations were supported by financial resources and dedicated teachers to help students meet those expectations. At TYWLS, all girls were expected to go to college. The school's foundation provided an onsite college counselor and that person was responsible for arranging visits to colleges for girls at all grade levels. In so doing, seventh graders became acquainted early in their schooling experience to the expectation that they would attend college. Moreover, a dedicated mathematics faculty provided, among other things, supplementary instructional support to students through Saturday and afterschool tutorial programs. In general, the mathematics faculty demonstrated that they cared about their students, both academically and personally.

A second implication is that students should be allowed to work collaboratively. An important part of the school culture at TYWLS was the establishment of a cooperative and supportive learning environment. The girls at TYWLS helped each other in every class. In their views, they were helping their "sisters." It was evident that this learning arrangement contributed to the girls' ability to debate with one another and their teachers about answers to mathematics problems.

A third implication involves the relationships established among the students and teachers. Students often referred to their teachers as being like parents. This co-parenting role points to the need to establish ethics of care within schools (Knight, 2003; Walker, 1996). At TYWLS, this process began as soon as students entered the seventh grade. The faculty viewed the advisory period as an opportunity to establish trusting relationships with their students, especially at a crucial time when students navigate the teenage years and experience mixed messages society sends daily. The ethic of care enacted itself in interpersonal discussions involving not only daily life topics (i.e., stress, family, friends), but also academics (i.e., mathematics, English, social studies, and other content areas).

This study highlights some of the factors that contributed to the Young Women's Leadership School's success with girls. In considering equity issues in the mathematics classroom, it is important to examine factors that make a school successful and incorporate those that are replicable into public schools. Raising expectations should become the norm and not the exception in schools so that all students can learn.

9

Looking Back
and Some Recommendations
for Further Research

Richard S. Kitchen

> Furthermore, I want all kids to know that the heritage of academia—in-
> cluding calculus—belongs to them as much as to anyone else. And they
> won't learn this by shying away from such fields, especially in a culture
> that has traditionally put off-limits signs on academic subjects for the least
> advantaged of our fellow citizens—"Sorry, but this is not meant for you."
>
> —*Meier* (1995, p. 167)

A guiding principle for this study was that highly effective schools serving high-poverty communities possess desirable characteristics and engage in instructional practices that less effective schools would want to replicate. This study focused on the instructional environment in which students learn, teacher practices (e.g., Martin et al., 2000), and teacher conceptions of the academic subjects they teach. Following the literature on effective teaching (Brophy & Good, 1986; Good et al., 1983) and on school restructuring (V. E. Lee & Smith, 2001; Newmann & Associates, 1996), we hypothesized that highly effective secondary schools in mathematics could be distinguished by policies and practices that characterize them as highly effective. Furthermore, we speculated that the nine schools that participated in this study had a greater concentration of highly effective teachers that would have a cumulative positive impact on their students' learning and achievement. Thus, studying highly effective teachers could provide insights into the salient characteristics of highly effective schools in general, and these teachers' conceptions and practices with regard to mathematics curriculum, instruction, and assessment in particular.

At all nine participating schools, the discipline policy, class schedule, student support services, and professional development objectives for teachers were established with one goal in mind: to positively impact student learning and achievement. Administrators, teachers, and, at a few schools, even parents had successfully worked together in powerful and innovative ways to make exceptional student learning their principal goal. One of the most tangible accomplishments of this work was that the cultures at the participating schools were the exact opposite of what is often found at less effective schools. Teachers came to school to teach and students came to learn. Student learning and teaching was priority one, particularly in the core subject areas. To maintain this focus, administrators and teachers regularly evaluated their progress and called into question school policies or practices that could detract from their primary objective.

Constructing a school culture in which teaching and learning took precedence over everything else compelled school administrators and faculty to think seriously about both classroom discipline and relationship building. A majority of the schools had discipline policies reinforcing the notion that learning was the top priority and obstructing the learning of others was a serious offense. We found that, for the most part, behavioral problems were minimal because of the steadfast focus on student learning at the schools. Students who interrupted the learning of others were reprimanded not only by teachers, but by peers as well.

A school culture where discipline formed a strong foundation for learning was exemplified by YES College Preparatory School and the two KIPP Academies where students signed a contract indicating their willingness to be subjected to strict behavioral norms. This contract stipulated that parents were also accountable for their students' conduct and learning at the schools. Through signing the contract, parents granted permission for faculty to decide if a student needed to stay after school for additional academic assistance. This meant that even after an extended school day, students would sometimes stay late. For example, at KIPP Academy Houston, students stayed at the school as late as 8 p.m. for additional tutoring and parents were expected to be supportive, given that they had signed a contract allowing faculty the latitude to act on behalf of their child. Also, at participating charter schools, students were required to attend summer school sessions that focused heavily on acclimating them to strict behavioral expectations.

Given the importance placed on learning at the participating schools, punishment for students who interrupted the learning process was not necessarily removal from the classroom. Removing students from class was considered detrimental to their learning. At the three participating charter schools, disciplinary action included having students stand in the back of all their classes for a week with their school uniform shirts turned inside out, eating lunch separated from their friends, and having certain privileges removed (e.g., engaging in extracurricular activities).

At KIPP Academy Bronx, harsh disciplinary procedures were particularly evident in a sixth- grade mathematics class that was observed. During the classroom observation, several students began crying after being strongly berated and mildly humiliated in front of the class for an extended period of time. The teacher's goal was to stop the progress of any behavioral problems during a student's initial year at the school, and the mathematics classroom was identified as the best place to accomplish this objective. By signing the KIPP Academy Bronx contract, students and their parents granted permission to be subjected to such high behavioral expectations at the school. Although the contract and its subsequent strong disciplinary actions would be difficult to implement at more traditional public schools, they were deemed a great success at the KIPP Academies for curtailing student disruptions of the learning process.

Another characteristic of the highly effective schools was that relationship building among teachers and between teachers and students was highly valued. Teachers collaborated to devise well-thought-out academic goals for their mathematics students. The fact that we found such strong collaborations among mathematics faculty at all of the school sites was among the most powerful findings in the research study. Emerald Middle School faculty, in particular, had a lot to say about not waiting for an administrator to make the learning and teaching of mathematics at their school a primary goal. Instead, they went to their principal and told her that the school had made literacy its focus for long enough and that they would lead the effort to improve mathematics learning and achievement at Emerald. These teachers collaboratively took the initiative and made the mathematics education of their students a core goal at their school. In this way, they also demonstrated the power they had as professionals to influence their school's priorities.

Teachers at the participating schools also expressed a sincere interest in developing strong and authentic relationships with their students. Some teachers could relate to their students' socioeconomic backgrounds. In addition to expressing how they understood and were empathetic with their students' home situations, teachers often spoke about how much they cared for their students. As described in chapter 8, students at the Young Women's Leadership School spoke about how their teachers were like parents to them. One of the primary goals of the teachers at TYWLS was to develop respectful and trusting relationships with students when they entered the school in seventh grade. These relationships provided students with consistent access to academic counseling. More importantly, caring relationships fostered by teachers at TYWLS promoted genuine discussions about matters of great personal significance to students.

Although all the schools prioritized teaching and learning, the actual strategies schools implemented to be highly effective varied. Rockcastle County Middle School is located in a rural, southeastern Kentucky county that includes some of the poorest and most isolated areas in the state. Rockcastle County Middle School transformed itself from being among the lowest performing middle schools in the state to among the highest, a turnaround the teachers attributed to extensive and long-term collaborations over the course of a decade. Just in the 4 years prior to when this study was undertaken, the school's eighth-grade mathematics scores had increased by 38.9%. As part of their work, the mathematics faculty at Rockcastle devoted significant time after school discussing their curricula.

An alternative strategy employed by Ysleta Middle School to prioritize teaching and learning was the establishment of strong community outreach programs. Ysleta Middle School was located within a federally designated "Empowerment Zone," characterized as the sixth poorest area in the country in average per capita income, with 27% of its population living in poverty. In 2001–2002, 93% of the students qualified for free or reduced-price lunch, and 33% were English-language learners. Community outreach programs that existed at Ysleta Middle School included an afterschool program for the many students who came from single- parent homes and would have otherwise spent their afternoons unsupervised. During our visits to the school, it was not uncommon for us to regularly interact with parents who were themselves participants in programs that were specifically designed for them (e.g., parent-led literacy circles and English-language classes). The principal at Ysleta talked about how parental empowerment had evolved to the point where parents were regularly engaged in local and national political actions in which they advocated for the school and their community.

At Emerald Middle School, the mathematics faculty believed that work on interdisciplinary teams greatly contributed to their status as a high-achieving school. Emerald Middle School is a public, Title I urban school located in eastern San Diego County. The percentage of students who qualified for free or reduced-price lunch at the school during the 2001–2002 academic year was 78%. At the time this study was undertaken, the school's student population was highly diverse (more than 50% students of color) and the total number of languages spoken by students was 16. For the mathematics faculty to be able to meet and plan their academic goals on interdisciplinary teams, release time was regularly provided by the school's administration. Perhaps most importantly, however, the mathematics teachers at the school were the ones who drove the effort to make the school highly effective in their subject area.

A variety of other strategies designed to support the focus on teaching and learning were observed. The extended school days at the KIPP Academies and YES College Preparatory School, where the school day lasted from 7:30 a.m. until 5 p.m. daily, provided time for teachers to tutor students, collaboratively plan, and communicate with each other. At J. D. O'Bryant School of Mathematics and Science and Emerald Middle School, there existed strong collaborations between the schools and local universities. As part of these partnerships, undergraduate and graduate students in engineering, mathematics, and the sciences regularly tutored students at the schools. At the Young Women's Leadership School, teachers worked to create a collaborative learning environment in which all students were expected to succeed academically. Teachers at TYWLS believed the collaborative learning environment had a powerful affect on creating a supportive learning environment so that all the girls could succeed at the school.

As these examples make clear, the schools did not follow the same path to achieve their status as highly effective. Some of the non-charter schools, specifically Rockcastle County Middle School and Ysleta Middle School, even had to overcome historical legacies of profound underachievement. What all nine schools did have in common, however, was a commitment to student learning and the creation of the necessary support structures and conditions to prioritize student learning and achievement. For instance, extended periods of time were allotted for mathematics instruction at the middle schools so that gaps in students' mathematical backgrounds could be addressed. Teachers strongly believed that these extended class periods were essential to continue to address students' mathematical weaknesses, while moving them forward with a challenging curriculum.

At the majority of the participating schools, programs were readily available for students to receive supplementary instructional support. At the Young Women's Leadership School, student learning was supported through Saturday classes and afterschool tutorial programs. In addition, some of the schools had special programs for failing students. At YES College Preparatory School, failing students were placed on academic probation, which required them to seek even more additional academic support from their teachers during lunch periods or study hall. At Rockcastle County Middle School, students were required to attend Extended School Services if they received an F in any of their classes, a 2-hour afterschool tutorial session.

Students did not encounter "off-limits signs" to higher level mathematics at the nine schools that participated in this study. Like at Deborah Meier's school in Harlem (1995), teachers took seriously the charge of teaching a challenging mathematics curriculum to their students, some of whom came from among the most disadvantaged communities in their respective cities and states. As illuminated in depth for the teachers at YES College Preparatory School in chapter 4, teachers at participating schools exhibited an exceptionally high level of commitment to their work, particularly to teaching a demanding mathematics curriculum.

Across the nine schools, the teachers' commitment to students learning challenging mathematics was exemplified by how they planned their curricula. Teachers described using a backward planning approach to curriculum development in which the initial step was to identify big goals for students that needed to be accomplished by the end of a specific grade level. At all the middle schools, this big goal was for all students to successfully complete the equivalent of a rigorous first-year algebra course before they went on to high school. Once such a goal was identified, then the teachers began the process of working backward chronologically to identify specific learning objectives that needed to be met to make reaching the larger goal feasible.

If students were going to study the equivalent of a first year of algebra in eighth-grade, then they needed to study and understand well specific topics and concepts identified by the teachers that are traditionally taught in a pre-algebra course in seventh grade. To have success in this seventh-grade course, teachers came to realize that students needed remediation with skills traditionally taught at the primary school level that they did not possess, such as an understanding of and ability to apply the products of single digits. Moreover, in sixth grade, teachers focused extensively on developing students' understanding of proportional reasoning (e.g., the adding and subtracting of fractions), while moving students forward by challenging them to engage in problem-solving activities. For middle school teachers to be able to achieve these goals, they found the extended class periods previously discussed were absolutely necessary. This strategy, first identifying large instructional goals and then working backward to identify the specific learning objectives that needed to be accomplished to make the large goals attainable, was a powerful and effective approach that we found was commonly used across the schools.

In interview after interview, teachers across the highly effective schools spoke about how they worked with their colleagues to horizontally and vertically align curriculum, shared teaching ideas, discussed their students' mathematical strengths and weaknesses, and modified and wrote curriculum together. The strong collaborations that existed among teachers clearly supported the implementation of challenging mathematics curricula and instruction. At the charter schools, time was built into the daily schedule for the mathematics teachers to meet. At Ysleta Middle School, Emerald Middle School, and Rockcastle County Middle School, teachers were paid stipends from funded grants to meet after school and during summers to develop curriculum. Novice teachers at both Emerald Middle School and Ysleta Middle School said the support and mentoring they were provided allowed them to focus primarily on teaching, and minimally on behavioral problems.

Meetings of the mathematics teachers across the nine sites often revolved around standardized testing. For instance, the teachers reviewed students' performance on "the test," and designed instructional units to prepare students for success on the test. Unquestionably, great value was placed on student success on "the test" at participating schools. Students talked about the importance placed on the test at their respective schools. For example, at Rockcastle County Middle School, a student said the teachers talked about the test almost everyday and that "they [the teachers] have billboards and signs they take around the school and everything" reminding them of the test and its importance. To gear students up for the test, pep rallies were also held at Rockcastle prior to testing.

At Ysleta Middle School in Texas, teachers were highly accountable for students' scores on standardized tests to such a degree that teachers had left the school in recent years because of their students' poor performance on standardized tests. The focus on preparing students for high-stakes testing was also stressful for some students. The following quote expresses how stressed one student was about the test. In his state, students must pass the test to graduate from high school:

> I see teachers desperately wanting to teach their lesson plan, but they have to stop in order to take that test and give it to the students. Me personally, I was stressed out, I was going home, as soon as I would sit down on the couch I would fall asleep, you know. … I was thinking about well, my grades are pretty good, my GPA is pretty high, but if I don't pass this test then I'm not graduating and so, I can do pretty good in school but if I fail then I'm not getting a diploma.

We found that structures were in place at all nine schools so that students could be successful on the test. For instance, teachers engaged in test item analysis to identify students' weaknesses, conducted study sessions geared specifically to prepare students for the test, and wrote instructional units aligned with the test. At Latta High School, teachers devoted significant time to preparing instructional units aligned with state mathematics standards. This was also the case at Emerald Middle School, where faculty analyzed their students' test results as well.

On the other hand, teachers spoke about teaching beyond the test. Schools worked to prepare their students for success on standardized tests, but the test did not necessarily dictate mathematics curricula and instruction. Teachers described how they did not stop teaching 2 weeks before the test to engage students in test preparation. Instead, they maintained their focus on sustaining a challenging mathematics program for students throughout the academic year. A teacher at KIPP Academy Bronx summarized this finding in the following way: "If you're teaching correctly, everything applies to the test. A test is just a basic problem solving situation, so if you're teaching them problem solving you won't have to worry so much about teaching [to] the test" (KIPPB4, KIPP Bronx, 4/03). At the highly effective schools, high expectations for student learning coupled with support mechanisms for this learning led to high achievement. This finding is an important one given the high-stakes testing climate that currently exists in the United States.

In general, the focus on curriculum, testing, and standards motivated strong collaborations among mathematics faculties at the participating schools. Teachers were continually engaged with their colleagues in planning lessons, reviewing lessons, and modifying lessons with the sole goal of advancing student learning. There is little doubt that these collaborations were among the primary reasons why the participating schools were highly effective. Teachers often talked about how powerful these collaborations had been in creating a sense of camaraderie at their schools. The teachers were proud of what they had accomplished together and were committed to ensuring that their schools continued to be exceptional places for the teaching and learning of mathematics.

In addition to the support the teachers gave one another, we found that the majority of the highly effective schools employed someone on a part-time or full-time basis to write grant proposals to sustain a variety of school activities, including collaborative work engaged in by teachers. At all the charter schools, a full-time development officer was employed to raise funds for the many extracurricular activities that were offered (e.g., a trip to Washington, DC, travel to college campuses, and visits to national parks). The fund-raising activities at the charter schools were viewed as critically important to carry on the missions of these schools, which included introducing students to the culture of a college campus. Ysleta Middle School, Rockcastle County Middle School, and J. D. O'Bryant School of Mathematics and Science also had programs to support student visits to college campuses. Because many students at these schools had parents who had not attended a 4-year college (the charter schools and TYWLS prioritized admitting students who would be the first in their families to attend college), a goal at many of the schools was to acclimate students to the culture of higher education with visits to college campuses. In addition, because students may not have traveled widely, an additional goal at some of the schools was to expose students to unspoiled wilderness areas. In general, the nine highly effective schools were all in a constant search for funds to initiate, support, and sustain the many activities they offered students.

External grants had also funded some of the resource materials that were widely available at the schools. Teachers talked about how fortunate they were to have so many teaching resources. They also spoke about how when they needed something, they could simply open their closets and pull out the desired materials. These resources were available to support the primary goals at the schools: teaching and learning. In general, teachers did not feel they had to beg for materials to be effective at their jobs.

The nine schools that participated in the study were places with a tangible sense of hope. Teachers liked coming to work; they knew they could focus on teaching demanding mathematical content to students who were expected to take academics seriously. Students also knew they would be held accountable by multiple adults in the school building for their actions. It may come as a surprise to some that student resistance (Willis, 1981) to the high academic expectations they encountered at their respective schools was essentially nonexistent. In fact, students frequently talked about willingly responding to the academic challenges they faced. For instance, as noted in the YES College Preparatory School chapter, students at the school recognized and appreciated their teachers' academic and personal commitment to them. Interestingly, students at both the Young Women's Leadership School and the J. D. O'Bryant School of Mathematics and Science told us that they, not their parents, had chosen to apply and attend these schools. Students at the other four participating non-charter schools also often expressed pride in their respective school's recognition for its academic accomplishments and selection for participation in this study.

The schools that participated in this study were places where teachers wanted to work. Evidence for this included the fact that at the non-charter schools, the mathematics faculties were quite stable, with many of the teachers having taught at their respective schools for years. One factor contributing to teachers' feelings of satisfaction with their work environments was the lack of behavioral problems that allowed teachers to focus on the art of teaching. This, in turn, resulted in higher levels of learning and achievement that supported teachers' sense of pride in what they had accomplished. Teachers recognized they worked at unique schools where, for the most part, administrators supported the creation of stimulating and demanding learning environments.

Interestingly, teacher retention was not an important goal at the participating charter schools. Instead, the main concern was to impact the quality of students' educational opportunities now, not in the future. These schools originated in communities where the quality of public schools was particularly reprehensible. They took seriously their missions, which entailed addressing this historical injustice by providing their students with "a rigorous college-preparatory curriculum that prepares them for matriculation and success in college" (YES College Preparatory School).

Achieving high academic goals at the charter schools necessitated an overwhelming workload, which led to teacher burn-out. However, these schools were able to effectively recruit highly motivated individuals to replace teachers because of their celebrated status. All three participating charter schools were quite successful at recruiting individuals who had recently completed a teaching assignment through the "Teach for America" program. Although many of these prospective teachers did not hold teaching degrees or licenses, the "Teach for America" program is well-known for recruiting individuals with a passion "to provide leadership in the movement to eliminate educational inequity" (http://www.teachforamerica.org/) at schools that serve high-poverty communities throughout the United States. Similar to "Teach for America," teachers at the three charter schools were being asked to make large personal sacrifices to meet their students' immediate academic needs.

Prospective teachers were also attracted to these schools because they were perceived to be places where teachers were making a profound difference in their students' lives. Concrete evidence supporting such perceptions included the fact that many graduates of the KIPP Academies were matriculating at prestigious private high schools or were high achievers at local, public high schools.[6] Similarly, YES College Preparatory School graduates were being accepted at and attending eminent universities throughout the country. Finally, although much was expected of them at the charter schools, prospective teachers were attracted to these schools because they could also expect much of their students.

As the authors of this book have found during numerous presentations made on this study at professional conferences, most teachers want to work at schools where they can focus on teaching and where they will have attentive students who come to school to learn. In this research project, we discovered that such public, secondary schools exist in high-poverty communities in the United States. These schools were celebrated by both teachers and students. A teacher at the Young Women's Leadership School summarized well the gratification that, for the most part, teachers and students expressed for their respective schools: "In a lot of schools, there are a lot teachers out there who are judged by the time they are at the school because that's where they are. But I think that everybody here wants to be here." Furthermore, "I think when they [the students] come here, they're going to learn and they want to be here to learn."

EXAMINING THIS STUDY'S FINDINGS VIS-À-VIS THE RESEARCH LITERATURE

It seems natural at this point to ask how the findings from this study of the nine highly effective schools can inform us with regard to the mathematics education reform movement and the notion of "teaching for diversity." The first construct has to do with the teachers' implementation of standards-based recommendations in their classrooms (see NCTM, 1989, 2000; NSF, 1996). Did many of the teachers regularly utilize a National Science Foundation-funded mathematics curriculum? Did we find instruction that aligned with standards-based recommendations at the highly effective schools that promoted such things as the development of students' mathematical reasoning? To what extent did teachers at the nine highly effective schools systematically promote a skills-based attitude to the teaching of mathematics versus problem-solving approaches? With regard to the second construct, teaching for diversity, the following questions will be addressed: Was the creation of equitable learning opportunities in

---

[6]Students could complete only through 8th grade at KIPP Academy Bronx and KIPP Academy Houston when this study was undertaken.

mathematics for all students highly valued by participating teachers? Was there a focus on developing students' capacities in mathematical literacy to think critically about mathematics and how mathematics is used?

Did Schools Utilize an NSF-Funded Mathematics Curriculum?

Whereas only a few of the schools regularly utilized NSF-created materials, many made use of some of these materials on a part-time basis. A strong research finding was that at all of the schools, teachers regularly engaged in modifying existing curricular materials and even created on a small-scale (with the exception of KIPP Academy Bronx, where teachers were writing a mathematics curriculum for use at all the KIPP Academies across the country) mathematics units and lessons. The lesson here appears to be that at these highly effective schools, the mathematics curriculum is a dynamic work in progress.

As a result, at all the nine schools it was not uncommon to observe teachers using both "traditional" and "standards-based" materials during the same lesson. Teachers used textbooks and supplemented these books regularly with one goal in mind: to positively impact their students' learning of challenging mathematical concepts and ideas. One could not help but notice how teachers at the highly effective schools generally did not teach mathematics by following a textbook "one page at a time." Teachers were regularly engaged, often collaboratively, in considering the scope and sequence of the mathematics curriculum. Mathematics curricula were a work in progress, modified and even created by teachers who systematically thought about the mathematics they wanted their students to learn.

Was Instruction Aligned With Standards-Based Recommendations?

To respond to whether instruction at the nine participating schools was aligned with standards-based recommendations, it is helpful to turn to the classroom observation ratings. Our original hypothesis was that at the highly effective schools we would be more likely to find instruction that aligned with standards-based recommendations (see NCTM, 1989, 2000; NSF, 1996). The subscales of our classroom observation protocols were designed to align closely with these standards-based recommendations in five areas: intellectual support, depth of knowledge and student understanding, mathematical analysis, mathematical discourse and communication, and student engagement. In calculating the means of the five classroom observation subscales (appendix C), we found engagement was rated highest ($M = 4.04$), followed by intellectual support ($M = 3.41$), mathematical discourse ($M = 2.80$), depth of knowledge ($M = 2.77$), and mathematical analysis ($M = 2.57$).

It may be surprising to some that engagement was the highest rated sub-scale ($M = 4.04$) of the five areas assessed during classroom observations. After all, these were middle school and high school students studying mathematics; what interest do the majority of teenagers have in mathematics? Nonetheless, students were highly engaged in studying mathematics in class. A rating of 4 in engagement means that: "Engagement is widespread; most students (50%–90%), most of the time (50%–90%), are on-task pursuing the substance of the lesson; most students seem to be taking the work seriously and trying hard" (see appendix B for descriptions of the five subscales rated). Although the high mean rating for engagement could be attributed to the scale's inability to reliably discern student indifference to mathematics, it seems more likely that students were genuinely interested in the mathematics that they were being taught. This is an impressive tribute to the teachers across the schools who participated in this study.

One theme emerging from the analysis of teachers' narratives as presented in chapter 5 was that teachers' asserted that they worked to engage students in mathematical communication and inquiry in class. Surprisingly, however, the average of the classroom observation ratings across all schools for mathematical discourse was less than three ($M = 2.80$). A mean of 2.80 in mathematical discourse suggests that just under half of the lessons observed most likely received a rating of three or above. A rating of 3 implies that: "There is at least one sustained episode of sharing and developing collective understanding about mathematics that involves: (a) a small group of students or (b) a small group of students and the teacher. Or, brief episodes of sharing and developing collective understandings occur sporadically throughout the lesson." Therefore, it could also be argued that it was not uncommon to observe participating teachers engaging students in at least one sustained or brief episode of sharing and developing mathematical ideas together during mathematics class. Therefore, it is likely that although teachers spoke about how they valued student discourse, we found they engaged their students in classroom talk at levels that would be considered less than what is valued in the classroom observation protocol.

Examining these classroom ratings further, mathematical analysis received the lowest mean ratings in all but two of the schools. In addition, the mean for depth of knowledge at the eight schools where classroom observations were made[7] was less than 3 at five of the eight schools. For both mathematical analysis and depth of knowledge, a rating of 3 means that: "There is at least one significant activity involving mathematical analysis in which some students (10%–20%) engage" and "deep understanding of some mathematical concepts is countered by superficial understanding of some other ideas," respectively. The low mean ratings for these two obser-

---

[7]Classroom observations were not conducted at KIPP Academy Houston. Observations and ratings were carried out at the Young Women's Leadership School in the spring 2003, but not during the fall 2002.

vation subscales suggests that students did not consistently engage in mathematical analysis in class nor did they regularly understand the depth of mathematical ideas presented during lessons.

It is important to clarify that whereas we found variations among each of the five ratings across the eight schools as would be expected, we also found that the largest variations existed for mathematical analysis and depth of knowledge. For mathematical analysis, the mean ratings ranged from a high of 3.34 at one school to a low of 1.86 at another. For depth of knowledge, the mean ratings varied from a high of 3.6 at one school to a low of 1.93 at another. The means for both subscales were less than two at one participating school, but they were well-above 3 for depth of knowledge at three schools and above 3 for mathematical analysis for two schools. Moreover, a particular school's mean ratings for depth of knowledge and mathematical analysis tended to be quite similar. For example, at one participating school the means ratings for these two subscales were 2.56 and 2.5, respectively, whereas for another they were 1.93 and 1.86. So, simply taking the average of the means across the eight schools muddies the waters considerably in our analyses of the ratings for these two subscales.

What does emerge more clearly is that there were, in fact, obvious differences among classroom lessons observed across the eight schools. Thus, although the ratings for depth of knowledge and mathematical analysis were not uniformly high, the means for these two subscales for several schools were quite respectable. That is, students pursued the mathematical content of their lessons in greater depth and engaged in mathematical analysis or higher order thinking more frequently at a subset of participating schools (see appendix C for an in-depth analysis of the classroom ratings).

This finding can also be understood from the standpoint of how both skills-based instruction and mathematical problem solving were highly valued at the participating schools. The observation instrument was designed to align with recommended standards-based instruction in mathematics (see NCTM, 1989, 1991, 2000; NSF, 1996) that stresses problem-solving approaches to promote students' reasoning skills. Thus, schools with higher ratings in mathematical analysis and depth of knowledge were more ardently promoting problem-solving instruction than at schools where the means for these two subscales were lower. From this perspective, instruction at a handful of schools was more aligned with standards-based recommendations than at other schools.

We also aggregated each of the five subscales from the individual classroom level: first comparing middle school and high school lessons observed, and second comparing charter school and non-charter school lessons observed over all the classroom observations made during the fall and spring visitations. Our analyses of the classroom observation ratings demonstrate that instruction in middle school classrooms and charter school classrooms was more closely aligned with recommended standards-based instruction than was the instruction observed in high school classes and non-charter school classrooms, respectively. Whereas the middle school ratings were higher than the high school ratings for all of the sub-scales, engagement was the only subscale whose mean was significantly different. Charter school ratings were higher than non-charter school ratings for all of the subscales. Furthermore, the differences in the means between these school types were statistically significant for all the subscales except intellectual support.

A possible interpretation of the higher ratings found at the charter schools is that these schools had several advantages over the non-charter schools. For instance, at all the charter schools (both KIPP Academies and YES College Preparatory School), students wanted to attend the school and had to engage in an application process. Although these schools accepted students through a lottery system and enrolled many who were low-performing before they entered the schools, the students and their parents were required to sign a contract that committed them to adhere to high behavioral and academic standards. If students did not hold to this agreement, they could be threatened with expulsion to attend the "regular" public school in their neighborhood. Thus, the charter schools did not have to serve all students who wished to attend these schools.

Furthermore, the participating charter schools had extended school days, as well as mandatory Saturday classes and summer school. As part of the commitment students made to attend these schools, they understood they would be in school, on average, 65% longer than their counterparts in non-charter schools. Teachers at participating charter schools also signed contracts committing them to long 9½-hour days at school, to teach Saturday classes and summer school, and to be available to tutor students at night via a school assigned cell phone.

A philosophy at the KIPP Academies and YES College Preparatory School was that students needed the extra support now, not only to catch up academically with students from more affluent neighborhoods, but to be able to "completely dominate," as a teacher at KIPP Academy Houston put it, once they entered high school. Teachers at the charter schools worked extremely long days, weekends, and summers to both provide students with remediation and to challenge them with a rigorous, problem-solving mathematics curriculum. Clearly, teacher retention was not highly valued at these schools. Instead, the immediate needs of the students were prioritized. This is not a trivial insight. These schools took very seriously their charge to impact the educational needs of their students now, given that their students had historically been educationally marginalized and never "given the educational opportunities they need to achieve at high levels" (National Research Council, 2001a, p. 4).

Skills-Based Instruction Versus Mathematical Problem Solving

Whereas the participating schools were concerned about students' specific mathematical skills such as recall of products of single-digit whole numbers, they also prioritized mathematical problem solving throughout the curriculum. Interestingly, "drill-and-kill" instruction of mathematics facts took place in classrooms across the schools as did mathematical problem solving. Teachers did not view basic skills instruction and mathematical problem solving as incompatible. In fact, it was widely believed across schools that students should memorize their "math facts," as well as utilize and make sense of these facts in problem-solving contexts.

It was often the case during lessons observed that students were solving mathematics problems and making sense of mathematical ideas. However, we also observed classes in which the focus was memorization of basic skills (e.g., sums of two single-digit numbers). The importance teachers placed on both skills-based instruction and mathematical problem solving suggests that both are vitally important aspects of the secondary mathematics curriculum. This finding inspires one to consider viewing teachers' perspectives of mathematical knowledge such as characterized by A. Thompson (1992) as not irreconcilable. That is to say, perhaps in practice, Thompson's three dominant characterizations of mathematics knowledge as an isolated body of discrete skills and rules (e.g., instrumentalist), as a body of connected and unified knowledge (Platonist), and as a discipline of inquiry that is continuously expanded by human creation (problem solving) are not necessarily mutually exclusive.

Mathematics teachers at the highly effective schools appear to have been very flexible in their philosophical orientations. At times they placed great emphasis on students being able to recite their mathematical facts. For example, at KIPP Academy Bronx, teachers regularly had their students chant mathematical raps. On the other hand, teachers spoke eloquently and frequently about the importance they placed on their students' developing the capacity to problem solve and think critically about mathematics. A question in need of research that emerges from this finding is: How and why do effective teachers of mathematics develop flexibility in their philosophical perspectives of mathematical knowledge?

The classroom observation ratings provide additional insight into the differences found in instruction across the participating schools. As discussed in the previous section, analyses of the classroom ratings completed demonstrated that differences existed in the level at which classroom lessons across schools visited aligned with standards-based instruction. Mean ratings for two indicators of standards-based instruction, depth of knowledge and mathematical analysis, were higher at a subset of participating schools. At these particular schools, teachers were observed more often engaging students in solving challenging mathematical problems than at schools where the means for these two subscales were lower. Thus, although skills-based instruction and mathematical problem solving were both highly valued across the participating schools, differences were found among how much teachers at participating schools implemented these two forms of instruction. Teachers at schools where the mean ratings for depth of knowledge and mathematical analysis were higher were more likely to engage their students in challenging problem-solving activities that required them to apply their knowledge of mathematical facts.

Creating Equitable Learning Opportunities for All Students

As described further in appendix C, we found that intellectual support ($M =$ 3.41) was among the highest rated of the five classroom observation subscales. Intellectual support for student learning means "the teacher supports students by conveying high academic expectations for all students. These expectations include that it is necessary [for students] to take risks and try hard to master challenging academic work, that all members of the class can learn important knowledge and skills, and that a climate of mutual respect among all members of the class contributes to achievement by all."

The finding that intellectual support was among the highest rated of the five classroom observation subscales strongly supports the primary finding from the qualitative analyses that participating schools highly valued rigorous student learning. To accomplish this goal, high expectations and support mechanisms to achieve this objective were present across all the schools. Most importantly, we did not find that a "pedagogy of poverty" (Haberman, 1991) existed at any of the schools. Instead of focusing on classroom control and teaching students that little was expected of them (Knapp & Woolverton, 1995), we observed teachers of students from high-poverty communities dedicate themselves to fostering their students' high-level thinking skills in mathematics. Clearly, high academic expectations (see Ladson-Billings, 1994; Lipman, 1998; Sheets, 1995; Zeichner, 1996) coupled with strong tutorial services and programs were the primary means by which the highly effective schools improved the mathematics teaching of students who had historically been underserved in their schooling.

Another aspect of the intellectual support subscale is that "a climate of mutual respect among all members of the class contributes to achievement by all." At the highly effective schools, it was not uncommon to observe teachers fostering a learning environment in which students were expected to actively engage during classroom lessons, share ideas with one another, and respect each others' contributions to class.

Further evidence for the successful creation of equitable learning opportunities across the nine schools is reflected in the ratings for engagement. As summarized earlier, engagement was the highest rated of the five classroom observation subscales. Student engagement during mathematics lessons can be "identified by on-task behavior that signals a serious psychological investment in class work; these include attentiveness, doing the assigned work, and showing enthusiasm for this work by taking initiative to raise questions, contribute to group tasks and help peers." Across all the lessons observed at eight schools over both the fall and spring visits, the mean for student engagement was above 4 on the 5-point scale. When one considers the minimal student resistance to learning that was observed during classroom lessons and how students talked about the pride they had for their schools' accomplishments, the high levels of engagement that were consistently observed validates the notion that teachers implemented highly engaging and equitable instructional strategies. How else can the consistent engagement and student enthusiasm for learning mathematics documented in the classroom ratings be explained?

Equitable learning opportunities were also evidenced through teachers' desires to develop their students' facility to communicate mathematically. As detailed in chapter 3 and all the case study chapters (chaps. 4, 6, and 8), teachers across the highly effective schools talked often about the importance they placed on developing students' capacities to communicate mathematically. As previously argued, we found in the classroom observations conducted that, on average, teachers engaged students in at least one sustained or brief episode of sharing and collectively developing mathematical ideas during mathematics lessons.

Developing Students' Capacities to Think Critically About Mathematics

Although we did not conduct an in-depth analysis of mathematics curricula taught, there was little evidence that critical perspectives, such as social justice or mathematical literacy (see, e.g., Ernest, 1991; Frankenstein, 1987; Gutstein, 2003; Skovsmose, 1994), were valued or put into practice at the schools. In lessons observed and interviews conducted, we found that the focus at the highly effective schools was teaching a challenging mathematics curriculum that developed students' critical thinking capacities through problem solving. Whereas teachers did talk about adapting the curriculum to students' needs (see the YES College Preparatory School case in chap. 4 and the Young Women's Leadership School case in chap. 8), these adaptations had more to do with addressing the gaps in students' learning (e.g., providing additional time to understand a concept) than with incorporating students' cultures, or socioeconomic and political realities in the curriculum.

Teachers across the highly effective schools did talk about the socioeconomic challenges their students faced. For the most part, they were well-aware of the trying conditions in which their students lived. Undoubtedly, they were empathetic with their students' difficult home situations, some of them even described their commitment to their students precisely because they had also grown up in challenging circumstances. Nevertheless, teachers consistently expressed their strong belief that all of their students could still succeed in mathematics. As a matter of fact, teachers at the highly effective schools often repeated their belief in slogans such as "No Excuses;" that is, there is no excuse for failure. Particularly at participating charter schools, teachers emphasized a sort of tough love approach to teaching and learning. They frequently stressed that students, despite the fact that many lived in tough socioeconomic and social circumstances, still had no excuse for not learning and achieving at high levels. So, with regard to students' economic, social, and cultural backgrounds, a tough love strategy was strongly embraced at most of the highly effective schools.

Teachers highlighted that they did not ignore students' home situations; they did everything they could at their respective schools to create high-level learning environments that included the support mechanisms that were needed for students' academic success. Given the opportunities that they had created for this success, administrators and teachers at the highly effective schools had consciously decided to focus on the structures they had created to support student learning in mathematics rather than students' circumstances that were beyond their control. They adamantly believed that they had created exceptional academic opportunities for their students, and tirelessly encouraged students to take advantage of the opportunities afforded them. For instance, at the Young Women's Leadership School, one of the primary goals of the faculty was the establishment and maintenance of a culture of success at the school. All the girls attending the school were expected to complete pre-calculus as a minimum requirement for graduation. Across the participating schools, teachers and administrators passionately believed that the opportunities they provided their students, in concert with the attitudes for success they worked to instill in their students, were such that students were simply not allowed to fail. Alternatively stated, teachers' complete and total commitment to student learning was so profound, particularly at several of the participating schools, that students had no option other than to achieve at high levels.

This points once again to perhaps the most important lesson that can be learned from this study: When teachers and administrators start with the idea that all students can learn challenging mathematical content and work to structure their school's policies and practices to do just this, then this goal can be accomplished. Of course, this entails all concerned to learn how to truly and actively cooperate with others and, most importantly, to be open to do whatever is necessary to help students learn deep mathematical ideas and achieve at high levels.

Finally, teachers and administrators at the schools understood that although much of their work went largely unnoticed, they were creatively transforming the educational landscape in innovative and uncharted ways. The schools' incredible successes were directly impacting the communities they served. The focus of this study was at the classroom and school levels, however we could not help but learn about the pride the participating schools fostered in their communities and about the life-changing opportunities they were providing students. These schools were making a profound difference in their students' lives, while powerfully addressing the historical injustices of public schooling in the communities they served.

RECOMMENDATIONS FOR FURTHER RESEARCH

The requirements imposed by the HP High-Achieving Schools Grant Initiative mandated that schools had specific technical capacities in place to be considered for participation in this study. These requirements included possessing a technical infrastructure at the school to support the maintenance and use of the HP Wireless Mobile Classroom. The technology infrastructure requirement alone meant that many other highly effective schools that serve high-poverty communities could not be considered for participation in this study. In addition, the fact that those schools selected to participate in the project received the HP Wireless Mobile Classroom that included 30 laptop computers and other equipment likely influenced which schools responded to the HP HAS Request for Proposals (RFP). Undoubtedly, schools that placed little emphasis on the integration of technology did not apply to participate. Lastly, the fact that the majority of the participating schools had a development officer or someone who worked part-time to write grant proposals suggests that schools with less support to seek outside funding sources may have been less likely to respond to the HP HAS RFP. Taking all of these things into consideration raises questions about how representative the nine participating schools are of highly effective schools that serve high-poverty communities across the United States. Additional research needs to be undertaken at other highly effective schools located in poor areas throughout the country to investigate the validity of the findings from this study.

High-stakes testing did not necessarily dictate what teachers taught, but testing had a strong influence on teachers' curricular choices and their conceptions of effective instruction. Taken together, these results suggest that high-stakes tests establish a baseline of what should be taught, press teachers to focus on a limited set of content to the exclusion of other content, and may limit the instructional practices teachers employ. Further research on how high-stakes testing influences curriculum content coverage and how, through that influence, it also affects student learning and achievement seems warranted.

Our working assumption that highly effective schools contain more classrooms that provide effective instructional environments for students needs to be tested. By sampling from a wider range of classrooms and increasing the number of observations, future studies may increase the statistical power, enable the use of more sophisticated statistical analyses (e.g., hierarchical linear modeling, HLM) of classroom observational data, and allow for analysis by various demographic variables (e.g., home language and culture) that were not possible in this study.

Effective instruction requires both content coverage and reform-oriented instructional environments. The fact that teachers in highly effective schools stated they taught more than what appeared on the test and that their conceptions of mathematics curriculum were highly elaborate suggests that future research should examine teachers' content coverage and mathematics instruction and seek to tie the content coverage to teaching practices.

Appendix A

Research Methods

Richard S. Kitchen

The research project described in this book was initiated in the summer of 2002. In August, teams of three from each of the nine participating schools that included a minimum of two mathematics teachers and an administrator came to Albuquerque, New Mexico, to participate in a 3-day institute. As part of the institute, participants learned about the research that the UNM research team[8] intended to undertake, and how to integrate the HP Wireless Mobile Classroom in the mathematics classroom to enhance student learning. During the institute, initial data about the participating schools were collected. The UNM research team also gathered artifacts from the schools and administrators from the schools completed a comprehensive survey.

In addition to the research that was undertaken at the nine participating schools described in this chapter, exemplary mathematics lessons were videotaped at KIPP Academy in Houston and the Young Women's Leadership School in the fall 2002. This videotaping was not part of the research project. Instead, these exemplary lessons were gathered for use by members of the research team for demonstration purposes in UNM methods classes.

PARTICIPANTS

This study examines (a) characteristics as identified by teachers, students, and administrators that distinguished their schools as highly effective in mathematics, and (b) teachers' beliefs and knowledge (conceptions) and practices about mathematics curriculum, instruction, and assessment. The

---

[8]The UNM research team consisted of Jonathan Brinkerhoff, Sylvia Celedón-Pattichis, Julie DePree, Pauline Goolsby, Richard Kitchen, and Sue Lloyd.

nine secondary-level (Grades 5–12), public schools that participated in this study were selected specifically because of their demonstrated effectiveness serving low-income communities. During the 2002–2003 academic year, the UNM research team visited all nine participating schools twice— once in the fall and once in the spring. Two members of the UNM research team traveled to each of the nine schools during both the fall and spring visits. In general, different members of the UNM research team went to each participating school during the two visits. The lead researcher, Richard Kitchen, was the only member of the UNM research team to visit every school. School-level and classroom-level data were collected at the participating schools through classroom observations, interviews with teachers, administrators, and students, and through survey instruments.

As a means to provide a more in-depth perspective of the school-level characteristics and classroom-level (teachers' conceptions and practices) characteristics that distinguished the nine schools as highly effective, case studies are provided in chapters 4, 6, and 8. The research methods employed in the case studies presented in chapters 4, 6, and 8 are consistent with the methods described here.

Classroom Observations

In the fall 2002 and spring 2003, classroom observations and interviews with individual teachers were undertaken at seven of the nine schools: Emerald Middle School, J. D. O'Bryant School of Mathematics and Science, KIPP Academy Bronx, Latta High School, Rockcastle County Middle School, YES College Preparatory School, and Ysleta Middle School. In the spring 2003, classroom observations and interviews with individual teachers were also undertaken at an eighth school, the Young Women's Leadership School (see chap. 8 for the TYWLS case study).

During the fall 2002 and the spring 2003, we observed four teachers at participating schools (seven schools in the fall and eight schools in the spring). The one exception was Ysleta Middle School, where there were only three mathematics teachers to observe during the two school visitations. The participating teachers were selected by a school administrator to participate in the study. We requested that the four teachers be representative of the teachers at the school who taught the "regular" mathematics classes across multiple grade levels. We specifically did not want to observe teachers who taught "honors" courses, or "developmental" or remedial courses. In general, the identical four teachers at each school participated in the research during both the fall and spring visits, although this was not the case for every school because there were some changes among the mathematics faculty at some schools. Maternity leave and/or extended illnesses were the primary causes of these changes. Before initial observations were made, teachers read about the goals of the research project and their right to cease participation in the research at any time. Teachers granted their permission to participate in the research by signing a consent form.

During a visit, a member of the research team observed the identical mathematics class on consecutive days. So, two classroom observations were made of each participating teacher. When possible, UNM researchers who were fluent in Spanish visited classrooms containing Spanish-speaking students. During each classroom visit, the observer obtained copies of academic tasks, such as handouts, used in instruction. These classroom artifacts were utilized to understand the classroom context and to examine teachers' conceptions and practices. Overall, a total of eight observations were made between the two researchers at all of the seven participating schools in the fall 2002 and all of the eight participating schools in the spring 2003.

For each lesson, the UNM research member made holistic judgments about the overall quality of instruction found in the classroom observed. To make those judgments, we employed a classroom observation instrument to examine mathematics instruction (see appendix B). The instrument investigated the extent to which students experienced reform-oriented instruction in mathematics.

The observation scales are designed to gather (high-inference) numeric indicators of the instructional environments that students' experience. These scales combine judgments about teachers' instructional practices with those about students' learning behaviors, and should not be thought of as passing judgment on the quality of teaching in the manner that some teacher effectiveness scales do (see appendix C for a summary of the classroom observation ratings).

The instrument focused on the intellectual quality that was taking place during mathematics instruction and was adapted from: the observation scales to measure authentic instruction developed by the Center for Organization and Restructuring of Schools (Newmann, Secada, & Wehlage, 1995) and the observation scales to measure reform-based instruction developed by the National Center for Research in Mathematical Science Education. The observation scales included: (a) intellectual support, (b) depth of knowledge and student understanding, (c) mathematical analysis, (d) mathematical discourse and communication, and (e) student engagement. Raters also provided structured, narrative field notes to support how each classroom's learning environment was rated. Examples were taken from events in the classroom as a whole so as to be consistent with how the observations were conducted.

Each of the observation scales uses a 5-point Likert rating system based on two criteria: the intensity with which something (e.g., intellectual support) is taking place and the number of students who are engaged in doing that thing. As a general rule, the five ratings indicate the following: no activity pertinent to the scale in question (Rating 1); minimal intensity, limited to the teacher or to a few students (Rating 2); greater and/or uneven intensity, comprising some students (Rating 3); substantial and high intensity, comprising many to most students (Rating 4); and very high intensity, comprising most or all students (Rating 5).

Faculty and Student Interview Protocols

Interviews were conducted with all four teachers observed during both fall and spring visits, all nine participating mathematics faculties in the fall 2002, and with a randomly selected group of students at each of the nine schools in the spring 2003. Finally, interviews were conducted with an administrator at each of the nine schools in the spring 2003.

During both the fall and spring visits, researchers conducted a 1-hour interview with each of the two teachers they had observed. All the interviews were audiotaped and transcribed. The majority of the time, these interviews were carried out after the two observations of the two distinct classes were completed. In addition, the UNM research team could refer to and reference tasks and activities collected during observations. This allowed the researchers to refer to specific events and to concrete tasks from a given lesson to illustrate something or to learn about the teacher's decisions and practices. By combining the observations and individual teacher interview during each visit, we could examine the relationship between teachers' practices (through observations) with conceptions (through interviews) within the context of what happened during the lesson. Overall, a total of four individual teacher interviews were conducted between the two researchers at all of the seven participating schools in the fall 2002 and all of the eight participating schools in the spring 2003. Table A.1 gives summary information about the numbers of teachers observed and interviewed.

The primary purpose of interviews conducted with individual teachers was to understand teachers' conceptions (knowledge and beliefs) about mathematics teaching and learning with linguistically and culturally diverse students (see appendix C for the fall and spring interview protocols). A secondary purpose was to use interview responses to verify or triangulate

TABLE A.1
Summary Information About Data Collected at Participating Schools

Semester	Number of Schools Visited	Observations Conducted	Interviews Conducted
Fall 2002	Seven (7) Schools	55/56[a]	28/28[b]
Spring 2003	Eight (8) Schools	64/64	32/32

[a] Read as 55 of possible 56 teacher observations were conducted; [b] Read as 28 of possible 28 teacher interviews were conducted.

classroom observations, as well as the administrator's survey responses. Each interview lasted about 45 minutes to1 hour.

The interview protocols were adapted from the research literature on mathematics education reform (see NCTM, 1989, 2000; NSF, 1996) and the observation scales. During both the fall 2002 and spring 2003, the interviews conducted with individual mathematics faculty members investigated teachers': (a) shared sense of purpose, (b) notions about administrative support and availability of teaching resources, (c) conceptions of integrating mathematics with student diversity, and (d) perspectives on why their school is high achieving.

In addition to collecting classroom artifacts, observing mathematics lessons, and interviewing individual teachers, an interview with the mathematics faculty was conducted. In the fall 2002, a structured 1-hour interview with the mathematics faculty at each of the nine participating schools was completed (see appendix D for the faculty interview protocol). This group interview explored the mathematics teachers': (a) collective sense of purpose, (b) values regarding the academic and personal support provided students, (c) perspectives on faculty collaboration, (d) notions about administrative support and availability of teaching resources, (e) conceptions about the importance of standardized testing, and (f) perspectives on why their school is high achieving.

During the spring 2003, a focus group interview was conducted at participating schools with groups of randomly selected group of 15–20 students. This interview took approximately 1 hour to complete. A teacher or administrator at the school assisted the UNM research team by selecting the students who participated in the focus group interview. We requested that of the students selected, both sexes be equally represented, that students of diverse ethnic and racial backgrounds be represented proportional to the student population, and that the students selected represent a range of ages and academic ability levels. Only students and the two researchers were present when the interview took place. Administrators and teachers from the school were not allowed to be present during the focus group interview so that students would not be constrained to express their opinions. The interviews were intended to examine students' general perceptions of: (a) their school's academic expectations, (b) the school's connection to their communities, (c) standardized testing, (d) school governance, and (e) availability of extracurricular activities. Questions were followed with probes. Parents of students who participated in the interviewed granted their permission for their child to participate in the research by signing a consent form.

Lastly, an interview was conducted with an administrator at all nine schools during the spring 2003 visit. These interviews investigated the administrator's: (a) goals for the professional development of teachers, (b) roles to support high academic achievement at their schools, (c) outreach efforts with parents and the community, (d) views on governance issues, and (e) perspectives on why their school is high achieving. These interviews were not audiotaped.

Data Collection and Analysis

Qualitative methods were used to identify major patterns and themes related to the salient features that distinguished the participating schools as high achieving in mathematics, and to the teachers' conceptions and practices about mathematics curriculum, instruction, and assessment (Miles & Huberman, 1984; Strauss & Corbin, 1990). All qualitative data were analyzed by an iterative coding process (Emerson, Fretz, & Shaw, 1995). Codes were generated during the initial review of the interview texts. Relationships among the codes were explored in subsequent readings of responses and broad themes emerged. This process continued until consistent themes were achieved. The themes reported had to be confirmed by two or more teachers at more than 50% of the participating schools (i.e., two or more teachers from five or more schools).

Rater Training

A 2-day training session with observers/interviewers on the UNM research team occurred in the fall 2002 in Albuquerque, New Mexico. Videotapes of secondary-level mathematics instruction were used to train for classroom observations. Discrepancies in ratings among observers were resolved through group discussion. In addition, all the raters observed the identical mathematics lesson at a local high school. Immediately following the lesson, discrepancies in ratings among observers were resolved through group discussion. The observers/interviewers also practiced with the teacher interview protocols. Finally, the entire research team traveled to the first school where observations and interviews were conducted in fall 2002. For each lesson observed, multiple researchers rated the lessons. After each lesson, discrepancies in ratings were resolved through group discussion.

Appendix B

Classroom Observation Instrument

INTELLECTUAL SUPPORT

To what extent is the classroom learning environment characterized by an atmosphere of high academic expectations for all students coupled with mutual respect and support among teacher and students?

Although a class may provide a safe haven and respectful environment, such an environment does not necessarily provide support for student learning. Intellectual support for student learning is present in classes when the teacher supports students by conveying high academic expectations for all students. These expectations include that it is necessary to take risks and try hard to master challenging academic work, that all members of the class can learn important knowledge and skills, and that a climate of mutual respect among all members of the class contributes to achievement by all. Mutual respect means that students with less skill or proficiency in a subject area are treated in ways that continue to encourage them and make their presence valued. If disagreement or conflict develops in the classroom, then the teacher helps students resolve it in a constructive way for all concerned.

Intellectual support can be undermined by teacher or student behavior, comments and actions that tend to discourage effort, participation, and taking risks to learn or express one's views. For example, teacher or student comments that belittle a student's answer, and efforts by some students to prevent others (e.g., talking during the class) from taking an assignment seriously serve to undermine support for achievement. Support can also be absent in a class when no overt acts like the aforementioned occur, but the overall atmosphere of the class is negative due to previous behavior.

Note: Token acknowledgments by teachers of student actions or responses do **not** constitute evidence of intellectual support. Similarly, high scores for classroom climate for physical safety does **not** automatically guarantee high scores for intellectual support.

Intellectual Support

1. Intellectual support is negative; action/comments by teacher or students result in put-downs of students' academic efforts; students interfere with one another's efforts to learn; and classroom atmosphere for learning is negative.

2. Intellectual support is mixed. Both negative and positive behaviors or comments by teacher or students concerning students' academic efforts are observed. The teacher fails to call on students who want to participate repeatedly.

3. Intellectual support is neutral or mildly positive. Evidence may be mainly in the form of verbal approval for student effort and work. However, such support tends to be given to students who are already taking initiative in the class, and it tends not to be given to those who are reluctant participants or less articulate or skilled in the subject.

4. Intellectual support from the teacher is clearly positive, and there is some evidence of intellectual support among students for their peers. Evidence of special efforts by the teacher take the form of expressions that convey high academic expectations for all, mutual respect, and a need to try hard and risk initial failure.

5. Intellectual support is strong; the class is characterized by high academic expectations, challenging work, strong effort, mutual respect, and assistance in achievement for all students. Both teacher and students demonstrate a number of these attitudes by soliciting and welcoming contributions from all students who are expected to put forth their best efforts. Broad participation may be an indication that low-achieving students receive intellectual support for learning.

DEPTH OF KNOWLEDGE AND STUDENT UNDERSTANDING

To what extent is mathematical knowledge treated deeply in the class? To what extent is knowledge treated in a shallow and superficial manner?

For students, mathematical knowledge is deep when they develop relatively complex understandings of the lesson's concepts. Instead of being able to recite only fragmented pieces of information, students develop relatively systematic, integrated, or holistic understandings of the mathematical content. Students may produce new knowledge by discovering mathematical relationships, solving problems, making conjectures, justifying their hypotheses, and drawing conclusions. They also may produce new knowledge when they connect mathematical topics to one another.

Mathematical knowledge is shallow, thin, or superficial when central ideas have been trivialized by the teacher or students, or is presented as nonproblematic. Knowledge is thin when students' understanding of important mathematical ideas remains superficial, such as when ideas are covered in a way that gives them only a surface acquaintance with their meaning. This superficiality can be due, in part, to instructional strategies, such as when teachers cover a large quantities of fragmented ideas and bits of information that are unconnected to other knowledge. Evidence of shallow understanding by students exists when they do not or cannot use knowledge to make clear distinctions, arguments, solve problems, and develop more complex understandings of other related phenomena.

In scoring this item, observers should note that depth of knowledge and understanding refers to the substantive character of the ideas that students demonstrate as they consider mathematical ideas. It is possible to have a lesson that contains substantively important and deep knowledge, but that students do not become engaged or they fail to show understanding of the complexity or the significance of the ideas. Observers' ratings should reflect the depth to which students pursue the content.

Depth of Knowledge and Student Understanding

1. Knowledge is very thin because concepts are treated trivially or presented as nonproblematic; students are involved in the coverage of information they are to remember.

2. Knowledge remains superficial and fragmented. Underlying or related concepts and ideas might be mentioned or covered, but only a superficial acquaintance or trivialized understanding of these ideas is evident.

3. Knowledge is treated unevenly during instruction; deep understanding of some mathematical concepts is countered by superficial understanding of some other ideas. At least one idea may be presented in-depth and its significance grasped by some (10%–20%) students, but in general the focus is not sustained.

4. Knowledge is relatively deep because the students provide information, arguments, or reasoning that demonstrates the complexity of one or more ideas. The teacher structures the lesson so that many students (20%–50%) do at least one of the following: sustain a focus on a significant topic for a period of time; or demonstrate their understanding of the problematic nature of information and/or ideas; or demonstrate understanding by arriving at a reasoned, supported conclusion; or explain how they solved a relatively complex problem.

5. Knowledge is very deep because the teacher successfully structures the lesson so that most students (50%–90%) do at least one of the following: sustain a focus on a significant topic; or demonstrate their understanding of the problematic nature of information and/or ideas; or demonstrate complex understanding by arriving at a reasoned, supported conclusion; or explain how they solved a complex problem. In general, students' reasoning, explanations, and arguments demonstrate fullness and complexity of understanding.

MATHEMATICAL ANALYSIS

To what extent do students use mathematical analysis?
The scale is intended to measure the extent to which students engage in mathematical analysis. Mathematical analysis can be thought of as higher order thinking that involves mathematics, that is, thinking that goes beyond mathematically recording or reporting mathematical facts, rules, and definitions or mechanically applying algorithms. Mathematical analysis involves searching for mathematical patterns, making mathematical conjectures, and justifying those conjectures. Analysis also includes organizing, synthesizing, evaluating, speculating, arguing, hypothesizing, describing patterns, making models or simulations, and inventing original procedures. In all of these cases, the content of the thinking is mathematics (or science).

Note: Mathematical analysis might take place almost accidentally or, seemingly, as an aside to the main flow of the lesson. For example, the teacher may ask a rhetorical question whose posing, if the question were taken seriously, would provide evidence of mathematical analysis. Even if some students call out the answer before the teacher has the opportunity to proceed with lesson, the mathematical analysis is a diversion from the lesson's real thrust.

Mathematical Analysis

1. Students receive, recite, or perform routine procedures. In no activities during the lesson do students engage in mathematical analysis.
2. Students primarily receive, recite, or perform routine procedures. But, at some point during the lesson, they engage in mathematical analysis as a minor diversion.
3. There is at least one significant activity involving mathematical analysis in which some students (10%–20%) engage. Or, mathematical analysis that is primarily diversionary in nature occurs throughout the lesson.
4. There is at least one major activity in which students engage in mathematical analysis; this activity occupies a substantial portion of the lesson; and many students (20%–50%) are engaged in it.

5. Most students (50%–90%), for most of the time (50%–90%), are engaged in mathematical analysis.

MATHEMATICAL DISCOURSE AND COMMUNICATION

To what extent is classroom discourse developed to create or negotiate shared understandings of mathematics?

This scale assesses the extent to which talking is used to learn and understand mathematics in the classroom. There are two dimensions to this construct; one involves mathematical content and the other involves the nature of the dialogue.

In classes characterized by high levels of mathematical discourse and communication, there is considerable teacher–student and student–student interaction about the mathematical ideas of a topic; the interaction is reciprocal, and it promotes coherent shared understanding. First, the talk is about mathematics and includes higher order thinking, such as making distinctions, applying ideas, forming generalizations, and raising questions, not just reporting experiences, facts, definitions, or procedures. Second, the conversation involves sharing ideas and is not completely scripted or controlled by one party (as in teacher-led recitation). Sharing is best illustrated when participants explain themselves or ask questions in complete sentences, and when they respond directly to previous speakers' comments. Third, the dialogue builds on coherently on participants' ideas to promote improved, shared understandings of a mathematical theme or topic (which does not necessarily require summary statements). In short, mathematical discourse and communication resembles the kind of sustained exploration of content characteristic of a good seminar where student contributions lead to shared understandings.

For fourth graders, mathematical discourse and communication may be composed of very short sentences. Also, students of limited English proficiency may rely only on their native languages. Alternatively, native language utterances may be incompletely translated into English; or English-language phrases or clauses may provide the accepted vehicles for students to explain themselves and to engage in discourse. Such conversations may (but need not) result in students needing to clarify what they mean to say to one another. To score high on this scale, however, mathematics must still be a substantial component of the ongoing dialogue.

In classes where there is little or no mathematical discourse and communication, teacher–student interaction typically consists of a lecture with recitation where the teacher deviates very little from delivering a preplanned body of information and set of questions; students typically give very short answers. Because the teacher's questions are motivated principally by a preplanned checklist of questions, facts, and concepts, the discourse is frequently choppy rather than coherent. There is often little or no follow-up of student responses. Such discourse is the oral equivalent of fill-in-the-blank or short-answer study questions.

Note: The use of mathematical terminology does not guarantee the existence of mathematical discourse; indeed, the inappropriate use of terminology may actually interfere with the development of collective understandings and shared meanings. Mathematical terms, when used, should be meaningful and appropriate, and they should help support the conversation.

In a whole-class setting, students could participate in mathematical discourse and communication by listening and being attentive to the conversations that take place. Students do not have to all take turns on each and every point of a lesson; such turn taking may interfere with communication. Rather, students may selectively make comments when they have something to add. In small group settings, mathematical communication is likely to be more broadly spread throughout the group. In both cases, the issue is one of balance; no one person should dominate the conversation. But there does not need to be the ritualistic taking of turns where everyone speaks, even when there is nothing new to add to the conversation. The teacher and students behave as if there are greed on rules for taking turns and talking about mathematics.

Mathematical Discourse and Communication

1. Virtually no features of mathematical discourse and communication occur, or what occurs is of a fill-in-the-blank nature.

2. Sharing and the development of collective understanding among a few students (or between a single student and the teacher) occur briefly.

3. There is at least one sustained episode of sharing and developing collective understanding about mathematics that involves: (a) a small group of students or (b) a small group of students and the teacher. Or, brief episodes of sharing and developing collective understandings occur sporadically throughout the lesson.

4. There are many sustained episodes of sharing and developing collective understandings about mathematics in which many students (20%–50%) participate.

5. The creation and maintenance of collective understandings permeates the entire lesson. This could include the use of a common terminology and the careful negotiation of meanings. Most students (50%–90%) participate.

STUDENT ENGAGEMENT

To what extent are students engaged in the lessons?

Engagement is identified by on-task behavior that signals a serious psychological investment in class work; these include attentiveness, doing the assigned work, and showing enthusiasm for this work by taking initiative to raise questions, contribute to group tasks, and help peers. To score high on this scale, students must be engaged in the lesson's actual content; that is, they cannot be engaged in reading comics, in another school subject, or in yesterday's or tomorrow's homework (unless that homework is the topic at hand).

Disengagement is identified by off-task behaviors that signal boredom or a lack of effort by students; these include sleeping, day dreaming, talking to peers about non-class matters, making noise, or otherwise disrupting the class. It is assumed these behaviors indicate that students are not taking seriously the substantive work of the class.

Note: Students can be engaged in content that, to the outside observer, seems to be contrived, trivial, uninteresting, and boring. Alternatively, students might be unengaged in content that is exciting, authentic, and interesting. Put such consideration aside when using this scale. The substance of the content is scored in other scales. The focus of this scale is on whether the class environment is or is not one of student engagement.

Student Engagement

1. Disruptive disengagement. Students are frequently off-task, as evidenced by gross inattention or serious disruptions by many students (20%–50%); this is the central characteristic during much of the class.

2. Passive disengagement. Students appear lethargic and are only occasionally on-task carrying out assigned activities; for substantial portions of time, many students (20%–50%) are either clearly off-task or nominally on-task but not trying very hard.

3. Sporadic or episodic engagement. Most students (50%–90%), some of the time (20%–50%), are engaged in class activities, but this engagement is uneven, mildly enthusiastic, or dependent on frequent prodding from the teacher.

4. Engagement is widespread. Most students (50%–90%), most of the time (50%–90%), are on-task pursuing the substance of the lesson; most students seem to be taking the work seriously and trying hard.

5. Serious engagement. Almost all students (90% or more) are deeply involved, almost all of the time (90% or more), in pursuing the substance of the lesson.

Appendix C

Summary of Classroom Ratings

Julie DePree

As detailed in appendix A (research methods), during the fall 2002 and the spring 2003, we observed four teachers at all participating schools (seven schools in the fall and eight schools in the spring). Each of the teachers was observed teaching the identical mathematics class on consecutive days. So, two observations and ratings were made of each participating teacher. A total of eight observations were made between the two researchers at all of the seven participating schools in the fall 2002 and all of the eight participating schools in the spring 2003.[9] Overall, 117 individual classroom observation ratings were conducted by the UNM research team.

During both the fall and spring classroom visitations, observations were scored using a whole-classroom observational instrument that consisted of five subscales: intellectual support, depth of knowledge and student understanding, mathematical analysis, mathematical discourse and communication, and student engagement. Each of the observation scales uses a 5-point Likert rating system (1—lowest, 5—highest) based on two criteria: the intensity with which something (e.g., mathematical analysis) is taking place and the number of students who are engaged in doing that thing (see appendix B for the classroom observation instrument).

THE RESEARCH FINDINGS OF THE CLASSROOM OBSERVATIONS

First, we aggregated the subscale scores for a classroom's two observations into a single set of subscales by averaging the two observational scores. We aggregated each of the five subscales (intellectual support, depth of knowledge and student understanding, mathematical analysis, discourse and

---

[9]As described previously in appendix A, some observations/ratings were not made because of teacher absences.

communication, and student engagement) from the individual classroom level for each of the participating schools over all the classroom observations made during the fall and spring visitations. Finally, we obtained a grand mean for each of the five subscales over the eight schools visited. Table C.1 provides the grand level mean for the five subscales, the grand level mean of the standard deviations, and the grand level mean of the ranges over both the fall and spring classroom observations.[10] The mean is the arithmetic mean or average of the classroom observation ratings by subscale. The standard deviation and range are reported as measures of spread or variability. The standard deviation measures how widely values are dispersed from the mean.

Across the eight schools where classroom ratings were conducted, intellectual support ($M = 3.41$) was more highly rated than three other subscales, mathematical analysis ($M = 2.57$), depth of knowledge ($M = 2.77$), and mathematical discourse ($M = 2.80$). Engagement was the highest rated subscale ($M = 4.04$). Mathematical analysis had the lowest mean rating of the five subscales ($M = 2.57$). Mathematical analysis received the lowest mean ratings in all but two of the schools. Similar to mathematical analysis, the means of the depth of knowledge and mathematical discourse subscales across the eight schools were less than three. In addition, the mean of depth of knowledge was less than three at all but three schools. The mean of mathematical discourse was less than three at all but two schools.

In addition to the descriptive statistics outlined in the previous sections, comparisons of middle schools and high schools, and charter and non-charter schools were conducted. Table C.2 shows which schools are middle schools, high schools, charter schools, and non-charter schools. It should be noted that the J. D. O'Bryant School of Mathematics and Science, YES College Preparatory School, and the Young Women's Leadership School (TYWLS) included both middle school and high school classrooms.

TABLE C.1

Aggregated Means, Standard Deviations, and Ranges Over Both Fall and Spring for All Participating Schools

All Schools	Intellectual Support	Mathematic al Analysis	Depth of Knowledge	Mathematic al Discourse	Engagement
Mean	3.41	2.57	2.77	2.80	4.04
Standard Deviation	.86	.91	.83	.81	.68
Range	2.75	2.63	2.5	2.63	1.88

[10]Classroom observations were made at the Young Women's Leadership School during spring 2003 only.

TABLE C.2

Schools by Type (Middle School, High School, Charter, and Non-Charter)

Middle Schools	High Schools	Charter Schools	Non-charter Schools
Emerald MS	J.D. O'Bryant	KIPP Bronx	Emerald MS
J. D. O'Bryant	Latta HS	YES College Prep	J. D. O'Bryant
KIPP Bronx	YES College Prep		Latta HS
Rockcastle MS	TYWLS	_	Rockcastle MS
YES College Prep		_	TYWLS
TYWLS	_	_	Ysleta MS
Ysleta MS			

We first aggregated each of the five subscales from the individual classroom level for both the middle schools and the high schools over all the classroom observations made during the fall and spring visitations. It was hypothesized that there would be no significant differences (at the .05 level of significance) in the ratings for intellectual support, mathematical analysis, depth of knowledge, mathematical discourse, and engagement between the middle schools and the high schools. The sample size for the middle schools was 80 for all analyses, and the sample size for the high schools was 37 for all analyses. Table C.3 provides the aggregated school-level means, standard deviations, and ranges over all classroom observations made for the middle schools and high schools. Figure C.1 displays the means for each of the five subscales for the middle schools and high schools.

TABLE C.3

Aggregated Means, Standard Deviations, and Ranges over Both Fall and Spring for All Middle Schools and High Schools

	Intellectual Support	Mathematical Analysis	Depth of Knowledge	Mathematical Discourse	Engagement
High Schools					
Mean	3.35	2.43	2.49	2.65	3.81
Standard Deviation	.89	.99	.99	.89	.97
Range	4	3	3	3	3
Middle Schools					
Mean	3.45	2.60	2.86	2.83	4.16
Standard Deviation	.99	1.03	.95	.99	.71
Range	4	4	4	4	3

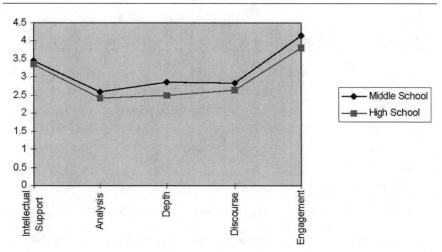

FIG. C.1.   Aggregated means for the five subscales by middle school and high school.

The means for the middle school ratings were higher than the means for the high school ratings for all of the subscales; however, engagement was the only subscale that was significantly different. The mean for the engagement subscale for the middle schools was 4.16 with a standard deviation of 0.71, whereas the mean for high schools was 3.81 with a standard deviation of 0.97. The means were significantly different at the .05 level of significance ($z = 1.965$, $p = .049$).

Lastly, we decided to aggregate each of the five subscales from the individual classroom level over all the classroom observations made for the charter schools and the non-charter schools. Like before, it was hypothesized that there would be no significant differences (at the .05 level of significance) in the ratings for intellectual support, mathematical analysis, depth of knowledge, mathematical discourse and engagement between the charter and non-charter schools. The sample size for the charter schools was 30 for all analyses, and the sample size for the non-charter schools was 87 for all analyses. Table C.4 provides the aggregated school-level means, standard deviations, and ranges over all classroom observations made for the charter schools and non-charter schools. Figure C.2 illustrates the means for the five subscales for the charter and noncharter schools.

The ratings for intellectual support produced a mean of 3.57 and a standard deviation of 1.01 for the charter schools. The mean for the non-charter schools was 3.37 and the standard deviation was 0.94. There was no significant difference ($z = .95$, $p = .34$) in the means for charter and non-charter schools in the area of intellectual support.

Mathematical analysis was also rated. The mean for mathematical analysis for the charter schools was 2.93 with a standard deviation of 0.98, and the

TABLE C.4

Aggregated Means, Standard Deviations, and Ranges Over Both Fall and Spring for All Charter Schools and Non-Charter schools

	Intellectual Support	Mathematical Analysis	Depth of Knowledge	Mathematical Discourse	Engagement
Charter Schools					
Mean	3.57	2.93	3.37	3.28	4.42
Standard Deviation	1.01	.98	.81	.87	.64
Range	4	4	3	4	2
Non-Charter Schools					
Mean	3.37	2.41	2.53	2.60	3.92
Standard Deviation	.94	.99	.94	.93	.82
Range	4	3	3	4	3

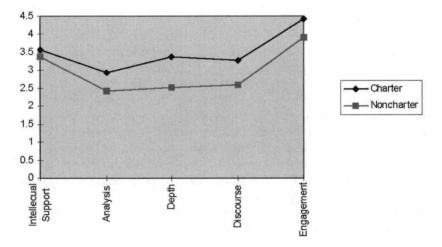

FIG. C.2. Aggregated means for the five subscales by charter and non-charter schools.

mean for non-charter schools was 2.41 with a standard deviation of 0.99. There was a significant difference ($z = 2.50$, $p = .012$) in the means for the charter and non-charter schools in the area of mathematical analysis.

A hypothesis test was also conducted to compare the depth of knowledge ratings of charter and non-charter schools. The mean for depth of knowledge for charter schools was 3.37 with a standard deviation of 0.81.

The mean for depth of knowledge of non-charter schools was 2.53 with a standard deviation of 0.94. The analysis indicated that there was a significant difference ($z = 4.69, p = .0000027$) in the means in the depth of knowledge subscale.

There was also a significant difference ($z = 3.63, p = .0003$) in the means for the mathematical discourse ratings. The charter schools had a mean of 3.28 with a standard deviation of 0.87, whereas the non-charter schools had a mean of 2.60 with a standard deviation of 0.93.

Engagement was another rating of interest. The mean for engagement for charter schools was 4.42 with a standard deviation of 0.64, whereas the mean for the non-charter schools was 3.92 with a standard deviation of 0.82. These data indicated that there was a significant difference ($z = 3.42, p = .0006$) between ratings for engagement in charter and non-charter schools.

SUMMARY OF FINDINGS

Overall, the engagement subscale had the highest means and the lowest standard deviations and ranges for all four school types, charter, non-charter, high school, and middle school. The low standard deviations and low ranges indicate that there was more consistency, or less variation, in the ratings for this subscale. In fact, the engagement subscale was the highest rated subscale at all eight schools. Mathematical analysis had the lowest mean rating of the five subscales ($M = 2.57$). Similar to mathematical analysis, the means of the depth of knowledge (2.77) and mathematical discourse (2.80) subscales across the eight schools were less than three.

The middle school ratings were higher than the high school ratings for all of the subscales; however, they were only significantly higher in the engagement subscale. The variation, as measured by the statistics, standard deviation and range, was fairly consistent for all the high school and middle school subscales. Also, mathematical analysis received the lowest ratings in both groups, high school and middle school, whereas engagement got the highest ratings for both groups.

For all five of the subscales, the charter school ratings were higher than the non-charter ratings. The differences in the means (charter vs. non-charter) were statistically significant for all the subscales except intellectual support. Mathematical analysis had the lowest mean rating for both charter and non-charter schools. Engagement and intellectual support had the highest means for the charter and non-charter schools.

DISCUSSION OF CLASSROOM RATINGS

An interesting finding was that middle schools and charter schools outperformed high schools and non-charter schools, respectively, in all areas, and in some areas the differences in performance were significant. The analysis of the classroom observation ratings found differences between middle schools and high schools (favoring middle schools) and charter and non-charter schools (favoring charter schools). The middle school ratings were higher than the high school ratings for all of the subscales, engagement was the only subscale that was significantly different. The charter school ratings were higher than the non-charter school ratings for all of the subscales, the differences in the means between these school types were statistically significant for all the subscales except intellectual support.

Our original hypothesis was that in the highly effective schools we would be more likely to find instruction that aligned with standards-based recommendations (see NCTM, 1989, 2000; NSF, 1996). Our findings demonstrate that instruction in middle school classrooms and charter school classrooms was more closely aligned with recommended standards-based instruction than was the instruction observed in high school classes and non-charter school classrooms, respectively.

Although the ratings demonstrate that participating middle schools[11] outperformed high schools in all areas, the middle school lessons observed were only statistically significantly higher in the engagement subscale. This means that in the middle school classes observed, students tended to be more actively engaged in learning mathematics than their counterparts in high school classroom. Of course, some of the aggregated means at some of the participating middle schools were lower than the aggregated means found at participating high schools. However, this finding does lend support to the notion that the highly effective middle schools provided more engaging instruction than was found in the high schools.

A possible interpretation of the differences found between the charter and non-charter schools is that the charter schools had several advantages over the non-charter schools. It was the case that at all the charter schools (both KIPP Academies and YES College Preparatory School), students wanted to attend the school and had to engage in an application process. Although these schools accepted students through a lottery system and enrolled many who may have been low performing before they entered the school, the students and their parents were required to sign a contract that committed them to adhere to high behavioral and academic standards put forth by the schools. If students did not hold to this agreement, they could be threatened with expulsion to attend the "regular" public school in their neighborhood. Thus, the charter schools did not have to serve all students who wished to attend these schools. Furthermore, the participating charter schools had extended school days, as well as mandatory Saturday classes, and summer school. As part of the commitment students made to attend these schools, they understood they would be in

---

[11]J. D. O'Bryant School of Mathematics and Science, YES College Preparatory School, and the Young Women's Leadership School included both a middle school and high school.

school, on average, 65% longer than their counterparts in non-charter schools. Teachers at participating charter schools also signed contracts committing them to long days at school (7:30 a.m.–5 p.m.), to teach Saturday classes and summer school, and to be available to tutor students at night via a school assigned cell phone.

A philosophy at the KIPP Academies and YES College Preparatory School was that students needed the extra support now, not only to catch up academically with students from more affluent neighborhoods, but to be able to "completely dominate" academically, as a teacher at KIPP Academy Houston put it, once they entered high school. Clearly, teacher retention was not highly valued at these schools. Instead, the immediate needs of the students were prioritized.

At all the participating schools, but particularly at the charter schools, teachers greatly valued problem solving (A. Thompson, 1992) and challenging students to think and reason. However, there was also an emphasis on instruction of mathematical facts and drill-and-practice approaches to teaching were used, although the instruction of mathematical facts was not the principal aim of instruction. Rather, at YES College Preparatory School and the KIPP Academies, teachers prioritized developing students' problem-solving skills and taught challenging mathematical content. This explains why we found higher levels of mathematical analysis in the charter school classrooms observed, instruction that focused on depth over coverage, and higher levels of mathematical discourse. These findings lend strong support to the notion that highly effective schools implement curriculum and instruction aligned with standards-based recommendations (see NCTM, 1989, 2000; NSF, 1996).

Appendix D

Participating Schools' Self-Reported Data on High Achievement

EMERALD MIDDLE SCHOOL, EL CAJON, CALIFORNIA

Emerald Middle School's commitment to promoting high achievement in mathematics is evidenced by the rich and challenging spectrum of mathematics classes offered at each grade level. Emerald offers both general math and pre-algebra classes in sixth and seventh grade. Algebra is also available in seventh grade and is required at the eighth-grade level, which is well in advance of California's 2003 mandate requiring all eighth-grade students take algebra. In Emerald's eighth grade, students may also take geometry, provided they have mastered algebra in the seventh grade. The algebra and geometry classes are high school equivalent courses.

Evidence of student high achievement is reflected in Emerald's SAT-9 scores over the past 4 years, which indicate a large majority of students at all grade levels achieving at or above the 50th percentile in Math Problem Solving and Math Procedures. In addition, upward trends in achievement scores have continued at each grade level over the same time period (see Table D.1 and Fig. D.1).

Student achievement is also reflected in Emerald's Academic Performance Index (API) scores. API scores are compared in two ways; Emerald's 2001 API scores are compared to all schools in the state, as well as to schools of similar demographics. In the statewide ranking of all middle schools, Emerald scored 6 out of 10, which continues to be above the average. When compared to other schools of like demographics in California, Emerald received a ranking of 9 out of 10. When compared to other middle schools in the Cajon Valley Union School District (CVUSD), Emerald was the only school to significantly improve its API score over the previous year, demon-

TABLE D.1

Percent of Emerald Students at or Above the 50th Percentile on SAT-9 in 1998–2001

Grade	1998	1999	2000	2001	3 yr. Change
Math Problem Solving:					
6	80%	88%	84%	92%	+12%
7	74%	86%	79%	84%	+10%
8	74%	81%	82%	84%	+10%
Math Procedures:					
6	73%	83%	84%	90%	+17%
7	79%	85%	85%	83%	+ 4%
8	71%	75%	76%	72%	+ 1%

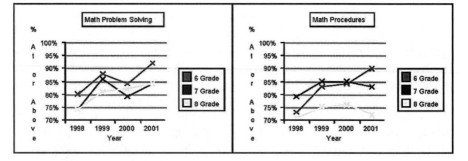

FIG. D.1.   Trends of Emerald students in math on SAT-9, 1998–2001.

strating an increase of 30 points. When looking at the subgroup scores for Emerald Middle School, the students met API growth goals in all categories for Hispanic, Socioeconomically Disadvantaged, and White students. Only one other middle school in CVUSD was able to meet these categorical API goals.

The state of California rewards schools that meet their projected API goals. Emerald Middle School achieved this goal and was awarded $62,000 for 2001. Emerald's faculty plans to use a portion of these funds to augment the High-Achieving Schools Grant if it is awarded. Specifically, release time funded by the API award will allow faculty members to attend training for the use of the HP Omnibook notebook computers, the Mindsurf Discourse Software, and to collaborate in the creation of interdisciplinary academic activities that incorporate this equipment.

A key factor contributing to student high achievement is Emerald's staff-developed, innovative programs for which they have received numerous awards. Some of these awards include: California Distinguished School and California Blue Ribbon Awards, two Golden Bell awards for its character education program "The Emerald Way" and Emerald's business education program EMCO, and local CBS affiliate KFMB's "Cool School Award" for utilizing technology in the classroom.

Another contributing factor to student high achievement is the high-quality staff at Emerald. Emerald staff members have received numerous individual awards, including California Middle School Principal of the Year, Classroom Technology Innovation Award, the Golden Disk Award from the Computer Using Educators organization, and numerous nominations for District Teacher of the Year. Many of Emerald's staff serve in mentor and support roles for teachers across the district or provide opportunities for preservice teachers from San Diego area universities.

Community and parent involvement are also seen as contributing factors to student success. Emerald's parents have logged over 1,000 volunteer hours in 2001–2002. In their support of the staff, parents have offered such services as written and oral translation for Spanish, Arabic, Chaldean, and Kurdish. They grade papers, prepare materials, and tutor individual students. Emerald parent volunteers include HP employees, one of which serves as vice president of the School Site Council.

As an Advancement Via Individual Determination (AVID) demonstration site for southern California, Emerald Middle School is committed to promoting a rigorous, challenging academic curriculum and environment. Emerald fosters this environment by organizing students and teachers into instructional teams. These teams provide opportunities for collaboration and integration of standards-based curriculum across the four core subject areas (math, English, science, history). Although Emerald's student–teacher ratio remains high, the instructional team structure allows greater student support through increased team communication. Emerald's instructional teams are identified and named according to university campuses, which is another way Emerald strives to promote successful college aspiration. The driving force behind this "college culture" is based on research that reports a direct correlation between successful college students and those who obtained high achievement in mathematics prior to attending college.

Another factor contributing to Emerald's high achievement is the availability of additional opportunities for academic support from a variety of sources. AVID provides tutors from San Diego State University 2 days per week. AmeriCorps provides six adult tutors on a daily basis to our low-achieving students during the regular school day and after school as a means to improve their reading and math skills. Formal, afterschool tutoring programs are also offered by credentialed Emerald teachers for assistance in pre-algebra, algebra, geometry, and English. Emerald's Homework Club meets daily for students who require less intensive assistance, or, need a place to complete homework.

JOHN D. O'BRYANT SCHOOL OF MATHEMATICS AND SCIENCE, BOSTON, MASSACHUSETTS

The Massachusetts Comprehensive Assessment System (MCAS) is the standardized testing program in the state of Massachusetts. The exam is administered to all 5th, 8th, and 10th graders in mathematics, language arts, composition, science, social studies, and technology, with a requirement that the exam must be passed to earn a high school diploma. At the J. D. O'Bryant School of Mathematics and Science, 8th graders and 10th graders were tested in 2001–2002. The school made tremendous improvements in its test scores from 1999 to 2001, as shown in Table D.2. In 2001–2002, the school ranked third in the city of Boston.

The graduation requirements for students at J. D. O'Bryant School of Mathematics and Science were more stringent than most of the other high schools in the city of Boston. In 2001–2002, students were required to pass 4 years of high school mathematics (system requirement is three courses), and all graduates were required to pass pre-calculus, calculus, or AP calculus. AP calculus students made tremendous improvements over the 3 years prior to 2001–2002 (see Table D.3).

The first characteristic that contributed to high achievement at the J. D. O'Bryant School of Mathematics and Science is the determination of the students. They are extremely hard working and goal oriented. In 2001–2002, most of the students at the school were first generation immigrants, with over 60% having a language other than English as their first language.

TABLE D.2

J. D. O'Bryant School of Mathematics and Science Test Score Performance From 1999 to 2001

	2001	2000	1999
Grade 8			
Failure rate	2%	21%	28%
Proficiency rate	48%	23%	5%
Advanced rate	6%	2%	0%
Grade 10			
Failure rate	4%	25%	33%
Proficiency rate	47%	25%	17%
Advanced rate	26%	17%	2%

TABLE D.3

**Test Performance on AP Calculus Test for Students
at J. D. O'Bryant School of Mathematics and Science, 1999–2001**

YEAR	# of students	% Scored 3 or higher	FRL
2001	24	73.7%	82%
2000	26	27.8%	87%
1999	25	24%	78%

The students understood that a college degree is essential for the success they want for their future. Prior to 2001–2002, more than 90% of the school's students went to college, with most being the first member of their family to attend college. Actually, many were the first in their family to graduate high school. They understand that hard work and good grades are their ticket to postsecondary education and, hopefully, scholarships. Although many are challenged by English-language acquisition, mathematics is a "language" all embrace.

A second characteristic that contributed to high achievement is programmatic. The administration funded and implemented necessary support programs, particularly in mathematics. Programs have been put in place to provide a wide range of support for students. In 2001–2002,

- There were daily tutoring programs, required by students with low standardized test scores, and recommended for all students who might benefit.
- The school had other after school programs such as "Gear-Up," which tracks students through the 8th, 9th, and 10th grades, providing academic support and enrichment experiences.
- There were mentoring programs, which match college students and interns with individual students to work on prescriptive programs.
- There were mentoring sessions between high-achieving upperclassmen and underclassmen.
- There was a MCAS Prep required courses in Grade 10 for students at risk of not passing this standardized exam.
- We had transitional programs for students at risk of not being promoted.

A third characteristic that contributed to high achievement was teacher driven. The mathematics department included many dedicated, hard-working professionals who were constantly retooling and upgrading their skills. There were endless professional development opportunities of which most take advantage. There were system mandated professional development activities that all were required to attend.

KIPP ACADEMY, BRONX, NEW YORK

For the past 4 academic years (1998–2002), KIPP Academy has been the highest performing middle school in the Bronx in terms of reading scores, mathematics scores, attendance, and improvement in test scores. Over 61% of the school is now reading above the national average, and 60% of the school scored above the national average in mathematics. The 96% daily attendance, which includes Saturday, and summer school, continues to be among the highest in New York State.

All KIPP eighth graders complete a 2-year algebra I course that puts them on par with their peers in the top private schools throughout the country. In 2000–2001, the eighth graders ranked seventh in the entire city in mathematics, 71% of them passed the ninth-grade Regents Exam in eighth grade. For the third consecutive year (which is every year we have had an eighth-grade class), over 70% of KIPP's eighth graders passed the High School Sequential I Algebra Regents. Likewise, the eighth-grade English curriculum is equally challenging. In 2000–2001, the eighth graders ranked 25th in the entire city in reading.

The KIPPsters success depends dramatically on the level of professional staff, as well as the programs offered at KIPP. Clearly, the academic improvements are a direct result of KIPP's unique structure and concerted effort to tailor curriculum to fit the needs of the students.

The data represents the academic performance of one class over 3 years, starting with sixth grade in 1998–1999 and finishing with eighth grade in 2000–2001. The group of students compared range from students enrolled in KIPP, District 7 middle schools in the Bronx, in all 313 New York City middle schools, and all New York State middle schools over the last 3 years.

The data in Table D.4 illustrates the high performance of KIPP students, particularly when compared to their peers in the local district schools and the middle schools citywide. Not only are KIPPsters performing above grade level, but the instruction at KIPP has allowed them to not only maintain that success but also annually improve it by a growing annual percentage, something not occurring in the patterns of statistics from the district and city. We believe that these test scores are a result of our five founding pillars of success: focus on results, more time, power to lead, high expectations, and choice and commitment.

KIPP's mission is to prepare students with the academic and character skills necessary for success in high school, college, and the competitive world beyond. KIPP students and their parents choose to enroll in KIPP instead of remaining at their zoned public school, thus attending school from 7:25 a.m. to 5:00 p.m. during the week, 4 hours on Saturdays, and 3 weeks

TABLE D.4
Test Performance of KIPP Academy, Bronx Students, 1998-2001

CTB Math Scores	1998–1999 (Students performing at or above grade level)	1999–2000 (Students performing at or above grade level)	2000–2001 (Students performing at or above grade level)	One-year Improvement
KIPP	58%	66%	73%	+11%
District 7	8%	9%	7%	−22%
New York City	23%	23%	23%	+0%
New York State	38%	40%	38%	−1%

during the summer, amounting to 67% more time in the classroom than the national average.

As previously mentioned, KIPP Academy has been the highest performing college preparatory middle school in the Bronx for 4 years running. KIPP is dedicated to ensuring that all students are successful in high school and college.

Before they leave KIPP, all students complete a 2-year, high school level algebra I class; study high school level literature, including works by Maya Angelou, Ayn Rand, J. D. Salinger, Shakespeare, Mark Twain, and Richard Wright; complete a 4-year physical, life, and earth science curriculum; learn to play an instrument and read music; participate in the 140-piece KIPP String and Rhythm Orchestra; and have the opportunity to travel to Washington, DC, Utah, Massachusetts, Pennsylvania, and California on class trips. KIPP to College's Director of High School Placement works intensively with KIPP students and parents to research and apply to appropriate high schools. In addition, KIPP to College employs a full-time director who works closely with KIPP Alumni to ensure that they follow their dreams to college. KIPP Alumni are expected to submit each of their report cards and maintain weekly contact with KIPP. KIPP to College includes PSAT and SAT preparation classes, tutoring, paid job internships, social events, college placement assistance, and any type of counseling or help that a student needs to be successful in high school and college.

The KIPP Orchestra helps KIPP students develop the academic and character skills needed to enter and succeed in top-quality high schools, colleges, and the competitive world beyond. We believe that the discipline and confidence developed in the KIPP Orchestra is transferable to the other academic disciplines such as reading and math. Subsequently, the skills and confidence learned in the academic disciplines can be transferred to the

KIPPsters lives. We have seen that the orchestra has helped students turn their entire lives around. All of the students at KIPP are part of the orchestra program. In 2000–2001, 96% of the eighth graders earned acceptances and scholarships to top-quality private and parochial high schools. Furthermore, we believe that the orchestra provides a clearly observable example for the entire school of the type of greatness that can be achieved if one is willing to put forth the required desire, dedication, and discipline.

Part of KIPP's success can be attributed the committed involvement and participation of KIPP's faculty members, parents, and students. Upon joining KIPP, parents, students, and faculty members sign a Commitment to Excellence Form, which outlines the expectations that are vital to individual student's and KIPP's overall success. Adherence to this contract leads to mutual respect between teachers, students, and parents and a strong family culture that has propelled the students toward academic success and high standards of achievement.

KIPP's structure and academic success serve as a model for other educators throughout the nation. Even more inspiring is that these achievements have been made despite statistics and stereotypes of low-income communities that say individuals in these communities *can't* learn and *don't* want to learn.

KIPP ACADEMY, HOUSTON, TEXAS

KIPP Academy in Houston has been recognized by the Texas Education Agency as an Exemplary School every year since its inception in 1995. However, approximately half the students that enter KIPP in fifth grade have failed the state's basic skills test, the Texas Assessment of Academic Skills (TAAS). After a year at KIPP, nearly 100% of students pass. The schoolwide TAAS passing rate for the 2001–2002 school year was 99.8% (see recent scores later). But beyond these basic skills, KIPP students go on to complete coursework far beyond their grade levels—many completing high school courses. In 2001–2002, eighth-grade students who completed KIPP's 2-year Algebra I curriculum earned a 91% passing rate on the State of Texas Algebra I End-of-Course Exam, a course normally taken in high school.

Moreover, eighth graders who finished the KIPP program in 1999–2001 have been accepted to the top public magnet school programs in Houston and have accepted scholarships totaling more than $7.5 million to help their families pay for a quality education in some of the most prestigious private high schools in Houston and the nation.

The TAAS scores for KIPP Academy in Houston for 2002, 2001, and 2000 are listed in Table D.5. Note that all students were tested and that no exemptions were claimed. Thus, the low-income and ethnic percentages of students tested in 2002 are identical to the demographics of the school in 2001–2002.

TABLE D.5

TAAS Scores for KIPP Academy in Houston for 2002, 2001, and 2000

	Math	Reading	Writing	Science	Social Studies
KIPP: 2002 Texas Assessment Of Academic Skills (TAAS) Results[a]					
5th Grade	100%	99%			
6th Grade	100%	100%			
7th Grade	100%	100%			
8th Grade	100%	100%	100%	100%	99%
KIPP: 2001 Texas Assessment Of Academic Skills (TAAS) Results[a]					
5th Grade	100%	97%			
6th Grade	100%	100%			
7th Grade	100%	100%			
8th Grade	100%	100%	100%	100%	100%
KIPP: 2000 Texas Assessment Of Academic Skills (TAAS) Results[a]					
5th Grade	97%	93%			
6th Grade	100%	98%			
7th Grade	100%	100%			
8th Grade	100%	100%	100%	98%	97%

[a] No student exemptions were claimed.

To provide a comparison of KIPP Academy's TAAS passing rates and the TAAS passing rates of the local school district, and one middle school in particular, the following districtwide averages for the Houston Independent School District (HISD) in 2000 are provided. The results in Table D.6 are for HISD non-special education students who tested in English.

The HISD zoned middle school that would have served the largest number of KIPP students (had they not chosen to come to KIPP) had the overall results listed in Table D.7 for 1999.

There are many factors that contributed to the success of KIPP Academy in Houston, but the primary factor is commitment. All students, parents, and teachers are required to sign the Commitment to Excellence Form that specifies attendance from 7:30 a.m. to 5:00 p.m. Monday through Friday, 4 hours most Saturdays, and 1 month each summer. The agreement obligates parents to reinforce the students' commitment, ensure attendance, and make sure the homework (2–3 hours) is completed each evening. This commitment alone encourages strong parental involvement and faculty and administration support, as we strive to prove that ALL OF US WILL LEARN.

TABLE D.6
Test Performance of Non-Special Education Students in Houston Independent School District Who Tested in English in 2000

	Math	Reading	Writing	Science	Social Studies
5th Grade	90%	85%			
6th Grade	79%	76%			
7th Grade	81%	74%			
8th Grade	84%	85%	77%	80%	57%

Note. All non-special education students who tested in English, of all income levels.

TABLE D.7
Test Performance of Middle School Students in Houston Independent School District

Math	Reading	Writing	Science	Social Studies
69.2%	65.7%	62.7%	N/A	N/A

Other important factors that promoted high achievement at KIPP are: more time on task (an extended-day, extended-week, and extended-year program), a culture of high expectations and success, a focus on measurable results, and the teachers' commitment to answer students' questions in the evening. All KIPP teachers were provided with a cell phone, and students were required to call if they had questions on the homework. This facilitated problem solving and ensured that students were caught up and not slowed down by problems that could be quickly resolved.

LATTA HIGH SCHOOL, LATTA, SOUTH CAROLINA

During the past 3 years and even before, Latta High School students have been consistently high achieving. This conclusion is based on a variety of data from different sources and belies the socioeconomic status. For example, for the last 3 years, students have performed above the state average on every Exit Exam category and Latta High was ranked the number two district in the state in 2001 Exit Exam scores. In addition, the school has shown significant improvement in every category over the past 3 years—except math in 2001, which was still 14% above the state average. Of those students taking the Exit Exam and participating in the free/reduced lunch program, 97.4% made a passing score. Only two students have failed to receive a diploma in the past 3 years due to Exit Exam results. SAT scores have also been above the state averages and have increased each year: 958 in 1999, 973 in 2000, and 1,006 in 2001. In 2001, 43% of seniors took the SAT and their average score of 1006 was the fourth highest in the state. In the first ever statewide school report card, Latta High was one of only 23 high schools in the state to receive an excellent rating in all three categories, which graded a total of 199 high schools. In 2001, 21.4% of seniors qualified to receive the SC Life Scholarship. Of those seniors participating in the free/reduced lunch program, 8.3% qualified for the SC Life Scholarship. For 2001, 78.6% of the students attempting advanced placement exams passed in comparison to a 40% median success rate in South Carolina.

Student achievement at Latta High was not attributed to just one or two strategies, but to a whole philosophy dedicated to improving learning. There were many aspects to this philosophy and each person involved—from administration to the classroom teacher to the parent—is responsible for a part of it. One factor that directly affected student achievement was parental involvement. In the 2001 school year, Latta High had 92.2% of parents attend conferences, as compared to the 60.1% median for schools in South Carolina. Increased parental involvement had a direct correlation to increased student performance. Another was the community atmosphere in the school. Teachers and administrators knew all the students and most of their parents and families. This high level of involvement made students realize that the school staff cared about their success and would do what it took to ensure that they had the opportunities that they needed to succeed. Another factor was a teaching staff that excelled in their relative disciplines. None of the teachers at Latta High School taught classes outside of their field and 46.2% hold advanced degrees. The teachers also put a lot of effort into working together to develop strategies that span classrooms and grade levels. This was especially true in the mathematics department, where good foundations in early classes had a big impact in higher level classes. This has been facilitated by the incorporation of standards-based learning into the curriculum and through the identification of specific objectives that led to student mastery of a subject. Ninth-grade students that demonstrated a weakness in reading or mathematics were given two semesters of the requisite course(s) instead of the typical one semester required in a 4 5 4 schedule. Latta High School also placed a big emphasis on maximizing instructional time during which students were actively engaged in the learning process. During the course of a school year, this added up to quite a substantial increase in prime instructional time that otherwise would be absorbed by other noninstructional-related activities. Student schedules were also refined to keep participation in study halls at an absolute minimum. Students were highly encouraged to participate in elective courses during blocks that were not filled with core courses. Administrative support was also apparent and extended up to the district level. District-level employees with jobs related to instruction played active roles in the daily routine of Latta High

School and their involvement ensured that policies and decisions affecting students were in their best interest.

ROCKCASTLE COUNTY MIDDLE SCHOOL, ROCKCASTLE, KENTUCKY

Rockcastle County Middle School improved in achievement in the several years preceding the 2001–2002 school year. In 2001–2002, scores reported for the state's accountability testing place the school in the top 15% of all middle schools in the state. It became a model for other middle schools throughout the state. In 2002–2003, the school was selected by the Charles A. Dana Center of the University of Texas at Austin for a study of high- achieving middle schools as one of only six middle schools in the nation. The mathematics department was also selected and invited by the Eisenhower Mathematics and Science Consortium as the only school in Kentucky to participate as a site to develop and implement research-based instructional strategies.

Kentucky's Commonwealth Accountability Testing System (CATS) tests all students in mathematics in the 5th, 8th, and 11th grades using a combination open response and multiple-choice test. The scores are reported as a scale score with the range being from 0–140. The state goal is for all students to be scoring 100, designated as proficient in the scoring sequence, or above by 2014. The scoring sequence consists of four levels. The levels are, in order of competence in the content area: novice, apprentice, proficient, and distinguished.

In 2001–2002, mathematics scores at Rockcastle County Middle School were well above the state averages. In the 3 years preceding 2001–2002, state averages in mathematics increased from 57 to 62, an 8.8% increase. The school's eighth-grade mathematics scores increased 38.9% in the same time period, from a score of 54 in 1999, to a score of 60 in 2000, to a score of 75 in 2001, which is a 38.9% increase. Kentucky school districts are divided into eight regions by the Kentucky Department of Education. The mathematics scores in Rockcastle County's region, the neighboring middle schools, increased from a score of 53 in 1999 to a score of 59 in 2001, which is a 10% improvement in test scores. The mathematics test scores at Rock County Middle School were well above those in the state and the region.

The Terra Nova, a nationally norm referenced test, was given in the third, sixth, and ninth grades. The Terra Nova represents less than 10% of Kentucky's accountability index score. State scores for the last 5 years prior to 2001–2002 in the sixth grade in mathematics increased from the 49th percentile to the 51st percentile, an increase of 4.1%. In the same 5-year period, the school's students increased their mathematics scores by 27.5% from the 40th percentile to the 51st percentile.

A comparison of 2000–2001 school year scores of those not participating in the free and reduced lunch program and those participating in the program in the state, the local region, and Rockcastle County Middle School revealed that Rock County's students in the free and reduced lunch program perform at a high level. All eighth graders in Kentucky schools take the mathematics portion of the CATS test, at the state level 41% participated in the free and reduced lunch program. Of these students, 48% scored at the novice level, 39% scored at the apprentice level, and 13% scored proficient/distinguished. In the local region, 57% of the students participated in the free and reduced lunch program, 47% scored at the novice level, 39% scored apprentice, and 14% were proficient/distinguished. At Rock County, 58% of the eighth-grade students participated in the free and reduced lunch program, 24% score at the novice level, 47% scored apprentice, and 28% scored proficient/distinguished. Of the students participating in the free and reduced school lunch program at Rockcastle County Middle School, about 14% fewer students than the students in the state and the local region scored in the novice category. More importantly, about 14% more of these students than students in the state and the local region scored at the highest level, proficient/distinguished.

Many characteristics of Rockcastle County Middle School contributed to the high achievement and the continuing improvement in achievement by students. The high achievement, particularly in mathematics, had occurred because of supportive leadership, district and school level, that was not afraid to share decision making or ask for help, thoughtful planning, collaboration, dedicated staff, and a commitment to increasing teacher capacity.

Rockcastle County Middle School developed partnerships that have been instrumental in supporting teachers of mathematics. The Appalachian Rural Systemic Initiative (ARSI), funded by the National Science Foundation, created a teacher partner position at the middle school for the 4 years prior to 2001–2002 who provided onsite and ongoing professional development for the mathematics and science teachers. The teacher partner worked one-on-one with teachers developing lessons, modeling teaching strategies, and serving as a resource teacher. Two years ago, the Eisenhower Regional Consortium for Mathematics and Science at AEL chose the middle school as the only site in Kentucky to receive intensive professional development one day per month. The project provided the means to implement research-based instructional strategies.

Through these programs and others, dedicated mathematics teachers at Rock County Middle School created a monthly study group. During these monthly meetings and others, teachers' professional development needs were identified by examining available data and by the teachers themselves. For the 2 years prior to 2001–2002, after reviewing the data, the group identified two areas of concern: the algebraic ideas strand and a curriculum emphasizing problem solving and higher order thinking skills, based on state and national standards. Previous to those years, the identified area was the geometry/measurement strand. The teachers collaboratively developed a plan for professional development in these areas. Because the district and the school valued teachers' time, they were compensated for using additional time to participate in professional development.

Teachers and students also worked diligently to improve skills in writing about mathematics. Writing about mathematics leads to a more in-depth understanding of mathematics concepts. Teachers collaboratively developed an approach to open response test items that included shared strategies and terminology within the mathematics content area. Students were assessed frequently using open response questions.

Students also received extra academic support. The grading policy required tutoring for students who received below a 70 in any class so that they learned the taught concepts. Tutoring was either during break times or elective classes such as physical education. The school offered other programs and strategies to increase students' academic success. These programs included mentoring programs, so students had close interactions with adults and afterschool programs that provided both tutoring and enrichment to further reinforce academic skills.

YES COLLEGE PREPARATORY SCHOOL, HOUSTON, TEXAS

At YES, college is not only a goal, but also a graduation requirement. The school's charter mandates that each student must receive a college acceptance letter in order to graduate from high school. By involving the community and setting high expectations, YES offers inner-city students the opportunity to experience a culture of achievement that prepares them for success both in and out of the classroom.

This success is most clearly seen in the test scores for the state-mandated TAAS exams. These exams are administered in 6th, 7th, 8th, and 10th grade. The Texas Education Agency (TEA) then rates the schools based on these scores and the school's attendance percentage. Out of approximately 180 charter schools in the state of Texas, YES is the only 6th- through 12th- grade school to receive an "Exemplary Rating" (the highest rating) from the TEA for the past 3 years. Table D.8 compares YES's passing rate in Math and English over the past 4 years to the 2001 results for "disadvantaged students" in Houston and Texas.

The table shows that YES students, since the school began in 1998, have maintained a consistently high passing rate on the state exams. The achievement is not limited, however, to the state tests. At the national level, on the advanced placement exams, students also performed at a high level of achievement. In 2001, 52% of the senior class took either the AB or BC Calculus exam; the average score for the students was a 3 out of 5. One student even received a 5 on the BC exam. Because of these passing scores, many seniors entered college with up to 6 hours of math credits and exemptions.

TABLE D.8

Passing Rate of Students at YES College Preparatory School in Math and English From 1999-2002 Compared to Other "Disadvantaged Students" in Houston and Texas

Grade	Subject	1999	2000	2001	2002	Houston	State
6	English	98%	100%	99%	98%	72.4%	77.4%
6	Math	99%	100%	100%	100%	81.5%	86.7%
7	English	91%	98%	100%	97%	78.6%	82.3%
7	Math	96%	99%	100%	100%	80.9%	84.3%
8	English	98%	100%	100%	100%	86.3%	86.5%
8	Math	93%	100%	100%	99%	86.0%	87.9%
10	English	95%	97%	100%	100%	80.0%	82.0%
10	Math	100%	97%	100%	100%	82.2%	83.0%

Perhaps the best way to track the students' achievement is to see how they measure up to YES's mission of college matriculation. In June 2001, YES graduated its first class of seniors. All 17 of those students were accepted to at least 4 colleges and universities around the country, including Stanford, Cornell, Rice, Smith, Texas A&M, and the University of Texas. The class received $1.1 million in scholarships and 85% were the first in their family to attend college. This year, YES will graduate 20 seniors. All of those seniors were also accepted to at least four colleges and universities, including Columbia, Brown, Loyola, Fordham, and Boston University. Ninety percent of these students will be the first in their families to attend college. These students are proving that the YES mission is obtainable for all students, regardless of race or socioeconomic background.

As is evident from the previous table, YES College Prep students not only outperformed HISD students in Houston's inner-city neighborhoods, but also surpassed state averages. The math scores reflect the emphasis YES places on this field of study. This achievement can be attributed to four distinct factors: the dedication of the families and YES staff, the YES schedule, the YES mathematics curricula, and the integration of technology into the mathematics curriculum.

The entire YES faculty works to create an environment of learning and achievement; in addition to the teaching staff, every administrator is required to teach at least one class. This not only keeps the administration in touch with the students, but also creates a student–teacher ratio of 15 to 1. YES teachers are even available to their students after regular school hours through the use of school-provided cell phones. The students' families are equally committed to the YES mission. This fall, over 90% of the parents attended YES's open house. In the spring, over 100 parents worked together to host a school carnival that raised over $25,000 for the students and the school. To date, the YES Parent Association has raised more funds than any single grant YES has received from a private donor or foundation.

YES asks much of its teachers, students, and families. Not only is the school day longer (from 7:50 a.m. to 5:00 p.m. daily), but students attend Saturday school twice a month and an extra month in the summer. A YES student spends 65% more time in school than the average public school student around the nation. This extra time enables all of the mathematics and English classes in middle school to meet for 90 minutes every day. In both the middle and high school, 45 minutes a day is allotted for "study hall": Every teacher is required to be on campus to provide one-on-one tutorials and instruction. With all of this additional time, teachers are able to present more interesting projects, as well as spend time working with those students who have been struggling with mathematics.

The mathematics curriculum is vertically aligned through the middle and high school program. The level of rigor and breadth of content covered in each class rivals any public or private secondary school in the city. Beginning in 6th grade, the students take pre-algebra. By the end of 8th grade, the students have spent 2 years mastering algebra I and developed fluency with the graphing calculator. In high school, the students begin with geometry in 9th grade, algebra II in 10th grade, pre-calculus in 11th grade, and ultimately AP calculus as seniors. In all of their high school classes, the students are expected to not just perform computations, but to also understand why certain mathematical principles must hold true. By the end of a unit, the students have become comfortable with the new material and are expected to solve "real-world" problems that include business, scientific, and technological applications.

By making the curriculum applicable to the students' lives, the school is able to motivate the students and create projects that integrate technology. This integration, which is still being developed, has enabled the students to expand their skills and increase their interest in mathematics. Some of these projects are detailed here:

- The 6th-grade class learns a programming language called Logo to draw geometric figures and create complex pictures and patterns.
- The 7th graders apply an Internet stock market program to analyze stock trends, and manage a portfolio. Later in the year, they again use

the Internet to research engineering pictures of bridges and build scale models.

- Computers are used in the 8th grade to help struggling students: They develop individualized mathematics tutorials and use an interactive quiz site, WebAssign, to create online quizzes that give students immediate feedback.
- The 9th-grade class become experts with the graphing calculators and use the advanced programs to create two- and three-dimensional graphs.
- The 10th- through 12th-grade computer science and math classes learn statistics, graphing, and data analysis with spreadsheet tools like MS-Excel.

THE YOUNG WOMEN'S LEADERSHIP SCHOOL

The Young Women's Leadership School (TYWLS) student performance has been strong, despite the fact that its students come from at-risk categories. As of the spring 2002, 100% of TYWLS students from the first two graduating classes had been accepted to a 4-year college. Average SAT scores for Math improved from 2001 to 2002 from 438 to 459 and were above the average for New York City and above the state average scores for African American and Latino students. In 2001, TYWLS had the second highest Regents scores of any public high school in Manhattan after Stuyvesant High School, the city's top magnet school. In 2001–2002, 79.2% of TYWLS girls were at or above grade level in math and 80.2% in reading, as compared to 63.1% and 49.6% citywide, respectively. In 2001–2002, the Young Women's Leadership School's New York State Regents Exam passing rates were 100% in English, 67% in Math, and 95% in Spanish. Each TYWLS teacher is focused on raising the school's capabilities in math, science, and technology. Although New York State only requires 2 years of lab science and 3 years of math, all TYWLS students are expected to go beyond the minimum requirements and take math and science through their senior year. In 2001–2002, 60% of TYWLS seniors were taking college-level courses on a City University (CUNY) campus.

Characteristics of the school that contribute to high achievement, particularly in math, include the support of the administration in attracting and retaining competent certified teachers and facilitating any and all opportunities for their ongoing professional development, both on the high school and middle school level. The administration ensures that the teachers have all the resources and supports required to maintain a high level of instruction. Lead teachers regularly plan and consult to maintain a productive plan of articulation and continuity to serve the entire spectrum of math students from weak to accelerated. During the 2002–2003 school year, TYWLS piloted a math acceleration strand for gifted eighth-grade students.

At TYWLS, parent involvement is the cornerstone of the students' progress and parental participation is an integral part of math instruction at the school (parent workshops, Math Fair) and at the district level (District 4 Family Math Saturdays).

New York State is in the national forefront of standards-based instruction and all curricula are standards-based. Teacher training is steeped in the math standards, which are displayed in every classroom and incorporated in every lesson.

The faculty at TYWLS is unusually committed to the school's mission and meets weekly on their own time to plan for advisory and instruction. The school is also supported by the Young Women's Leadership Foundation, which supports teachers in "putting the icing on the cake" of their curricula and resources by paying for offsite participation in training and conferences and purchasing supplies not available through the board of education. The foundation also funds a full-time college advisor, through the College Bound Program, who arranges college trips for all grades.

TYWLS has unusually small class sizes for a New York City public school with a student–teacher ratio of 18–22 to 1, and classes meet beyond the mandated 42-minute period (50 minutes and 84 minutes). In addition, the school serves as a lab for teaching and regularly has more than one adult in the classroom, such as student teachers, observers, and tutors from Columbia University Teachers College and Hunter College, two special education teachers and a paraprofessional who "push in" to content area classes, and mentoring and visiting senior or retired teachers. All classrooms are doing inquiry-based cooperative and applied learning to foster students' active participation and success. Classrooms are set up in small tables of four students each to facilitate cooperative learning and group work.

Alternative assessments are regularly incorporated into all evaluations. For example, in the math classes, TYWLS teachers use math, art, poetry, projects, research, journals, presentations, and portfolios in addition to the standard assessments that are required by the state and city to administer.

TYWLS has also made a sizable budgetary commitment to extra academic support in extended day small group tutoring, Saturday Regents prep, Academic Intervention Services, and standardized test prep.

YSLETA MIDDLE SCHOOL, EL PASO, TEXAS

Several factors contribute to student success at Ysleta Middle School. Consistent classroom procedures and routines maximize students' time for learning and minimize discipline issues. The school has a strict dress code policy, which allows student choice in what they wear to school (within the parameters of the policy) and makes school uniforms unnecessary. Although the school district has an alternative school for disruptive students,

Ysleta Middle students are rarely assigned to go there because the students are well behaved and successful. The school maintains a 97% daily attendance rate, which is the highest of all secondary schools in the district. Students clearly enjoy being in school, where they can participate in successful athletic, music, art, dance, and other enrichment programs.

Students attend classes that are 70 minutes long, allowing for sustained instruction, hands-on projects, and cooperative learning. The school has a warm, cheerful atmosphere where student work is proudly displayed in the classrooms and hallways. As middle schoolers, the students are already thinking ahead to college. Through their Career Investigations and Technology classes, they have conducted Internet research and prepared Power Point presentations about colleges they plan to attend. The school has maintained "Recognized" status from the Texas Education Agency for the past 5 years, based on student achievement on the Texas Assessment of Academic Skills.

Students have displayed high achievement, particularly in mathematics, as illustrated in Table D.9. In 2001–2002, 65% of the 8th graders who took the Algebra End-Of-Course Exam passed, as compared to 49.2% statewide. The highly trained math teachers at Ysleta Middle School use standards-based curricula and instruction. The district and campus administrators support the teachers by providing ongoing professional development and department planning time within the school day. From 1998 through 2000, the mathematics teachers participated in intensive professional development to align mathematics curriculum and instructional practices to state and national standards. They worked during the summer 1998 to rewrite the curriculum. They meet collaboratively on alternate days to plan instruction, analyze student work, and continue to refine their instructional practices. The most at-risk students are tutored in the afterschool program, where they used interactive CD-ROMs, games, and alternative assessments to learn mathematics. The entire faculty supports mathematics by integrating math into other content areas and teaching math curriculum during the daily "homeroom" period.

Providing engaging and meaningful opportunities for parents is integral to the school's mission and essential to student success. Ysleta Middle School provides a dynamic parent program to which parents respond enthusiastically. At least five or six parents are in the school every day, working on projects in the Parent Center, assisting students in the Learning Center, or helping teachers in the classrooms. Monthly Parent Academies are held in both mornings and evenings, and an average of 30 parents participate in each session. In these academies, parents learn strategies for helping with homework, understanding the recommended high school curriculum plan, accessing financial aid for college, and many other skills that empower parents to help their children reach their long-term goals. A group of 20 parents meet monthly in a Literacy Circle where they are reading *Raising*

TABLE D.9

Percentage of Students by Grade-Level at Ysleta Middle School Passing the Texas Assessment of Academic Skills Compared with other Subgroups, 1999–2001

	Campus	State	District	Group[a]	Disadv.
Grade 7					
Reading 2001	87.7%	89.4%	91.5%	84.6%	86.6%
Reading 2000	80.4%	83.5%	87.2%	72.7%	78.9%
Reading 1999	84.0%	83.6%	88.5%	70.0%	83.3%
Math 2001	94.8%	89.6%	94.4%	88.7%	94.4%
Math 2000	94.4%	88.1%	94.0%	83.2%	95.2%
Math 1999	93.0%	84.9%	92.6%	76.0%	92.5%
Grade 8					
Reading 2001	92.0%	91.9%	94.0%	88.0%	91.3%
Reading 2000	92.9%	89.6%	92.6%	81.8%	92.3%
Reading 1999	92.2%	88.2%	92.8%	79.9%	92.0%
Writing 2001	89.9%	85.8%	91.2%	81.8%	89.0%
Writing 2000	88.5%	84.3%	90.8%	74.5%	87.4%
Writing 1999	87.5%	85.7%	90.1%	78.4%	87.4%
Math 2001	97.0%	92.4%	95.8%	88.8%	96.7%
Math 2000	95.7%	90.2%	94.5%	84.3%	95.3%
Math 1999	91.4%	86.3%	91.4%	79.4%	90.8%

[a] Campus Group is the category of schools with similar demographics

Nuestros Niños, by Gloria G. Rodriguez, *The Middle School Years* by Michele A. Hernandez, and other works. Occasionally, the parents invite their children to participate in the circle and they read together.

The school celebrates each year with a student-led Conference Night, during which students showcase portfolios of their work to family members. In 2000–2001, 80% of the families attended the event. The others were contacted by the teachers and invited to come for the conference at a time convenient to them. Almost 100% of the parents eventually participated. The school's *Padres Unidos* parent program has received state and national recognition and has been featured in several videos.

Ysleta Middle School is sought out as a model of best practice in educating low-income students. The school is frequently visited by educators from across the country, including Sacramento, California; Lancaster, Pennsylvania; Portsmouth, New Hampshire; and even New Zealand. Researchers from Harvard University, the National Center for the Improvement of Educational Assessment, Just for the Kids, and others have conducted research in the school. Despite its many successes, the school recognizes the urgent challenge of preparing students for the future world of higher education and work in a technologically advanced society.

References

Abraham, J., & Bibby, N. (1988). Mathematics and society: Ethnomathematics and the public educator curriculum. *For the Learning of Mathematics, 8*(2), 2–11.

Adler, J. (1995). Dilemmas and a paradox—Secondary mathematics teachers' knowledge of their teaching in multicultural classrooms. *Teaching and Teacher Education, 11*(3), 263–274.

Adler, J. (1998). A language for teaching dilemmas: Unlocking the complex multilingual secondary mathematics classroom. *For the Learning of Mathematics, 18,* 24–33.

American Association of University Women. (1991). *Shortchanging girls, shortchanging America.* Washington, DC: AAUW.

American Association of University Women. (1992). *How schools shortchange girls: A study of major findings on girls and education.* Wellesley, MA: Center for Research on Women.

American Association of University Women. (1999). *Gender gaps: Where schools still fail our children.* New York: Marlowe & Company.

Annie E. Casey Foundation. (2004). City & rural kids count data book: Kids count special report. Retrieved from www.aecf.org/kidscount/rural_databook/entire_city_rural_databook.pdf

Apple, M. (1985). *Education and power* (ARK ed.). New York: Routledge.

Apple, M. (1990). *Ideology and curriculum* (2nd ed.). New York: Routledge.

Armstrong, J. M. (1981). Achievement and participation of women in mathematics: Results of two national surveys. *Journal for Research in Mathematics Education, 12,* 356–372.

Armstrong, J. M., & Price, R. A. (1982). Correlates and predictors of women's mathematics participation. *Journal for Research in Mathematics Education, 13*(2), 99–109.

Atweh, B., Bleicher, R. E., & Cooper, T. J. (1998). The construction of the social context of mathematics classrooms: A sociolinguistic analysis. *Journal for Research in Mathematics Education, 29*(1), 63–82.

Atweh, B., Forgasz, H., & Nebres, B. (2001). *Sociocultural research on mathematics education: An international perspective.* Mahwah, NJ: Lawrence Erlbaum Associates.

Ball, D. L., & Cohen, D. K. (1999). Developing practice, developing practitioners: Toward a practice-based theory of professional education. In L. Darling-Hammond

& G. Sykes (Eds.), *Teaching as the learning profession: Handbook of policy and practice* (pp. 3–32). San Francisco: Jossey-Bass.

Banks, J. (1993). Canon debate, knowledge construction, and multicultural education. *Educational Researcher, 22*(5), 4–14.

Becker, J. R. (1981). Differential treatment of females and males in mathematics classes. *Journal for Research in Mathematics Education, 12*(1), 40–53.

Boaler, J. (2002a). *Experiencing school mathematics: Traditional and reform approaches to teaching and their impact on student learning.* Mahwah, NJ: Lawrence Erlbaum Associates.

Boaler, J. (2002b). Learning from teaching: Exploring the relationship between reform curriculum and equity. *Journal for Research in Mathematics Education, 33*(4), 239–258.

Boaler, J. (2002c). Paying the price for "sugar and spice": Shifting the analytical lens in equity research. *Mathematical Thinking and Learning, 4*(2&3), 127–144.

Boswell, S. L. (1985). The influence of sex-role stereotyping on women's attitudes and achievement in mathematics. In S. F. Chipman, L. R. Brush, & D. M. Wilson (Eds.), *Women and mathematics: Balancing the equation* (pp. 175–198). Hillsdale, NJ: Lawrence Erlbaum Associates.

Bradbury, B., & Jantti, M. (1999). *Child poverty across industrialized nations.* Revised version of paper presented at the 25th general conference of the International Association for Research in Income and Wealth, Cambridge, England, and at the UNICEF-ICDC Workshop on Children in and Out of Poverty. Retrieved from http://www.lisproject.org/publications/liswps/205.pdf

Brandon, P. R., Newton, B. J., & Hammond, O. W. (1987). Children's mathematics achievement in Hawaii: Sex differences favoring girls. *American Educational Research Journal, 24*, 437–461.

Brenner, M. E. (1998). Adding cognition to the formula for culturally relevant instruction in mathematics. *Anthropology and Education Quarterly, 29*(2), 213–244.

Brophy, J., & Good, T. L. (1974). *Teacher–student relationships: Causes and consequences.* New York: Holt, Rinehart & Winston.

Brophy, J., & Good, T. L. (1986). Teacher behavior and student achievement. In M. C. Wittrock (Ed.), *Handbook of research on teaching* (3rd ed., pp. 328–375). New York: Macmillan.

Brown, J. S., Collins, A., & Duguid, P. (1989). Situated cognition and the culture of learning. *Educational Researcher, 18*(1), 32–42.

Carpenter, T. P., Fennema, E., & Franke, M. L. (1996). Cognitively guided instruction: A knowledge base for reform in primary mathematics instruction. *Elementary School Journal, 97*(1), 3–20.

Children's Defense Fund. (2004). *2003 facts on child poverty in America.* Retrieved from http://www.childrensdefense.org/familyincome/childpoverty/basicfacts.aspx

Civil, M., & Andrade, R. (2002). Transitions between home and school mathematics: Rays of hope amidst the passing clouds. In G. de Abreu, A. J. Bishop, & N. C. Presmeg (Eds.), *Transitions between contexts of mathematical practices* (pp. 149–169). Dordrecht: Kluwer.

Clark, I. (2004). Co-education and gender: The end of the experiment? *Education Policy Analysis Archives, 12*(41). Retrieved from http://epaa.asu.edu/epaa/v12n41/

Clewell, B. C., Anderson, B. T., & Thorpe, M. E. (1992). *Breaking the barriers: Helping female and minority students succeed in mathematics and science.* San Francisco: Jossey-Bass.

Cummins, J. (2001). Empowering minority students: A framework for intervention. *Harvard Educational Review, 71*(4), 649–675.

D'Ambrosio, U. (1983). Successes and failures of mathematics curricula in the part two decades: A developing society viewpoint in a holistic framework. *Proceedings of the fourth International Congress of Mathematics Education,* 362–364.

Darling-Hammond, L. (1993). Reframing the school reform agenda: Developing capacity for school transformation. *Phi Delta Kappan, 74,* 753–761.

Davis, P. J., & Hersh, R. (1980). *The mathematics experience.* Boston: Birkhauser.

Dunn, T. K. (2005). Engaging prospective teachers in critical reflection: Facilitating a disposition to teach mathematics for diversity. In A. J. Rodriguez & R. S. Kitchen (Eds.), *Preparing mathematics and science teachers for diverse classrooms: Promising strategies for transformative pedagogy* (pp. 143–160). Mahwah, NJ: Lawrence Erlbaum Associates.

Eccles, J. S., & Jacobs, J. E. (1986). Social forces shape math attitudes and performance. *Signs, 11,* 367–380.

Edmonds, R. (1979). Effective schools for the urban poor. *Educational Leadership, 37*(10), 15–24.

Emerson, R. M., Fretz, R. I., & Shaw, L. L. (1995). *Writing ethnographic fieldnotes.* Chicago: University of Chicago.

Ernest, P. (1991). *The philosophy of mathematics education: Studies in mathematics education.* London: Falmer.

Ethington, C. A., & Wolfe, L. M. (1984). Sex differences in a causal model of mathematics achievement. *Journal for Research in Mathematics Education, 15,* 361–377.

Fennema, E., Carpenter, T. P., Jacobs, V. R., Franke, M. L., & Levi, L. W. (1998). A longitudinal study of gender differences in young children's mathematical thinking. *Educational Researcher, 27*(5), 6–11.

Fennema, E., & Franke, M. L. (1992). Teachers' knowledge and its impact. In D. A. Grouws (Ed.), *Handbook of research on mathematics teaching and learning* (pp. 147–164). New York: Macmillan.

Fennema, E., & Nelson, B. S. (Eds.). (1997). *Mathematics teachers in transition.* Mahwah, NJ: Lawrence Erlbaum Associates.

Fennema, E., & Sherman, J. (1977). Sex-related differences in mathematics achievement, spatial visualization, and sociocultural factors. *American Educational Research Journal, 14,* 51–71.

Ferguson, R. F. (1998). Teachers' perceptions and expectations and the Black–White test score gap. In C. Jencks & M. Phillips (Eds.), *The Black–White test score gap* (pp. 273–317). Washington, DC: Brookings Institution.

Fox, L. H., & Cohn, S. J. (1980). Sex differences in the development of precocious mathematical talent. In L. H. Fox, L. Brody, & D. Tobin (Eds.), *Women and the mathematical mystique* (pp. 94–111). Baltimore: Johns Hopkins University Press.

Frankenstein, M. (1987). Critical mathematics education: An application of Paulo Freire's epistemology. In I. Shor (Ed.), *Freire for the classroom* (pp. 180–210). Portsmouth, NH: Boynton/Cook.

Frankenstein, M. (1995). Equity in mathematics education: Class in the world outside the class. In W. G. Secada, E. Fennema, & L. B. Adajian (Eds.), *New directions for equity in mathematics education* (pp. 165–190). New York: Cambridge University Press.

Freeman, C. E. (2004). *Trends in educational equity of girls and women: 2004.* Retrieved from http://nces.ed.gov/pubs2005/2005016.pdf

Freire, P. (1993). *Pedagogy of the oppressed*. New York: Continuum.

Gerdes, P. (1988). On culture, geometrical thinking and mathematics education. *Educational Studies in Mathematics, 19*, 137–162.

Goldman, W., & Blakely, E. (1992). *Separate societies: Poverty and inequality in U.S. cities*. Philadelphia: Temple University Press.

Good, T. L., & Grouws, D. A. (1979). The Missouri mathematics effectiveness project in fourth-grade classrooms. *Journal of Educational Psychology, 71*, 355–362.

Good, T. L., Grouws, D. A., & Ebmeier, H. (1983). *Active mathematics teaching*. New York: Longman.

Goodlad, J. I. (1983). *A place called school: Prospects for the future*. New York: McGraw-Hill.

Grant, C. A. (1989). Equity, equality, teachers and classroom life. In W. G. Secada (Ed.), *Equity in education* (pp. 89–102). London: Falmer.

Gutiérrez, R. (2002). Beyond essentialism: The complexity of language in teaching mathematics to Latina/o students. *American Educational Research Journal, 39*, 1047–1088.

Gutstein, E. (2003). Teaching and learning mathematics for social justice in an urban, Latino school. *Journal for Research in Mathematics Education, 34*(1), 37–73.

Guzman, B. (2001). *The Hispanic population 2000*. U.S. Concensus Bureau, U. S. Department of Commerce. Available at www.census.gov/prod/2001pubs/c2kbr01–3.pdf

Haag, P. (1998). *Single-sex education in grades K–12: What does the research tell us? Separated by sex: A critical look at single-sex education for girls*. Washington, DC: AAUW Educational Foundation.

Haberman, M. (1991). The pedagogy of poverty versus good teaching. *Phi Delta Kappan, 73*, 290–294.

Henningsen, M., & Stein, M. K. (1997). Mathematical tasks and student cognition: Classroom-based factors that support and inhibit high-level mathematical thinking and reasoning. *Journal for Research in Mathematics Education, 28*(5), 524–549.

Hersh, R. (1979). Some proposals for revising the philosophy of mathematics. *Advances in Mathematics, 31*, 31–50.

Hiebert, J., & Carpenter, T. P. (1992). Learning and teaching with understanding. In D. Grouws (Ed.), *The handbook of research on mathematics teaching and learning* (pp. 65–97). New York: Macmillan.

Huston, A. C., & Carpenter, C. J. (1985). Gender differences in preschool classrooms: The effects of sex-typed activity choices. In L. C. Wilkinson & C. B. Marrett (Eds.), *Gender differences in classroom interaction* (pp. 143–165). New York: Academic Press.

Ingersoll, R. M. (1999). The problem of underqualified teachers in American secondary schools. *Educational Researcher, 28*(2), 26–37.

Institute for Research on Poverty. (2005). *Who was poor in 2003?* Retrieved from http://www.irp.wisc.edu/

Jackson, A., & Davis, G. (2000). *Turning points 2000: Educating adolescents in the twenty-first century*. New York: Teachers College Press.

Jackson, C. (2002). Can single-sex classes in co-educational schools enhance learning experiences of girls and/or boys: An exploration of pupils' perceptions. *British Educational Research Journal, 28*(1), 37–48.

Jacobs, J. E., & Eccles, J. S. (1985). Gender differences in math ability: The impact of media reports on parents. *Educational Researcher, 14*(3), 20–24.

Johnson, J., Duffett, A., Vine, J., & Moye, L. (2003). *Where we are now: Twelve things you need to know about public opinion and public schools*. New York: Public Agenda.

Johnson, T. M. (1994). *A teacher's roles and calculator tasks in two twelfth-grade mathematics courses*. Unpublished doctoral dissertation, University of Wisconsin—Madison.

Jordan, M. L. R. (1995). Reflections on the challenges, possibilities and perplexities of preparing preservice teachers for culturally diverse classrooms. *Journal of Teacher Education, 46*, 369–374.

Kaestle, C. (1973). *The evolution of an urban school system*. Cambridge, MA: Harvard University Press.

Kamii, C., Lewis, B. A., & Livingston, S. J. (1993, December). Primary arithmetic: Children inventing their own procedures. *Arithmetic Teacher, 40*, 200–203.

Kellner, D. (1990). *Television and the crisis of democracy*. Boulder, CO: Westview Press.

Khisty, L. L. (1997). Making mathematics accessible to Latino students: Rethinking instructional practice. In J. Trentacosta & M. Kenney (Eds.), *Multicultural and gender equity in the mathematics classroom: The gift of diversity* (pp. 92–101). 97th Yearbook of the National Council of Teachers of Mathematics. Washington, DC: National Council of Teachers of Mathematics.

Kitchen, R. S. (2003). Getting real about mathematics education reform in high poverty communities. *For the Learning of Mathematics, 23*(3), 16–22.

Kitchen, R. S. (2005). Making equity and multiculturalism explicit to transform the culture of mathematics education. In A. J. Rodriguez & R. S. Kitchen (Eds.), *Preparing mathematics and science teachers for diverse classrooms: Promising strategies for transformative pedagogy* (pp. 33–60). Mahwah, NJ: Lawrence Erlbaum Associates.

Kitchen, R. S., & Lear, J. M. (2000). Mathematizing Barbie: Using measurement as a means for girls to analyze their sense of body image. In W. Secada (Ed.), *Changing the faces of mathematics* (pp. 67–173). Reston, VA: National Council of Teachers of Mathematics.

Knapp, M. S., & Woolverton, S. (1995). Social class and schooling. In J. Banks & C. Banks (Eds.), *Handbook of research on multicultural education* (pp. 548–569). New York: Macmillan.

Knight, M. G. (2003). It doesn't happen by accident: Creating successful cultures of college preparation for urban Latina/o youth. *Educators for Urban Minorities, 2*(2), 91–107.

Kozol, J. (1967) *Death at an early age*. New York: Bantam.

Kozol, J. (1991). *Savage inequalities: Children in America's schools*. New York: Crown.

Kozol, J. (2005). *The shame of the nation: The restoration of apartheid schooling in America*. New York: Crown.

Krupnick, D. (1985). Women and men in the classroom: Inequality and its remedies. On teaching and learning. *Journal of the Harvard Danforth Center*, 18–25.

Kulm, G. (1991). New directions for mathematics assessment. In G. Kulm (Ed.), *Assessing higher order thinking in mathematics* (pp. 71–78). Washington, DC: American Association for the Advancement of Science.

Kulm, G. (1994). *Mathematics assessment: What works in the classroom*. San Francisco: Jossey-Bass.

Ladson-Billings, G. (1994). *The dreammakers: Successful teachers of African American children*. San Francisco: Jossey-Bass.

Ladson-Billings, G. (1995). Toward a theory of culturally relevant pedagogy. *American Education Research Journal, 32*(3), 465–491.

Lakatos, I. (1976). *Proofs and refutations.* Cambridge, England: Cambridge University Press.

Lampert, M., & Ball, D. L. (1999). Aligning teacher education with contemporary K–12 reform visions. In L. Darling-Hammond & G. Sykes (Eds.), *Teaching as the learning profession: Handbook of policy and practice* (pp. 33–53). San Francisco: Jossey-Bass.

Leder, G. C. (1987). Teacher student interaction: A case study. *Educational Studies in Mathematics, 18,* 255–271.

Leder, G. C. (1992). Mathematics and gender: Changing perspectives. In D. A. Grouws (Ed.), *Handbook for research on mathematics teaching and learning* (pp. 597–622). New York: Macmillan.

Lee, O. (1999). Equity implications based on the conceptions of science achievement in major reform documents. *Review of Educational Research, 69*(1), 83–115.

Lee, V. E., & Bryk, A. S. (1986). Effects of single-sex secondary schools on student achievement and attitudes. *Journal of Educational Psychology, 78*(5), 381–395.

Lee, V. E., & Marks, H. M. (1990). Sustained effects of the single-sex secondary school experience on attitudes, behaviors, and values in college. *Journal of Educational Psychology, 82* (3), 579.

Lee, V. E., & Smith, J. B. (2001). *Restructuring high schools for equity and excellence: What works.* New York: Teachers College Press.

Leedy, M. G., LaLonde, D., & Runk, K. (2003). Gender equity in mathematics: Beliefs of students, parents, and teachers. *School Science and Mathematics, 103*(6), 285–292.

Leonard, J., & Dantley, S. J. (2005). Breaking through the ice: Dealing with issues of diversity in mathematics and science education courses. In A. J. Rodriguez & R. S. Kitchen (Eds.), *Preparing mathematics and science teachers for diverse classrooms: Promising strategies for transformative pedagogy* (pp. 87–118). Mahwah, NJ: Lawrence Erlbaum Associates.

Lincoln, Y. S., & Guba, E. G. (1985). *Naturalistic inquiry.* Newbury Park, CA: Sage.

Lipka, J. (1994). Culturally negotiated schooling: Toward a Yup'ik mathematics. *Journal of American Indian Education, 33*(3), 14–30.

Lipman, P. (1998). *Race, class, and power in school restructuring.* Albany, NY: State University of New York.

Little, J., & Dorph, R. (1998). *California's school restructuring program: Lessons about comprehensive school reform and its effects on students, educators, and schools.* Berkeley, CA: University of California, Berkeley.

Lockheed, M. E. (1985). Some determinants and consequences of sex-segregation in the classroom. In L. C. Wilkinson & C. B. Marrett (Eds.), *Gender influences in classroom interaction* (pp. 167–184). New York: Academic Press.

Louis, L. K., & Miles, M. B. (1990). *Improving the urban high school.* New York: Teachers College Press.

Lubienski, S. (2000). Problem solving as a means toward mathematics for all: An exploratory look through a class lens. *Journal for Research in Mathematics Education, 31*(4), 454–482.

Ma, L. (1999). *Knowing and teaching elementary mathematics.* Mahwah, NJ: Lawrence Erlbaum Associates.

Martin, D. B. (2000). *Mathematics success and failure among African-American youth: The roles of sociohistorical context, community forces, school influence, and individual agency.* Mahwah, NJ: Lawrence Erlbaum Associates.

Martin, M. O., Mullis, I. V. S., Gregory, K. D., Hoyle, C., & Shen, C. (2000). *Effective schools in science and mathematics: IEA's Third International Mathematics and Science Study*. Boston: International Study Center, Lynch School of Education, Boston College. Retrieved from http://timss.bc.edu/timss1995i/TIMSSPDF/T95_ EffSchool.pdf

McKay, S., & Wong, S. (1996). Multiple discourses, multiple identities: Investment and agency in second-language learning among Chinese adolescent immigrant students. *Harvard Educational Review, 66*(3), 577–608.

McKinnon, J. (2001). *The Black population 2000*. U.S. Census Bureau, U.S. Department of Commerce. Retrieved from www.census.gov/prod/2001pubs/c2kbr01-5.pdf

McLaughlin, M. W., Shepard, L. A., & O'Day, J. A. (1995). *Improving education through standards-based reform: A report by the National Academy of Education Panel on Standards-Based Education Reform*. Stanford, CA: Stanford University, National Academy of Education.

McNeil, L. (1986). *Contradictions of control: School structure and school knowledge*. New York: Routledge & Kegan Paul.

Meier, D. (1995). *The power of their ideas: Lessons for America from a small school in Harlem*. Boston: Beacon Press.

Mellin-Olsen, S. (1987). *The politics of mathematics education*. Dordrecht: Reidel.

Merriam, S. B. (1998). *Qualitative research and case study applications in education* (2nd ed.). San Francisco: Jossey-Bass.

Meyer, R. J. (2005). Invisible teacher/invisible children: The company line. In B. Altwerger (Ed.), *Reading for profit: How the bottom line leaves kids behind* (pp. 96–111). Portsmouth, NH: Heinemann.

Miles, M. B., & Huberman, A. M. (1984). *Qualitative data analysis: A sourcebook for new methods*. Beverly Hills: Sage.

Moschkovich, J. N. (1999). Supporting the participation of English language learners in mathematical discussions. *For the Learning of Mathematics, 19*(1), 11–19.

Moses, R., & Cobb, C., Jr. (2001). *Radical equations: Math literacy and civil rights*. Boston: Beacon Press.

National Center for Education Statistics. (2005). Average mathematics scale scores, by student eligibility for free/reduced-price lunch. Retrieved from http://nces.ed.gov/nationsreportcard/mathematics/results2003/lunch.asp

National Council of Teachers of Mathematics. (1989). *Curriculum and evaluation standards for school mathematics*. Reston, VA: Author.

National Council of Teachers of Mathematics. (1991). *Professional standards for teaching mathematics*. Reston, VA: Author.

National Council of Teachers of Mathematics. (2000). *Principles and standards for school mathematics*. Reston, VA: Author.

National Poverty Center. (2005). *Poverty in the United States: Frequently asked questions*. Retrieved from http://www.npc.umich.edu/

National Research Council. (1996). *National science education standards*. Washington, DC: National Academy Press.

National Research Council. (2001a). Adding it up: Helping children learn mathematics. In J. Kilpatrick, J. Swafford, & B. Findell (Eds.), *Mathematics Learning Study Committee, Center for Education, Division of Behavioral and Social Sciences and Education*. Washington, DC: National Academy Press.

National Research Council. (2001b). *Educating teachers of science, mathematics and technology: New practices for the new millennium.* Washington, DC: National Academy Press.

National Science Foundation. (1996). *Indicators of science and mathematics education 1995.* Arlington, VA: Author.

Newmann, F., King, M., & Rigdon, M. (1998). Accountability and school performance: Implications from restructuring schools. In *Cool thinking on hot topics: A research guide for educators* (pp. 34–66). Cambridge, MA: Harvard Educational Review.

Newmann, F. M., & Associates. (1996). *Authentic achievement: Restructuring schools for intellectual quality.* San Francisco: Jossey-Bass.

Newmann, F. M., Secada, W. G., & Wehlage, G. G. (1995). *A guide to authentic instruction and assessment: Vision, standards and scoring.* Madison, WI: Center on Organization and Restructuring of Schools, Wisconsin Center for Education Research.

Newmann, F. M., & Wehlage, G. G. (1995). *Successful school restructuring: A report to the public and educators.* Madison, WI: Center on Organization and Restructuring of Schools, Wisconsin Center for Education Research.

Oakes, J. (1990a). *Lost talent: The underparticipation of women, minorities, and disabled persons in science.* Santa Monica, CA: RAND Corporation. (ERIC Document Reproduction Service No. ED318640)

Oakes, J. (1990b). Opportunities, achievement, and choice: Women and minority students in science and mathematics. In C. B. Cazden (Ed.), *Review of research in education* (Vol. 16, pp. 153–222). Washington, DC: American Educational Research Association.

O'Day, J. A., & Smith, M. S. (1993). Systemic school reform and educational opportunity. In S. H. Fuhrman (Ed.), *Designing coherent educational policy: Improving the system* (pp. 250–311). San Francisco: Jossey-Bass.

O'Day, J., Goertz, M., & Floden, R. (1995). Building capacity for education reform. *CPRE policy briefs: Reporting on issues and research in education policy.* New Brunswick, NJ: Rutgers University.

Olsen, L. (1994). *The unfinished journey: Restructuring schools in a diverse society.* San Francisco: California Tomorrow.

Parker, R. (1993). *Mathematical power: Lessons from a classroom.* Portsmouth, NH: Heinemann.

Patton, M. Q. (1990). *Qualitative evaluation and research methods* (2nd ed.). Newbury Park, CA: Sage.

Perie, M., Moran, R., Lutkus, A. D., & Tirre, W. (2005). *NAEP 2004 trends in academic progress: Three decades of student performance in reading and mathematics.* Retrieved from http://nces.ed.gov/nationsreportcard/pdf/main2005/2005464.pdf

Peterson, P. L., & Fennema, E. (1985). Effective teaching, student enjoyment in classroom activities, and sex-related differences in learning mathematics. *American Educational Research Journal, 22*, 309–335.

Powell, A., Farrar, E., & Cohen, D. (1985). *The shopping mall high school: Winners and losers in the educational marketplace.* Boston: Houghton Mifflin.

Purkey, S., & Smith, M. (1983). Effective schools: A review. *Elementary School Journal, 83*(4), 427–452.

Resnick, L. B. (1992). From protoquantities to operators: Building mathematical competence on a foundation of everyday knowledge. In G. Leinhardt, R.

Putnam, & R. A. Hattrup (Eds.), *Analysis of arithmetic for mathematics teaching* (pp. 373–429). Hillsdale, NJ: Lawrence Erlbaum Associates.

Richardson, V., & Placier, P. (2001). Teacher change. In D. V. Richardson (Ed.), *Handbook of research on teaching* (4th ed., pp. 905–950). Washington, DC: American Educational Research Association.

Riordan, C. (1990). *Girls and boys in school: Together or separate.* New York: Teachers College Press.

Riordan, J., & Noyce, P. (2001). The impact of two standards-based mathematics curricula on student achievement in Massachusetts. *Journal for Research in Mathematics Education, 32*(4), 368–398.

Rodriguez, A. J., & Kitchen, R. S. (Eds.). (2005). *Preparing mathematics and science teachers for diverse classrooms: Promising strategies for transformative pedagogy.* Mahwah, NJ: Lawrence Erlbaum Associates.

Romberg, T. A. (1992). Problematic features of the school mathematics curriculum. In P. W. Jackson (Ed.), *Handbook of research on curriculum* (pp. 749–788). New York: Macmillan.

Roy, F. (2002, February). *Searching for a knowledge base to inform mathematics teacher education: Preparing teachers to meet the needs of all students.* Paper presented at the 2002 annual meeting of the American Association of Colleges of Teacher Education, New York.

Roy, F., & Kitchen, R. (2005, April). *Teachers' conceptions about mathematics and diversity in two urban districts: Results from an effective schools study.* Paper presented at the annual meeting of the American Educational Research Association, Montreal, Canada.

Roy, F., & Rousseau, C. (2005). Student thinking as a context for high expectations. *For the Learning of Mathematics, 25*(2), 16–23.

Rury, J. (1993). The changing social context of urban education: A national perspective. In J. Rury & F. Cassell (Eds.), *Seeds of crisis: Public schooling in Milwaukee since 1920* (pp. 10–41). Madison: University of Wisconsin Press.

Sadker, D., & Sadker, M. (1985). Sexism in the classroom of the 80s. *Psychology Today, 19,* 54–57.

Sadker, D., & Sadker, M. (1986). Sexism in the classroom: From grad school to graduate school. *Phi Delta Kappan, 67*(7), 512–515.

Sadker, D., & Sadker, M. (2001). Gender bias: From colonial America to today's classroom. In J. A. Banks & C. A. McGee Banks (Eds.), *Multicultural education: Issues and perspectives* (pp. 125–151). New York: Wiley.

Sadker, M., & Sadker, D. (1994). *Failing at fairness: How America's schools cheat girls.* New York: Scribner's.

Schifter, D., & Fosnot, C. T. (1993). *Reconstructing mathematics education: Stories of teachers meeting the challenge of reform.* New York: Teachers College Press.

Schoenfeld, A. H. (2002). Making mathematics work for all children: Issues of standards, testing, and equity. *Educational Researcher, 31*(1), 13–25.

Schwartz, W., & Hanson, K. (1992). *Equal mathematics education for female students.* Newton, MA: Education Development Center. (ERIC Document Reproduction Service No. ED344977)

Scott, R. M. (1995). Helping teacher education students develop positive attitudes toward ethnic minorities. *Equity & Excellence in Education, 28,* 69–73.

Secada, W. G. (1992). Race, ethnicity, social class, language, and achievement in mathematics. In D. A. Grouws (Ed.), *Handbook of research on mathematics teaching and learning* (pp. 623–660). New York: Macmillan.

Secada, W. G. (1995). Social and critical dimensions for equity in mathematics education. In W. Secada, E. Fennema, & L. B. Adajian (Eds.), *New directions for equity in mathematics education* (pp. 146–164). New York: Cambridge University Press.

Sheets, R. H. (1995). From remedial to gifted: Effects of culturally centered pedagogy. *Theory Into Practice, 34*(3), 186–193.

Skovsmose, O. (1994). *Towards a philosophy of critical mathematics education.* Dordrecht: Kluwer.

Sleeter, C. E. (1994). White racism. *Multicultural Education, 1*(4), 5–8, 39.

Stage, E., Kreinberg, N., Eccles, J., & Becker, J. (1985). Increasing participation and achievement of girls and women in mathematics, science, and engineering. In S. Klein (Ed.), *Handbook for achieving sex equality through education* (pp. 237–269). Baltimore: Johns Hopkins University Press.

Strauss, A., & Corbin, J. (1990). *Basics of qualitative research: Grounded theory procedures and techniques.* Newbury Park, CA: Sage.

Szatjn, P. (2003). Adapting reform ideas in different mathematics classrooms: Beliefs beyond mathematics. *Journal of Mathematics Teacher Education, 6*, 53–75.

Tate, W. F. (1995). Economics, equity, and the national mathematics assessment: Are we creating a national tollroad? In W. G. Secada, E. Fennema, & L. B. Adajian (Eds.), *New directions for equity in mathematics education* (pp. 191–208). New York: Cambridge University Press.

Tate, W. F. (1997). Race-ethnicity, SES, gender, and language proficiency trends in mathematics achievement: An update. *Journal for Research in Mathematics Education, 28*(6), 652–679.

Tatum, B. D. (1992). Talking about race, learning about racism: The application of racial identity development theory in the classroom. *Harvard Educational Review, 62*, 1–24.

Thompson, A. (1992). Teachers' beliefs and conceptions: A synthesis of the research. In D. Grouws (Ed.), *Handbook of research on mathematics teaching and learning* (pp. 127–146). New York: Macmillan.

Thompson, C. L., & Zeuli, J. S. (1999). The frame and the tapestry: Standards-based reform and professional development. In L. Darling-Hammond & G. Sykes (Eds.), *Teaching as the learning profession: Handbook of policy and practice* (pp. 341–375). San Francisco: Jossey-Bass.

Tymoczko, T. (1986). *New directions in the philosophy of mathematics.* Boston: Birkhauser.

U.S. Census Bureau. (2001). *Poverty in the United States.* P-60, No. 219. Washington, DC: U.S. Government Printing Office.

U.S. Census Bureau. (2003, August). *Income, poverty and health insurance coverage in the United States: 2003.* Current population reports. Washington, DC: U.S. Government Printing Office.

U.S. Department of Education. (1994). *Single-sex schooling: Perspectives from practice and research.* Washington, DC: Office of Educational Research and Improvement.

U.S. Department of Education. (1998). *No more excuses: The final report of the Hispanic Dropout Project.* Washington, DC.

U.S. Department of Education, Office of Elementary and Secondary Education. (2002). *Testing for results: Helping families, schools and communities understand and improve student learning.* Retrieved from http://www.ed.gov/nclb/accountability/ayp/testingforresults.html

Walker, V. S. (1996). Interpersonal caring in the "good" segregated schooling of African-American children. In D. Eaker-Rich & J. A. Van Galen (Eds.), *Caring in an unjust world* (pp. 129–146). New York: SUNY Press.

Wallis, J. (2005). What the waters revealed. *Sojourners Magazine* (November).

Wehlage, G., Rutter, R., Smith, G., Lesko, N., & Fernandez, R. (1989). *Reducing the risk: Schools as communities of support.* Philadelphia: Falmer.

Wiggins, G. P. (1993). *Assessing student performance: Exploring the purpose and limits of testing.* San Francisco: Jossey-Bass.

Willis, P. (1981). *Learning to labor: How working class kids get working class jobs.* New York: Columbia University Press.

Wilson, S. M., & Berne, J. (1999). Teacher learning and the acquisition of professional knowledge: An examination of research on contemporary professional development. In A. Iran-Nejad & P. D. Pearson (Eds.), *Review of research in education* (Vol. 24, pp. 173–209). Washington, DC: American Educational Research Association.

Winfield, L. F. (1986). Teacher expectations and low-achieving students. *The Urban Review, 18*(4), 253–268.

Winfield, L. F., & Manning, J. B. (1992). Changing school culture to accommodate student diversity. In M. E. Dilworth (Ed.), *Diversity in teacher education* (pp. 181–214). San Francisco: Jossey-Bass.

Zeichner, K. M. (1996). Educating teachers to close the achievement gap: Issues of pedagogy, knowledge, and teacher preparation. In B. Williams (Ed.), *Closing the achievement gap: A vision for changing beliefs and practices* (pp. 56–76). Alexandria, VA: Association for Supervision and Curriculum and Development.

Author Index

Subject Index